"Keir Giles has explained with clarity, concision, and deep knowledge why Russia cannot be understood by Western criteria alone. His book is a much-needed antidote to simplistic judgements. It should be required reading for all who deal with Western policy towards Russia."
—SIR RODERIC LYNE, *UK ambassador to Moscow 2000–04*

"*Moscow Rules* makes an important contribution to understanding the different viewpoints that exist in Russia and how Russia's state system and influencing traditions differ from those of Western democratic countries in ways that have not always been comprehended. This is essential to understanding how the West can learn to distinguish real threats relating to Russia from those that only look like a threat but are not."
—HANNA SMITH, *Director of Strategic Planning and Responses at Hybrid CoE (The European Centre for Excellence for Countering Hybrid Threats)*

"Keir Giles has written the essential 'go-to' book for anyone, everyone—in government, the media, business, the military, or academia—who works with Russia or on Russia, or who needs to understand Russia to do their job. In a commendably clear, compelling, straightforward, and highly readable way, Giles explains not only how Russia thinks and works, but how it got there and why. His expert, sympathetic treatment of the subject is eminently practical and immediately applicable. I hope that every Western politician and political commentator will read and act on this book. Doing so would immediately put our relationship with Russia on firmer and safer ground."
—CHRIS DONNELLY, *Co-Director, The Institute for Statecraft*

MOSCOW RULES

Providing new perspectives and knowledge on an increasingly complex, uncertain, and interconnected world.

The Chatham House Insights Series
Series Editor: Caroline Soper

The Insights series provides new perspectives on and knowledge about an increasingly complex, uncertain, and interconnected world. Concise, lively, and authoritative, these books explore, through different modes of interpretation, a wide range of country, regional, and international developments, all within a global context. Focusing on topical issues in key policy areas, such as health, security, economics, law, and the environment, volumes in the series will be written accessibly by leading experts—both academic and practitioner—to anticipate trends and illuminate new ideas and thinking. Insights books will be of great interest to all those seeking to develop a deeper understanding of the policy challenges and choices facing decision makers, including academics, practitioners, and general readers.

Published or forthcoming titles:

Amitai Etzioni, *Foreign Policy: Thinking Outside the Box* (2016)

David Lubin, *Dance of the Trillions* (2018)

Nigel Gould-Davies, *Tectonic Politics: Global Risk in an Age of Transformation* (forthcoming)

Chatham House, the Royal Institute of International Affairs, is a world-leading policy institute based in London. Its mission is to help governments and societies build a sustainably secure, prosperous, and just world.

Chatham House does not express opinions of its own. The opinions expressed in this publication are the responsibility of the author(s).

MOSCOW RULES

What Drives Russia to Confront the West

KEIR GILES

BROOKINGS INSTITUTION PRESS
Washington, D.C.

CHATHAM HOUSE
The Royal Institute of International Affairs
London

Copyright © 2019
First published in Great Britain in 2019 by
Royal Institute of International Affairs
Chatham House
10 St James's Square
London SW1Y 4LE
www.chathamhouse.org
(Charity Registration No. 208223)

Distributed worldwide by
THE BROOKINGS INSTITUTION
1775 Massachusetts Avenue, N.W., Washington, D.C. 20036
www.brookings.edu

All rights reserved. No part of this publication may be reproduced
or transmitted in any form or by any means without permission
in writing from the Brookings Institution Press.

The Brookings Institution is a private nonprofit organization devoted to research, education, and publication on important issues of domestic and foreign policy. Its principal purpose is to bring the highest quality independent research and analysis to bear on current and emerging policy problems. Interpretations or conclusions in Brookings publications should be understood to be solely those of the authors.

Library of Congress Cataloging-in-Publication data are available.
ISBN 978-0-8157-3574-8 (pbk : alk. paper)
ISBN 978-0-8157-3575-5 (ebook)

9 8 7 6 5 4 3 2 1

Typeset in Adobe Garamond

Composition by Elliott Beard

This book is dedicated to all those career U.S. government officials who are working hard to build and deliver a sensible policy on Russia while hoping that President Trump doesn't notice.

Moscow Rules (*n., intelligence, apocryphal*)—the specific set of assumptions, approaches and procedures that must be adopted as an essential precondition for successful operations in Russia (formerly, in the Soviet Union).

Contents

Acknowledgments xiii

Introduction xv

Part I
Russia's Place in the World

ONE A World Apart 3

TWO Great Power and Empire 13

THREE Russia under Threat 35

FOUR Winning the Cold War 59

Part II
Russia's Internal System

FIVE Ruling Russia 71

SIX The Individual and the State 87

Part III
Russia's Inheritance

SEVEN Russia's Moral Framework 103

EIGHT History Matters 117

Part IV
Prospects for Change

NINE Opposition, Protests, and Discontent 127

TEN Change from Within 139

Conclusion
The Way Forward 159

Notes 175

Index 227

Acknowledgments

Writing *Moscow Rules* was made possible by a grant from the Smith Richardson Foundation, whose assistance is acknowledged with deep gratitude.

Credit for the genesis of *Moscow Rules* must go to James Nixey of Chatham House's Russia and Eurasia Programme, who asked me to come up with an idea for a new and original book on Russia, and only later explained that he actually wanted me to write it as well.

Also within Chatham House, Ľubica Polláková has overseen the project with her customary patience, which as always has at times been sorely tested. And I am indebted to Julia Friedrich for painstakingly checking and updating every web address referenced in the book.

Lincoln Pigman and Jaroslava Barbieri provided essential support tracking down interviewees, obscure quotations, and references.

A particular thank you is due to the Kremlin press office for permission to use the image of Vladimir Putin on the front cover, and to Angel Sin for adapting the image to fit the czarist banknote.

Margaret May and Marjorie Pannell were the book's highly professional editors, working on behalf of Chatham House and Brookings, respectively. They have rescued me from more than one error of misquoting or misinterpretation, but any errors of fact that remain are of course entirely my own.

Important corrections and contributions to the book came from a group of Russia experts convened in October 2017 to discuss the first draft. Duncan Allan, Mathieu Boulègue, Elena Fell, Ivan Kurilla, Edward Lucas, Eugene Rumer, Carl Scott, and Hanna Smith were kind enough not only to read the draft but then also to gather at Chatham House to offer useful—often vital—suggestions for improvement. Other respected colleagues, including Andrew Monaghan, Tomas Ries, Sulev Suvari, Nigel Gould-Davies, and Shima Keene, also offered helpful reviews and comments. In particular, Carolina Vendil Pallin overfulfilled the plan by contributing a magnum opus of corrections, recommendations, and discussion that would have made a substantial research paper on its own.

But the ideas and arguments presented in this book date not only from the last two years, but instead from all of the three decades that I have spent observing and studying Russia. As such, the greatest credit must go to the dozens of senior colleagues from Russia, Europe, and North America and from across the worlds of politics, diplomacy, the military, and academia who have listened to me, guided and corrected me, and given unstintingly of their time, knowledge, and insights over that period. They are, unfortunately, too many to name (and many would indeed prefer not to be named). But their importance to this book is every bit as great as the grand names of Russia studies, from this century and previous ones, who are cited repeatedly in its chapters.

Introduction

This book is written for anybody who cannot understand why Russia and its leaders behave as they do.

Western minds, especially liberal educated ones, rebel against national stereotypes. The taint of orientalism causes them to reject explanations for personal or national behaviors that are based on psychological constructs or worldviews that are specific to a given people or culture. The notion that a nation will behave in a given way because that is how it has always done is a hard sell in academic circles.

It is even harder when that nation, like Russia, superficially resembles the West. The fact that Russia is not only contiguous with Europe but often describes itself as an integral part of Europe makes it harder to succeed in a coherent explanation of consistent profoundly un-European behavior by the country, its rulers, and its subjects. When Russians borrow Western terminology to describe their political system, and when the majority of them are outwardly indistinguishable from white members of the Euro-Atlantic community, an additional mental step is required to assess whether they might be guided by a view of their country and the world around it that is very distinct from that of Western Europeans or North Americans.

And yet throughout the centuries, Russia's leaders and population have displayed patterns of thought and action and habit that are both internally consistent and consistently alien to those of the West. The distinctive relationship between the ruler, the state, and its subjects in Russia, and consequently the manner of interaction between those subjects, shows features today that echo back through history—and throughout history, they have spilled over into how Russia as a state in its various incarnations has interacted with its neighbors and the rest of the world.

Each new circle of confrontation with Russia causes surprise and disarray in the West, but this is usually not the result of any change of policy in Moscow. Consistent Russian state behaviors and demands can be traced not just to Soviet times but back to czarist foreign and domestic policy, and further to the structure and rules of Russian society. In this respect, what surprises some Western observers so much about Moscow's current behavior is simply Russia reverting to type. But this also gives the West pointers for how to behave—and how not to—in order to construct an effective relationship with Russia, based on past experience of both successful and unsuccessful engagement.

However, this requires recognition of a Russian approach to thinking and a Russian view of the world. In descriptions of Russia's current politics, the worldview expressed by the Russian leadership is often referred to as a "narrative." But as political analyst Maria Lipman points out, it is "not a narrative but a sphere of symbols and symbolic practices that are intuitively understood and accepted by the majority rather than rationally learned." These include the assumptions that

> Russia is a great power, and the West is hostile to it; the supreme leader is the only source of authority and the pillar of the correct and appropriate state order; the state is omnipotent, and its citizens depend on it; "might makes right" is a legitimate concept, and injustice is an inevitable part of life which is taken for granted. . . . These beliefs are not necessarily articulated but are implicitly present in the world view of most Russians.[1]

Each of these assumptions provides a source of misunderstanding of Russia—or, if accepted as the prism through which to view Russia, of understanding it. Consequently, each of these is explored in this book.

This exploration includes highlighting the remarkable consistency of specific features of Russian life over time. Themes are drawn from historical descriptions of Russian society, philosophy, and worldview and related to present-day examples to show how they still inform the Russian approach to both domestic and foreign policy. While it is important always to resist determinism and overstating the role and importance of historical parallels, the undeniable continuity of these aspects of Russian life throughout the imperial, Soviet, and post-Soviet periods does lead to conclusions about key aspects of Russia's current and future relationship with the West.

This book does not criticize or condemn Russia, still less Russians. Some of the actions and attitudes described here may be considered reprehensible in Western societies, and indeed among the politer and better-educated social substrata of Russia itself. But this merely emphasizes the importance of not assessing Russia or trying to predict its behavior according to Western criteria; instead, the key to engagement lies in recognizing that it constitutes a culture apart, one in which the written and unwritten rules and assumptions of the West do not apply. Consequently, the distinct manifestations of "Russianness" described here are presented dispassionately; the aim is to understand them rather than pass moral judgment on them.

The book draws heavily on direct quotations from observations of Russia made over several centuries, not only by Russians writing about their own country but also by foreign travelers and residents. Russia has always polarized opinions, and commentary by foreigners has tended to fall into two categories—either fiercely critical or, especially from the early twentieth century on, and under the influence of political motivations, fawning. To the fawning, little fault could be found with Russia, and even Stalin was "positively softhearted (except to Shaw, who saw him as the timely scourge of the incompetent)."[2] To the fiercely critical, Russia had nothing to recommend it: "Go to Russia. It is a journey that would be beneficial to every foreigner; for whoever has really seen Russia will find himself content to live anywhere else."[3] Objective and dispassionate witnesses to the internal state of Russia in past years are hard to come by; but they do exist, and the combination of their intimate acquaintance with Russia and their detachment often allows them to describe it more objectively than Russians writing about their own country. Consequently their descriptions are drawn on extensively in this book to illustrate key themes.[4]

This book is about how Russia sees the West. Russia has, and always has had, relationships with many parts of the world. How Russia interacts with other nations and regions, especially China, will be critical for the country's long-term development. But it is by measurement against the West in particular that Russia has historically defined itself and continues to do so, and this therefore gives context and foundation for many of the persistent behaviors described here.

At the same time, this is a book about Russia, not about the West. Not everything said in this book is peculiar to Russia, and in some cases not only contrasts but also comparisons could be drawn with phenomena from other countries, with or without attempts at moral judgment. But this is not an exercise in comparing, or measuring Russia against any other nation or group of nations; readers can draw their own parallels with features of life in other countries or the conduct of other states. The aim of this book is simple: to address the problem of consistent incomprehension of Russia when viewed from abroad by describing and explaining specific features of its history and worldview that affect its interactions with the West.

Similarly, this is emphatically not an academic text. Academic readers of an early draft of this book searched for a theoretical construct within which to place it and proposed labels including "constructivist," "essentialist," "structuralist," and more. But any resemblance to academic theory, present or outmoded, is purely coincidental. It is true that some features of Russia's domestic policy are common to authoritarian systems and that some features of its foreign policy are common to declining great powers. But again, that is not what this book is about. Instead of seeking a pattern into which to fit Russia, it describes the country and its foreign and domestic trajectories as they are (or, often, would wish to appear to be) and uses the understanding gained to arrive at practical recommendations on how to deal with Moscow.

Throughout the book, "Russia" is often referred to as a single homogeneous entity—"Russia says," "Russia does," and so on. This is a monstrous and deliberate oversimplification that masks enormous diversity. Even using the word "Russian" in English is insufficient to distinguish between the two adjectives it can be used to translate, each with its own specific implications—*russkiy*, meaning ethnically or linguistically Russian, and *rossiyskiy*, meaning belonging to the Russian state. Within these two categories, too, generalization must be employed with caution. A *rossiyskiy* view of the world can be expressed by the state, using a wide and perhaps contradictory range of mechanisms from leadership and protocol statements, through officially approved commentary, to the delivery of messages by means of Russia's expansive array of information warfare tools. And even without considering the substantial proportion of Russian citizens who are not of Russian ethnicity, a *russkiy* view of the world also includes a vast array of shades and variations expressed by different people whose life experiences have been vastly distant from one another, separated by generation, income, geography, and more; some of these differences are unpicked in later chapters. Overall, it would be impossible in a book of this scope to explore every variation and nuance of each of the Russian views and behavior described; instead, the dominant trend, tone, or tenor is used as a guide to Russian official or social consensus where it can be said to exist.

"The West" too is shorthand, masking not only a variety of national approaches to Russia but also a variety of needs by different communities for understanding it. Policymakers, defense planners, concerned citizens, journalists, academics, and others will all have their own reasons for seeking a greater understanding of Russian behaviors and of the country's apparent perpetual inability to join what Europe and North America understand as the modern community of nations. One vital interest that is common to all, however, is avoiding the current state of confrontation with Russia spilling over into open hostilities. At the time of writing, Russia perceives itself to be already engaged in conflict with the West, led by the United States, regardless of whether this conflict is recognized by the adversary or not. It is this perception that drives the background noise of hostile actions by Russia in a wide range of domains—in cyberspace, in disinformation campaigns, in assassinations of its own and foreign citizens abroad, in military interventions in third countries. The debate over whether in doing so Russia believes it is defending itself against an actual and genuine threat from the West or is simply expressing its nature as an unreconstructed expansionist power is perpetual.[5] But whatever the reasons, the danger is present, and the potential consequences are inestimable.

With all this in mind, this book seeks answers to two key questions. What misconceptions about Russia cause persistent failure to achieve a productive and cooperative relationship with the West? And what can the West learn from both Russian history and contemporary society to begin to address these misconceptions, and hence foster a less crisis-prone relationship with Moscow?

To answer these questions, the book considers Russia from four distinct perspectives. Part 1, "Russia's Place in the World," looks at how Russia views its relationship with the West, including its perception of its own status as a great power, and in particular the persistent and critically important presumption that Western states are perpetually conspiring against Moscow.

Part 2, "Russia's Internal System," looks inside Russia, at how its distinctive form of government, often indistinguishable from ownership of the country by its leaders, has influenced not only the lives and rights of Russia's subjects but also its interaction with other states with fundamentally different traditions of governance.

Part 3, "Russia's Inheritance," introduces some specific features that derive from Russia's distinctive history and the distinctive moral framework that has developed as a result, again considering the implications when these collide with fundamentally different beliefs about both history and, in some cases, ethics and morality held in the West.

Part 4, "Prospects for Change," discusses the nature of change in Russia. The cycles of Russian history, through liberalism followed by repression, rapprochement with the West followed by renewed disillusion and confrontation, are so consistent in their repetitiveness that they start to resemble inevitability. Each time hopes for substantial change in Russia have been raised, they have been dashed as the country reverts to its historical pattern. But at the time of writing, there are signs of entirely new phenomena emerging within the youngest generation of Russian society, unprecedented in the country's history, which may finally provide the basis for a realistic optimism that Russia may achieve a functional and durable relationship with the West.

The book's concluding chapter brings together key lessons from the preceding parts to suggest an interim way forward in dealing with Russia. The overall conclusion, based on the history not only of the last twenty-five years but of centuries before it, is that hopes for a better relationship with Moscow must not be based on the assumption that Moscow will change in the short term. Instead, the fundamental requirement for a stable and realistic relationship is recognition that Russia is not, and never has been, part of the West, and thus does not share its assumptions, goals, and values.

PART I

Russia's Place in the World

ONE

A World Apart

Europe and Russia

Let us begin with this evident fact: Russia does not belong at all to Europe, but to Asia. It follows that judging Russia and the Russians by our European standards is a mistake to be avoided.

—GONZAGUE DE REYNOLD, *1950*[1]

In methodological terms, one should de-Europeanise any analysis of Russian policy.

—THOMAS GOMART, *2006*[2]

The superficial resemblance of Russia to a Western country, and of the majority (not all) of its people to white Europeans and North Americans, presents an obstacle to objective understanding of the country because it takes an effort of mind to grasp and remember the underlying differences. An assumption based on appearances that Russians are not so different, and that they see the world and react to events in the same way as Westerners, has obstructed understanding of those ideals, values, prejudices, hopes, fears, and motivations that are shared by many Russians but are distinctive or alien to the West.[3]

This misconception has real and important implications for managing the relationship with Russia as a country. The assumptions and preconceptions of its leadership are so much at odds with what is taken for granted as common ground in the Euro-Atlantic community that a false impression of similarity provides fertile ground for misunderstandings, miscommunication, and miscalculation. In particular, Western audiences often struggle to understand why Russia's ruling elite still has such a different worldview from the West's more than twenty-five years after the end of the Soviet Union.[4] This difficulty is compounded by an apparent commonality of terminology to describe Western and Russian politics. Russia borrows Western terms to describe its own system—"president," "parliament," "elections," "Liberal Democratic Party"—but none of these terms means quite what it implies in a Western context, and any assumption that it does, though on the face of it reasonable, only leads to further confusion for the unwary.

Paradoxically, the sector of Russian society that the West finds easiest to understand constitutes a further barrier to understanding the country as a whole. Russia's liberal, educated, cosmopolitan class can communicate easily with the West because it shares the West's general views, values, and esteem for democracy. But because the message sent to the West is comprehensible and amenable, it tends to be enormously overstated in assessments of Russia overall. As put by one representative of this class, Professor Ivan Kurilla, "Many primary sources about Russia came to the West from people like myself—relatively educated, Western-connected, mostly opposition-minded people. They tend to look at Russia like Westerners do."[5] But this is misleading. Russia's liberals say things that the West would like to hear, but their views are not representative of attitudes in the country as a whole.

The story of the liberal intelligentsia is an integral part of the story of Russia. But it is not a part that has any bearing on the country's current trajectory except insofar as it stimulates state policy to suppress its political inclinations. Still, the predominance of this group in Western sources of information about Russia, and especially the repeated appearance of a very limited number of well-known Russians of liberal or Western orientation in interviews with Western writers, commentators, and journalists, not only distorts the West's image of Russia but also exacerbates the inclination to mirroring—to assuming that Russians see the world in the same way and with the same points of reference and historical and conceptual framework as Westerners do.[6]

It is therefore essential to look beyond the individuals most widely quoted in Western descriptions of Russia. This necessarily involves leaving behind descriptions that are comforting and familiar and instead considering those elements of Russian behaviors and worldviews that are less palatable to Western sensitivities. To consider Russia as a whole requires noting the vastly different attitudes deriving from the vastly different impact of recent history and social development on each of the "four Russias." This term, formulated by geographer Natalia Zubarevich, divides Russians into categories by location, urbanization, education, and income, arriving at four groups with very distinctive views of their country and, by extension, the rest of the world.[7] Zubarevich's First Russia is urban, educated, and relatively affluent; the Second Russia is urban and industrial; the Third Russia is rural, apolitical, and impoverished; and the Fourth Russia is ethnically non-Russian and primarily concentrated in the southern republics.[8] Importantly, the liberal, Western-leaning Russians encountered by foreigners in person or through the media tend to come almost exclusively from the First Russia, but even then they represent only a relatively small subset of it. This leaves aside the great majority of Russians holding a distinctly non-Western set of historical beliefs, attitudes, presumptions, and values.

At times, the dawning realization of these different values has caused Western writers on Russia to recoil in horror and resort to emotive language to try to convey the alien nature of the culture they are describing. In the early stages of the Cold War, the U.S. Army noted that "the characteristics of this semi-Asiatic are strange and contradictory. . . . The Russian is subject to moods which to a westerner are incomprehensible; he acts by instinct."[9] A decade later the South African author and traveler Laurens van der Post attempted to understand and rationalize the Russian cultural phenomena he encountered by placing them within a familiar frame of reference, repeatedly comparing Russians to "the primitive black people of Africa."[10] It has even been suggested that under the influence of their history, Russians as a people are not motivated by the same needs and drivers as other human beings. The U.S. Army general Walter Bedell Smith served as ambassador to Moscow, and later as director of Central Intelligence. In his view, "It is not enough and basically it is not true to say, as so many have said to me, that the Russian people are like people everywhere and only the Government is different. The people, too, are different. They are different because wholly different social and political conditions have retarded and perverted their development and set them apart from other civilizations."[11] Russian authors too can write angrily and damningly of their own country's psychological peculiarities, and "diagnose 'manic-depressive psychosis . . . acute megalomania, persecution complex and kleptomania' [even if] foreigners who write like this are accused of Russophobia."[12]

These differences become most evident when Russia and the West encounter each other without the filters of distance. Even before Soviet times, the deceptive superficial resemblance between Russians and Europeans did not long survive first contact. Henry Kissinger notes that on Russia's arrival in European politics after the defeat of Napoleon, "Western Europeans . . . viewed with awe and apprehension a country whose elites' polished manners seemed barely able to conceal a primitive force from before and beyond Western civilization."[13]

Today the stark differences between one side of the Russian border and the other are especially striking in northern Europe. The Estonian border town of Narva and its Russian counterpart, Ivangorod, are a case in point. To the British novelist Gerald Seymour, visiting in 2017, the border crossing represented "a collision point in two worlds, tectonic plates, where great forces either tolerated each other and stayed apart, or collided."[14] There are persistent alarmist claims that Moscow might create and exploit discontent among the largely Russian-speaking population of Narva to attempt to destabilize the Estonian government. This view tends to discount local reality, where the advantages of living peacefully in Estonia—even if expressed only in terms of quality of life and public services—are immediately obvious to residents on both sides of the border.[15]

But in the front-line states along Russia's western periphery, it is the memory of Russian domination and occupation that echoes most strongly. This memory too can reinforce national stereotypes that border on racism. Intermingled with the knowledge that neighboring peoples have been subjected to repression, deportations, and mass murder at the hands of Russians are more recent portrayals of Russians in the post-Soviet era as remaining chaotic, primitive, brutalized, and insanitary.[16] Although with the passing of generations, the direct memory of being under Russian rule may fade, the consciousness of stark societal differences at the Russian border is still strong.[17] Few cultural artifacts speak of this divide as clearly as the Russian-language signs at Finnish truck stops explaining the correct way to use a Western toilet.

These differences are highlighted still further on the rare occasions when Russia welcomes large groups of foreigners who may previously have had little interest in or knowledge of the country. It was normal and natural that the Olympics hosted by Russia, whether in Moscow in 1980 or in Sochi in 2014, were preceded by a frenzy of beautification so that visitors would receive as little exposure as possible to the natural state of the country and its infrastructure; the same applied in full measure, for instance, to the London Olympics in 2012. But cultural trivia such as—again—the notorious twin toilets and other lavatorial oddities[18] combined with more sinister reminders of state control, such as official references to surveillance cameras in the showers, to emphasize just how far European and North American visitors were from home.[19] The Sochi Olympics could have been an effective instrument of soft power for Russia, and were promoted as demonstrating the country's attraction, hospitality, and openness to the world, but instead they became known as a case study in corruption and gross mismanagement, the high point of Russia's state-sponsored doping program, and a precursor to the annexation of Crimea.[20] They also provided many foreigners with their first understanding of how profoundly different Russia is from Europe—not least in the country's lack of self-awareness in how it presents itself to the rest of the world.

By the time of the soccer World Cup four years later in the summer of 2018, there were signs that Russia had at least recognized that it had an image problem. The Russian leadership went to considerable lengths to create "an image of Russia as a country that is safe, modern and open to the world."[21] Russian police and security forces were at pains to tone down their normal level of response to expressions of public enthusiasm for the duration of the tournament, with one regular visitor to Russia expressing surprise that they resorted to "polite requests rather than baton charges."[22] But other steps taken to make Russia seem less alien and more inviting served to highlight still further the cultural differences between the host nation and its visitors. Volunteers tasked with escorting and assisting fans had been sent to classes in which they were taught how to appear friendly, including the art of smiling (a display of friendliness in much of Europe and North America but in Russia a cause for suspicion).[23] According to travelers' reports, these efforts had widely varying results.[24]

Nevertheless, the difficulties experienced by the West in grasping the nature of Russia are not insurmountable. To the Western mind, Russia abounds in contradictions and paradoxes derived from its unique history and its precarious balance between Europe and Asia in terms of politics, culture, social development, and simple physical geography. But these contradictions can be resolved, or at least accommodated and lived with, if Western preconceptions of history, truth, and logic are left behind. According to the American author and long-term Russia correspondent David Satter, "Understanding Russia is actually very easy, but one must teach oneself to do something that is very hard—to believe the unbelievable. Westerners become confused because they approach Russia with a Western frame of reference, not realizing that Russia is a universe based on a completely different set of values."[25]

Above all, Russia should not be treated as fundamentally inexplicable or impenetrable, or comprehensible not through rational analysis but only through mystical invocations of the Russian soul.[26] Instead, in order to understand the roots of the persistent failures in the multiple relationships between Moscow and the West, Russia "has to be treated not as a monstrous, unfathomable apparition to be contemplated helplessly, but as one country among others (with startling peculiarities, of course)."[27] Later chapters of this book seek to explore, and if possible explain, some of these peculiarities.

Russia and Europe

> "Mount up! On the road! To Europe now, and seize it!" . . . The way winds on across an unknown, unknowable planet.
> —ALEKSANDR SOLZHENITSYN, Prussian Nights[28]

Problems of alienation and mutual incomprehension also apply in reverse; the same complex of "otherness" in large part governs how Russia views the West. The notion that there are special, eternal cultural qualities of the Russian people that distinguish them fundamentally from other peoples, in particular from those of Western Europe, means the West ordinarily serves as the constituting "other" for Russian nationalist sentiment.[29]

Historically, this use of the West as a benchmark against which Russia measures itself has referred to Europe; the relatively recent emergence of North America as a center of values and power has not diluted the role of geographic proximity in Europe's traditional role as both a model to emulate and an opponent to be feared or hated.[30] In one of the many instances of repetitive cycles in Russian history, this ambivalent view of Europe, alternately or simultaneously envied and despised, has swung back and forth according to a familiar pattern, all the while providing not only Russia's principal foreign policy dilemma but also a substantial part of the philosophical preoccupation of thinking Russians.

The perennial debate between the *Zapadniki* or Westernizers, who saw integration with the West as Russia's only hope, and the Slavophiles, who preferred to retreat from Europe and stand apart as a distinctive and unique people, was an expression of this combination of allure and hatred. Naturally enough, this debate has tended to peak after periods of increased contact or interaction with the West. After the Napoleonic Wars, suggestions that the West enjoyed a superior system of government were displaced by explanations of Russian moral superiority to liberal Europe. A similar pattern could be observed following Russia's defeat in the Crimean War in the 1850s, and again at the end of the nineteenth century. On each occasion, as described by historian Tibor Szamuely, the blend of "admiration and hatred, envy and contempt, superiority and inferiority, that has so often characterized the Russian attitude towards Europe [meant that] their standing in the world had to be measured by Western yardsticks, even while stressing their differentness, yet to feel truly proud of their country they had to be assured that they were not merely as good, but even better than 'abroad.' "[31]

Eventually, with the return of Russian self-confidence, it became axiomatic that Europe was effete, played out, and convulsed by insoluble social problems.[32] This view continues today: according to Aleksey Levinson of the Levada Center polling organization, polls asking Russians whether they are Europeans or not show constantly changing results. During the 1990s the majority wanted to be European. By 2017 the majority said they did not. In part, of course, the difference in poll results reflected unambiguous direction from the state aimed at stimulating nationalist feeling. But the Levada Center's director, Lev Gudkov, adds that the recent "propaganda-driven patriotic surge among Russian citizens goes hand in hand with the open and envious hostility toward the West. The collective consciousness always paints an ambivalent picture of the West."[33]

When Russian government or society has recognized the necessity of reform, be it in law, industry, the economy, or social relations, the West has been available as a model and a source of innovations. But every time the Russian government addresses the task of stabilizing the country, suppressing social unrest, or just holding on to power, and consequently turns more conservative or autocratic, the West is portrayed instead as a danger and a menace, and a force working to sabotage Russian achievements.[34] Another persistent driver for the rejection of Europe is the perception that even when it is a positive role model for modernization, Europe is a negative one in terms of culture and values—and seeks constantly to impose its culture and values on Russia. Foreign Minister Sergey Lavrov has compared this tendency unfavorably with the country's centuries-long domination by the Mongols, who, he argues, allowed Russians to retain their customs, language, and religion.[35] And yet the submission and regular deliveries of tribute that the Mongols demanded, together with the rise in fortunes of those Muscovite princes who allied themselves with them, shaped Russian history more profoundly than any influence from the distant West ever has.

The conflict between these irreconcilable views of Europe, and hence of Russia's place in it, reinforces Russians' views of their country's own exceptionalism and singularity.[36] Deciding that it is neither of the West nor of the East leads to a compromise conclusion of uniqueness.[37] The other available approach is to reject compromise and attempt to resolve the issue of whether Russia is Western or not by simply declaring that it is. Repeatedly throughout history, Russia's rulers have attempted at times to demonstrate to themselves or their audience that Russia is an integral part of Europe. In President Putin's annual address to the Federal Assembly of the Russian Federation in 2005, he suggested that Russia was "a major European power" that had

> for three centuries . . . together with the other European nations passed hand in hand through the reforms of the Enlightenment, the difficulties of emerging parliamentarianism, municipal and judiciary branches, and the establishment of similar legal systems. Step by step, we moved together toward recognizing and extending human rights, toward universal and equal suffrage, toward understanding the need to look after the weak and the impoverished, toward women's emancipation, and other social gains. I repeat—we did this together, sometimes behind and sometimes ahead of European standards.[38]

A World Apart 11

And yet few outside Russia would recognize this description of Russian history or of Russia's relationship with Europe, any more than two and a half centuries earlier they recognized Catherine the Great's categorical assertion, with far less attempt at justification, that "Russia is a European country."[39] Instead it is the persistent desire throughout history to "prove" that Russians are Europeans that is most telling. If it were true, it would not need to be proved.

In any case, just over a year after Putin's appeal to commonality with Europe, increasing frustration and alarm at Western behavior had already led Russia to begin to seek another path.[40] In fact, this same cycle of aspiring to and then rejecting the West had already played out under the previous president, Boris Yeltsin, at the very start of the post-Soviet period. While serving as foreign minister of the Russian Socialist Federative Soviet Republic (the Soviet predecessor of the Russian Federation), Andrey Kozyrev suggested that Russia should join the developed countries of the West, and structure Russian foreign policy and diplomacy in such a way as to seek "entry into the world community."[41] The implication that Russia itself was a backward, undeveloped supplicant was hard to swallow and incompatible with the conflicting notion that Russia as a historical great power automatically deserved respect. Consequently, the idea of a Russian "return to civilization" quickly fell out of favor in the debate over the state's relationship with Europe. This was evident as early as January 1993, when Yeltsin remarked that while "Russia's independent foreign policy started with the West," it was now time to "build relations with any country, be it from the West or East, Europe, or Asia."[42]

The issue of respect is a recurring obstacle to Russia's reaching mutual understanding with the West. While it is true that many Russians perceive not only that Western countries boast higher standards of living and opportunities for social mobility but also that life and social order in those countries are organized more humanely and justly than in Russia, this observation in itself is not sufficient to seek to be one of them.[43] The admiration must be returned, and due homage must be paid to the image of a mighty Russia. As André Gide observed in the 1930s: "What really interests them is to know whether we admire them enough. What they are afraid of is that we should be ill-informed as to their merits. What they want from us is not information but praise."[44] "Do you respect me?" is one of the classic existential Russian questions, traditionally associated with advanced stages of vodka consumption; but it is consistently addressed en masse to the West as well as individually to drinking partners. Time and again, Russia takes offense when its feelings are not requited, and retreats into contemplation of its own unique destiny and the comfort of doctrines like Eurasianism, with its implicit rejection of the West.[45]

At the same time, "respect" is another term with far more implications in Russian than its simple translation into English suggests. Westerners might, for example, hold Russia in high esteem for its cultural achievements; but this has little in common with what the Russian state envisages when it makes its demands for respect. Instead, Russia equates respect with fear, and expression of respect by other nations with ensuring that Russia is consulted—and deferred to—on all major aspects of international affairs. Failure to display this deference prompts another reaction from Russia, one that is more dangerous than simple rejection of the West: it fosters the instinct to insist on Russia's own perceived status as a great power, and to seek to assert this status in confrontation with the West.

TWO

Great Power and Empire

The View from 1914

We have two complaints against the West; firstly that you have not given us the aid that was promised, secondly that you do not accord us the respect due to a Great Power.

—RUSSIAN ACADEMICIAN, *speaking in the United Kingdom, 1994*[1]

A crucial element of Russia's self-perception that determines how it interacts with the outside world is an obsessive belief in its right to be treated not as a "normal country" but as one of the two or three most important nations in the world. Western analysts may point out that Russia is far from being a leading nation when judged by its relatively small GDP, its underdeveloped economy, and the limited focus of its influence in the world. This is true, but it is not necessarily the prism through which state power is viewed by the Russian leadership, including President Putin and those whose advice he trusts.

Mark Galeotti, a leading scholar of Russian power politics, summarizes Russia's understanding of great-power status according to three key criteria: possession of a buffer zone of dominions between the great power itself and its adversaries, a voice (in effect meaning a veto) that carries globally, and a get-out clause—an exemption from the rules that ordinarily govern interstate behavior.[2] In fact, among many persistent features of the Russian worldview over centuries, the concept of Russia as a state with greater rights than others has remained one of the most constant.³ In this as in many other things, Russia is far from unique—plenty of other nations have convinced themselves of their special destiny and birthright of leadership. But incomprehension between Moscow and the West stems from the two very different ways in which their concept of what it means to be a leading nation developed in the twentieth century. In effect, while the West, and in particular Western Europe, moved on to a postnationalist view of international relations, Russia retained the 1914 understanding of itself as a great power. Very soon after the end of the Soviet Union it became clear that these imperial great-power attitudes had been preserved through seventy years of communism, bolstered by the special role of the Russian Soviet Federative Socialist Republic (RSFSR) in the USSR, and of the USSR itself in the Eastern bloc, and were now reemerging into a changed world and reasserting themselves.⁴ As Russia rediscovered and embraced its czarist past, it also embraced the older and deeper national tradition of imperial rule over its neighbors, to the extent that the idea of its being a great power was almost the only stable element in Russia's political identity in the immediate post-Soviet years.⁵ The result has been to emphasize still further that although the westernmost areas of Russia may in formal geographic terms be a part of Europe, in terms of attitude and worldview the country as a whole stands very much apart *from* Europe.

Moscow looks to great-power status not only as a source of pride but also as a potential guarantee of security in a world that is fundamentally threatening and challenging from Russia's point of view. Political analyst and former military intelligence officer Dmitriy Trenin echoes President Putin when he says that "Russia is nothing if not a great power." But he goes on to explain that Russia views this assertiveness as essential for its security: "In other words, no one will step forward and protect Russia the way the United States [protects] so many other great countries that depend on the United States for existential issues. Russia depends on itself for existential issues."⁶ Yet another assumption underlying the belief of ordinary Russians in their country's special status, and one that is even less apparent in the West, is that Russia and its peoples have repeatedly suffered on behalf of others and therefore are owed recognition and a debt of gratitude. The idea that Russia has saved Europe at great cost to itself dates back to invasions from the east, during which, according to Aleksandr Pushkin, "the barbarians did not dare to leave an enslaved Rus behind their lines and returned to their Eastern steppes. The developing Enlightenment was saved by a ravaged and dying Russia."[7] But most recently in modern Russian historical consciousness it refers to World War II. In all instances the suffering of the Russian people has been tragic and undeniable, but the fact that so much of it has been self-inflicted rather than at the hands of foreign invaders does not in any way dilute the belief that it confers a kind of moral superiority and an enduring right to deference from other nations.[8]

The net result is that the notion of great-power status and superiority among nations is a key component of Russian national identity, and one that at present it appears impossible to relinquish. The depth and tenacity of this belief were evidenced by the visceral response by President Putin and the Russian political establishment to Barack Obama's 2014 characterization of Russia as a "regional power" acting out of weakness.[9] But how Russia goes about convincing others of its privileged status is a continuing challenge in an era when the traditional metric, military power, is no longer considered an attribute of greatness in many of the countries it is seeking to convince. In the twenty-first century even possession of nuclear weapons, formerly an attribute of a superpower and one still cherished by Russia, is now just as likely to indicate status as a rogue state. Consequently, Russia has found alternative means of meeting its perceived needs.

During the period of its greatest weakness in the late 1990s and early 2000s, before increased revenues from rising oil prices fed through into enhanced levers of international power, Russia sought to boost the perception of its status in the world through relatively risk-free, "soft" actions. It used a number of supranational organizations to both support and exercise its claim to great-power status. The Commonwealth of Independent States (CIS), whether or not it was an abortive attempt to resurrect the Soviet Union, in some ways constituted a continuation of the Russian Empire: Russian border policy in the 1990s gave only the CIS's external perimeter the full status of an international border, the rest being regarded as internal administrative boundaries.[10] The CIS also served as a mechanism through which Western states could be invited or persuaded to recognize the Russian Federation's special position, and other member states as Moscow's privileged zone of interest.[11] Leadership of the Collective Security Treaty Organization (CSTO) and the creation of assorted other international structures in the former Soviet space—eventually culminating in the aim of forming a Eurasian union—fell within this category.[12] Similarly, during this period Putin devoted time and energy to summits with the leaders of the BRICS (Brazil, Russia, India, China, and South Africa), even though it steadily became apparent that these countries had very different interests and were not going to form an alliance. Since 2014, the BRICS project has been increasingly superfluous to Russia's needs and has accordingly been allotted a much lower priority.

In previous decades the USSR had employed similar means of legitimation. The Council for Mutual Economic Assistance (COMECON) was in part designed to lessen resistance to economic and other plans devised in Moscow, since Prague, Budapest, or Warsaw could more readily accept Soviet instructions if they came through a notionally multilateral organization than if they were issued direct from Moscow. The Warsaw Pact filled a similar role in the military domain. Both are replicated today in the organizations established by Russia on the territory of the former Soviet Union, serving much the same purpose: the CSTO is the new but much-reduced Warsaw Pact, and the Eurasian Economic Union (EEU) fills the role of COMECON. According to Russian academic Tatiana Stanovaya, the intent of these and other integrationist projects is "maintaining the influence of Russia on the post-Soviet space not by 'ruling', but by forming a single strategically united space for issues of defence policy, trade and the economy. In the same way the US and EU have closely aligned strategic interests, but this does not mean that the US 'rules' Europe."[13] Nevertheless, the defining element of these projects is the central and driving role of Russia, and its instrumentalization of them is intended to bolster its own security and status.

A related vital facet of Russia's status anxiety is the unshakable belief that Russia matters and is relevant—everywhere, at all times, and under all circumstances. The actual condition or strength of Russia at any given time does not have any bearing on this sense of entitlement. As described by Henry Kissinger, "When it was strong, Russia conducted itself with the domineering certainty of a superior power and insisted on formal shows of deference to its status. When it was weak, it masked its vulnerability through brooding invocations of vast inner reserves of strength. In either case, it was a special challenge for Western capitals used to dealing with a somewhat more genteel style."[14]

In fact, Moscow's changing fortunes through history mean that the presumption of Russia's centrality has had to be flexible and agile, shifting at times between leadership of Orthodox civilization, of the Slavic world, of global communism, or now of the post-liberal order.[15] Beyond Russia's neighborhood and the Slavic lands, it is vital to this belief that Russia should be seen not only as a ubiquitous power in regional systems across the world, but also as an indispensable counterpart in international affairs whose interests have to be taken into account even when they are purely obstructive. The urge to demonstrate Russia's centrality to world dealings whether or not this has any basis in reality leads to bizarre fictions, such as editing President Putin into images from the July 2017 G-20 meeting to show him as the central figure.[16] In this view, everything anywhere is all about Russia, up to and including transient Western consumer fads like Pokémon Go[17] and fidget spinners.[18] As put by Jeffrey Mankoff, a leading analyst of Russian foreign policy, "The continued centrality of the United States to Russian foreign policy thinking can make it difficult for Russians to understand that the United States no longer makes policy decisions solely on the basis of Moscow's reaction."[19] Even Western-leaning Russian academics can assume that the admiration is mutual and that Russia features just as prominently in the West's domestic rhetoric as the West does in Russia's.[20]

The result is the assumption of Russian involvement in problems where other states may not necessarily perceive any relevance to Moscow at all. Foreign policy analyst Dmitriy Suslov notes that "Russia's objection to US involvement in Syria was the same as its objection to bombing Serbia—that Russia was not consulted."[21] In both cases, the United States would have been hard put to find any possible reason why it should be. However, Russia's interventions in Ukraine and Syria have demonstrated clearly that it is to some extent able, and definitely willing, to mount military operations both in its immediate neighborhood and farther afield. As a result, even if Russia has not achieved widespread recognition of its pretensions to leading-power status, it has at least ensured that others are paying it attention and are wary of its reactions. This is not the first time that Russia's claims to special status were not taken seriously in the West until the country became militarily strong enough to assert them—at which point they became a genuine concern. Tibor Szamuely in 1974 described the Russian government's perennial pretensions to the leading place among the nations of the world. Already in the reign of Ivan the Terrible the incipient national megalomania had reached a stage where not only the monarchs of Poland, Sweden, England and France, but even the German Emperor were, one by one, declared unfit to be treated as equals by the ruler of Muscovy. . . . It should be noted that these delusions of grandeur, coinciding, as they did, with the nadir of Russian fortunes in the field, caused more amusement than annoyance among the European Courts. . . . However, with the growth of Russia's military might, her sweeping claims to worldwide moral and political leadership became a source of constant anxiety.[22]

Threats and Bluster

Look at me! Don't you look away from me! Why are you looking away? . . . Don't you dare insult Russia again.
— RUSSIAN DEPUTY ENVOY TO THE UNITED NATIONS, *April 2017*[23]

Frustration over not earning respect, or indeed an audience, through other means provides at least part of the explanation for Moscow's bellicose rhetoric even during periods when the West considers that relations are stable, and is hence repeatedly taken by surprise. Threatening language from Moscow, as exemplified in President Putin's extended paean to advanced nuclear weapons systems in his March 1, 2018, address to the nation, is often considered a recent development; in fact, a constant feature of the post-Soviet period has been what was described in 1999 as "sporadic paroxysms of belligerent anti-Western rhetoric, with the illusory hope of making 'them' respect Russia."[24]

In 2019, Russia's military threats are taken more seriously after a decade of Moscow pouring money into reorganizing and upgrading its armed forces.[25] Military power may be the only area of state influence where Russia's strength is currently growing—but this is a less uncomfortable position than it would be for Western powers, since military power is how Russia defines strength as a state. In another example of attitudes frozen in 1914 and preserved to defrost in 1991, leaving the rest of Europe bemused, despite superficial adjustments to the language of national security documentation Russia never ceased to see its national security primarily in military terms.[26] Military security is the only aspect that is regarded as indispensable.[27] As a result, the armed forces are not only stronger but also more influential today than at any time since the end of the Soviet Union. Senior Russian military officers may like to joke that "we may not have a Foreign Ministry with a defense policy, but we definitely have a General Staff with a foreign policy;" but since the establishment of the National Defense Control Center, a mechanism for all government ministries coming under the command of that same General Staff in time of crisis, they are only half joking.

The result of this attitude, now that funding is available to enable it, is an overall renewed militarism in Russian society.[28] The armed forces are enjoying unprecedented prestige, popularity, and salaries. Russian children can, if desired, start military training in kindergarten.[29] The military is there to be used, and used for offensive purposes: if Russian troops present in a given area are intended only for defense, for Russia this counts as the area being "demilitarized."[30] And according to a Russian foreign policy forecast, it is "logical to regard the use of military power by Russia as a tool of coercion"; furthermore, and perhaps counterintuitively for a Western readership, "limited use of military tools by Russia for political purposes makes its behaviour more predictable."[31]

This phenomenon is linked to an element of Russian social interaction that carries through into international relations: namely, a prevalent lack of understanding that respect can be earned in any way other than by making threats and demonstrating brute force. "Respect" is one of Russia's fundamental demands from the rest of the world. But so little of what Russia does earns it respect anywhere except at home. This paradox cannot be resolved, because to do so would involve breaking the traditional Russian equation of respect with fear. Hence the message delivered by threats and bluster is ordinarily received, but not necessarily understood, and achieves the opposite effect to that intended. It may produce apprehension at the likelihood of Russian military adventurism, but unlike in Russia, in contemporary European terms fear does *not* equate to respect.[32] And this cycle is self-perpetuating: as veteran observer of Russia Fiona Hill points out, "Western leaders habitually completely miss the core message that Putin is trying to transmit. This frustrates Putin and causes him to think that he has to deliver the message again; but even more forcefully—or even forcibly, by backing up his words with military action. In doing so, he merely alienates his interlocutors in the West even more."[33]

Western societies are baffled still further by the confusing and contradictory nature of Russian threats. Russia is quite content to assure its neighbors that it poses no threat and simultaneously make bombastic boasts of the power of Russian armaments to destroy them.[34] An authoritative Russian foreign policy forecast can place descriptions of Russia preparing for war alongside complaints of "paranoia" by Western nations, with no apparent recognition of the irony: "Russia openly, and notably at the top level, welcomes the strengthening of its (national) military might and the demonstration of it. But through this type of coercion the Kremlin has at the same time revived paranoid, phantom fears among its neighbours and amplified the Western distrust toward Russia."[35]

In a way, this inherent contradiction is nothing new. As described by scholar of strategy and military culture Dima Adamsky:

> Soviet foreign and defense policy, in rhetoric and in action, often expressed a puzzling combination of contradictory attitudes. In frames of the security context, scholars argue, in Russian strategic mentality "both an inferiority complex and a superiority complex can be simultaneously on display: defensiveness bordering on paranoia, on the one hand, combined with assertiveness bordering on pugnacity, on the other." The Soviet mentality saw no contradiction in combining a very aggressive military strategy with pursuit of peaceful political aims and accepted this ambiguity without intellectual embarrassment.[36]

Russia's current leadership appears more comfortable with these apparently conflicting approaches than its Western counterparts. An assessment of Russian security thinking published in 2009 noted: "Many who have reached the top in Russia are not only accustomed to dealing with contradictions, but chaos. To the rationalist mindset, chaos makes purposeful activity impossible; to the Leninist mindset which Russia's *siloviki* have inherited, chaos is merely a medium for realising one's objectives."[37]

Confrontational approaches by Russia, even when considered entirely inappropriate by the other side, serve a clear purpose. As put by U.S. academic Kimberly Marten, "Russian diplomats sometimes use angry tirades and insults as negotiating tactics. . . . Being confrontational [is] a way to test a partner and look for psychological weaknesses or cracks in the opposing team's unity that could be exploited."[38] An unusually public example of this occurred at the UN Security Council in April 2017, when Russia's deputy permanent representative Vladimir Safronkov fell back on the language of street brawls to insult other members—behavior later described by the Kremlin as entirely normal.[39] But on occasion, threats from Moscow not only have a specific and clearly discernible objective but can be directly counterproductive, achieving the exact opposite result. For example, Russia has failed to understand that repeated direct threats against Finland and Sweden, warning of the consequences in military terms if these two states join NATO, entirely defeat their purpose because they only serve to demonstrate how NATO membership is essential for protection for as long as Russia is incapable of the normal good-neighborly relations typical of the rest of Europe in the twenty-first century. When the Swedish government ruled out an application for NATO membership in the foreseeable future[40] but nevertheless was directly threatened by Russia days later to reinforce the point,[41] Russia demonstrated only that it had once again misjudged its audience: the result was that shortly afterward, support for NATO membership in Sweden for the first time outweighed opposition.[42]

Proceeding from their own views of international security, the United States and other Western powers assumed by default that Russia would recognize that it was not under threat, and consequently would learn to live with its vulnerabilities—or at least find ways of dealing with them that did not threaten its neighbors.[43] But this is not compatible with Russian views of national security, summarized in the so-called "security dilemma" and complaints by Foreign Minister Lavrov against the West that "strengthening one's own security [comes] at the expense of the security of others."[44] The practical effect of this approach means that Russia feels secure only when all others are at risk. The post–Cold War enlargement of NATO is often blamed as a significant and unprecedented factor in aggravating Russia; but this view overlooks that any efforts by Western nations to protect themselves are denounced as aggressive by an aggrieved Moscow—including the very signing of the explicitly defensive North Atlantic Treaty even before any practical steps at setting up NATO as a defensive alliance were taken.[45]

Cooperation and Disruption

> I cannot comprehend why Western experts who have spent so much time studying Russia fail to detect this genetic trait of Russian political mentality: the more the West calls for compromise, the more it provokes the assertiveness of the Russian System.
>
> —LILIA SHEVTSOVA, *2016*[46]

The foundering of hopes for a new partnership between Russia and the West at the end of the Cold War began a repetitive cycle of attempted cooperation with Russia followed by disappointment.[47] Offers of cooperation are severely challenged by an underlying Russian assessment that peaceful cooperation for the common good is not a normal and natural state of affairs. In his famous "Long Telegram," the U.S. diplomat George Kennan noted that Russian leaders "have learned to seek security only in patient but deadly struggle for total destruction of rival power, never in compacts and compromises with it."[48] Henry Kissinger has observed how this runs counter to what is taken for granted in Europe:

> In the Westphalian concept of order, European statesmen came to identify security with a balance of power and with restraints on its exercise. In Russia's experience of history, restraints on power spelt catastrophe. . . . The Peace of Westphalia saw international order as an intricate balancing mechanism; the Russian view cast it as a perpetual contest of wills, with Russia extending its domain at each phase to the absolute limit of its material resources.[49]

This assumption is echoed in literature, where Russian visions of Utopia, far from being peaceful, were founded on "military victories, the incorporation of new territories, acquiring spheres of influence and eliminating geopolitical enemies."[50]

The essential precondition for working with Russia that is repeatedly forgotten when NATO seeks "partnership" is that cooperation for its own sake is of no interest to Moscow. Russia continues to interpret concessions as weakness and an invitation to demand more rather than to soften a stance. Reaching international agreement through compromise and cooperation that goes beyond direct self-interest is not in the spirit of Russian public diplomacy, and apparently not in President Putin's nature. Or, as put more succinctly by the distinguished Russia scholar James Sherr: "One good turn deserves another. Is not a Russian proverb."

In Western social interaction, cooperation and mutual assistance when required is entirely normal, even, under the right circumstances, between complete strangers, and furthermore it is generally assumed that public services work, even in countries where their level of efficiency appears intolerable to visitors from northern Europe or North America. In Russia, by contrast, there can be no assumption of cooperative behavior; instead, the assumption is that it has to be bought, earned, or forced, up to and including through bribing or coercing state officials to carry out the functions they are notionally paid to provide. Similarly, Western contracts are based on the presumption of honest dealing, both sides entering into the agreement in good faith with every intention of carrying out their obligations. Russian contracts, by contrast, are drawn up on the basis of a presumption of dishonesty, with sanctions specified for breaches of contract that are expected rather than exceptional.[51] The parallel in international relations is the Russian assumption that offers of collaboration or cooperation for its own sake, with no evident direct furthering of Russian state or leadership interests, are part of a ploy or trap.

The instinctive rejection of cooperative solutions is reinforced by the belief that all great nations achieve security through the creation and assertion of raw power. In this view, one side's gain is automatically the other side's loss, and win-win situations are not envisaged.[52] The consequence is that Russia negotiates seriously only when it feels that the adversary holds some advantage and is willing to act on it.[53] In addition, concessions to find a mutually acceptable settlement are precluded by what security commentator Pavel Baev calls "the inescapable logic of confrontation according to which every de-escalatory move amounts to giving up to Western pressure."[54]

Russia's belief that the insecurity of others makes Russia itself more secure depends on the dubious principle that there is only a finite amount of security in the world. But it also prompts Russia to engage in subversion and destabilization of states it perceives as adversaries, even if there is not necessarily a final objective in mind: since simply weakening them will in relative terms make Russia stronger.[55] In addition, it implies that to realize its aspirations to great-power status, Russia must necessarily diminish the power and status of competitors. Consequently, the return of Russia to the position of global influence and power it consistently craves is dependent on challenging the West in general and the United States in particular. According to veteran Russia-watcher Don Jensen, although Russia's anti-U.S., anti-Western attitude "has now broadened to anti-globalization, the inclination throughout is simply to disrupt and cause chaos."[56] During 2017, as part of the ongoing investigations into Russian attempts to influence the U.S. presidential elections the previous year, it emerged that the Kremlin had purchased targeted advertising on social media that focused on amplifying divisive social and political messages across the ideological spectrum, exploiting topics as diverse as LGBT and race issues, immigration, and gun rights.[57] In addition, Russia had used social media to organize divisive events in real life in the United States.[58] The approach of simply sowing or stoking discord in U.S. society is entirely consistent with previous practice during the Cold War. As observed by Edward Crankshaw in 1957, Moscow hoped that "by using every device and trick to disrupt the Western powers internally . . . a universal chaos will ensue from which they alone will profit. Certainly they are behaving as though they believed this."[59]

At times, acting as the disruptor can serve a secondary objective of achieving recognition for Russia, or the start of negotiations in which Russia can enjoy the status of being seen as an equal partner with the United States—if necessary, at the same time as it continues to function as the spoiler. When Russia demands everything, the West treats it as a success if Moscow is eventually satisfied with only half of everything. Russia can exploit this attitude by creating a destabilized situation in order to then offer the "solution"—as in the case of dangerous behavior risking collisions at sea and in the air, where the more appropriate solution than negotiations with Russia on new rules would be for Russia to abide by existing agreements and once more instruct its aircrew and seamen to conduct themselves professionally.[60] This is a typical example of Russia behaving egregiously and then demanding accommodations from others in order to restore relations—summed up in the words of President Putin: "We, as a people, say don't hold a grudge and we are ready to meet halfway, but that can't be a one-sided game."[61]

The desire to involve the United States in direct bilateral talks reveals the significance of Russia's insistence on being treated as an equal to the United

States. But Russia has previously often rejected offers of equality from the West because of its profoundly different understanding of the term. NATO treats Russia as an "equal partner" with NATO nations, including at the NATO-Russia Council, which it sees as an indicator that Russia's status as a necessary interlocutor is recognized. But when Russia asks for equality with NATO, it means with the organization as a whole—not with individual states such as Luxembourg. The failure of an EU offer of "equality" similarly resulted from a different failure of understanding the word. The "Four Common Spaces" initiative was intended to be an agreement of "equal partners." But the Russian interpretation of "equality" was that both Moscow and Brussels would make reciprocal concessions and compromises, rather than Russia alone modifying its standards, procedures, and rules to get closer to Europe.[62]

All these considerations together suggest that the 2009 "reset" in relations between the United States and Russia delivered entirely the wrong messages to Moscow. Despite the good intentions and firm policy basis of the reset, by implying equal status for Russia and normalizing relations with no conditions required of Moscow, the United States rewarded Russia for its conduct during the armed conflict with Georgia the year before. This provided strong grounds for Russia to believe, six years later when it was contemplating seizing Crimea, that there would be few adverse consequences.

The End of Empire, Postponed

> The search for a "lost kingdom" as a phenomenon of European history is hardly unique to Russia. . . . But a particular feature of the Russian story is that its search for the "lost kingdom," coupled with its longing for imperial expansion and great-power status, is still going on.
> —SERHII PLOKHY, 2017[63]

Whatever the state of its power or political fortunes, Moscow has always maintained a very expansive view of what constitutes Russian territory. From the earliest possible opportunity, Moscow claimed that "all Russian land of old," including the very tenuously related territory of Kievan Rus', had belonged to Russia since time immemorial. Russian leaders would describe adjacent territories as their *votchina,* or patrimony, asserting spurious claims by unspecified ancestors, and this same language was used to justify claims to Baltic and Finno-Ugric territories that were not even remotely related to the putative Kievan inheritance.[64] More recently, claims made by Russia within the context of the conflict with Ukraine have suggested similarly that "Russia did not just want to protect its own [borders] but also return 'the historic Russian territories,' "[65] no matter how spurious the claim to entitlement might be. This is not a principle that Russia would wish to see applied by anybody else; besides the impossibility of recognizing past territorial claims in the rest of Europe, it would also mean Russia renouncing Kaliningrad, Karelia, and other territories, including vast swaths of Siberia once China began to assert claims.

Where claims were not recognized, continued expansion by direct conquest or colonization has been Russia's default option since the foundation of the Muscovite state. Formerly, as now, this acquisition of new territory could be dressed up as essential for maintaining stability, a pretense scorned by Lev Tolstoy as "efforts to maintain the peace so dear to [the czar's] heart (efforts which express themselves in the seizing of other people's lands and in the strengthening of armies for the defence of those stolen lands)."[66] With this consistency of practice, driven by considerations of national security and national prestige that have also remained consistent over time, there is no reason to doubt that Moscow would have sought control over Eastern Europe in the post–World War II period even if there had been no Soviet regime.[67] This expansion, of course, no longer necessarily involves annexation, colonization, or even temporary occupation; Russia is content to exert control remotely, including organizing state capture without any military intervention at all.[68]

This attitude is related to the permanent and persistent belief throughout history that Russia's land borders present a critical vulnerability and that in order to protect itself, Russia must exert control far beyond them. This has direct and unfortunate consequences for Russia's European neighbors, including those that are allies of the United States. Russia demands a veto over security arrangements within its self-declared sphere of influence. But it asserts this right with no basis, as an absolutist demand for a substantial degree of control over some domestic and most major foreign policy decisions made by other countries.[69] According to Tatiana Stanovaya, "Putin is absolutely convinced that the West also operates according to the same logic: there is the US, and there are countries within the US zone of influence (Europe, Canada, Australia). Putin has been trying to insist that Russia should enjoy the same right."[70]

The result is a fundamental divergence of understanding between Russia and the West over the concept of a sovereign independent state. As explained by Alina Polyakova:

> The Kremlin does not believe that countries like Ukraine, other countries it considers in its sphere of influence, [and] the people in those countries have the right to determine their own future and the direction they want to head in democratically. . . . And of course countries like the United States and other Western countries think that the people of Ukraine, of Georgia, Moldova, et cetera, should have the right to determine their own path, wherever that may lead. . . . The idea of national sovereignty from a Russian point of view is completely different than what the idea of national sovereignty is from a Western point of view.[71]

The key difference in this respect is the Russian presumption that only great powers can be sovereign. Smaller, less powerful states like Ukraine or, say, the United Kingdom are simply objects of different degrees of influence wielded by states like Russia and the United States. And these tiers of sovereignty imply a differentiation of rights. Russia has consistently maintained that it has a right to limit the sovereignty of small nations in its periphery.[72] The result of this attitude for Ukraine has been summarized by Russian foreign policy expert Dmitriy Suslov: "Ukraine's internal politics were unacceptable to Russia. Russia has a role in establishing the status quo in Ukraine."[73] Putin's "Crimea Speech" in March 2014 asserted repeatedly in varying forms that Ukrainian "state stability and territorial integrity" were conditional on Russian interests,[74] and Russian state bodies are not averse to treating Ukrainian affairs as falling within their purview.[75] But Ukraine is just one example of how Russia defines its own security through the insecurity of its neighbors. This stance inevitably brings it into confrontation with Western states that view those neighbors as sovereign nations that in some cases are entitled to protection. In this context, the notion of peaceful cooperation in the marches of Europe is unlikely to appear viable to Russian security planners, should it even occur to them, without a dramatic adjustment in attitudes and assumptions. Given this basic incompatibility of views of security, argues former U.S. ambassador to NATO Robert Hunter, "it is unlikely that anything the West could have proposed would have made possible a workable similarity of interests between NATO and Russia, even if Vladimir Putin had not come to power."[76]

The idea of distance as deterrence might seem outdated. In an era when power is projected by cruise missiles launched from hundreds of kilometers away and covert preparations by Western nations for large-scale conflict are next to impossible, the physical proximity of a NATO border to St. Petersburg is of greatly reduced military significance. Nevertheless, Russia's attitude that domination over its neighbors is a security imperative has persisted unchanged, including through periods of Russian weakness and retreat.[77] On each such occasion, after an interval Russia has sought to reassert its dominion. The most recent interval, the 1990s, saw a proliferation of references to the phrase used by Prince Aleksandr Gorchakov, the nineteenth-century foreign minister, to describe Russia gathering its forces after a defeat in order once again to launch a drive for expansion: "La Russie ne boude pas; elle se recueille" ("Russia is not sulking, she is composing herself")—rendered in Russian for modern consumption as *"Rossiya sosredotachivayetsya"* ("Russia is concentrating" or "Russia is focusing").[78]

The rationale and claim to legitimacy for expansion may change over time, but the ambition to expand has remained consistent.[79] Despite a more recent perception that Russia became a danger only after the 1917 revolution, European powers in Russia's neighborhood were in no doubt as to the potential threat this posed for them as far back as the time of Peter the Great.[80] The events of 1917–18 in fact marked one of the periods of pause and even retreat that occurred when Russia did not have the power or resources to expand,[81] but after a period of postrevolutionary weakness and readjustment, Moscow resurrected the power of the Russian Empire in the form of the Soviet Union both by direct annexation of neighboring territories and by indirect governance of Eastern Europe, preserving it for several more decades until the USSR's eventual collapse. As such, the process of relinquishing pretensions to empire did not start for Russia at the end of the two world wars, as it had for the Ottoman and European empires, but only after the end of the Cold War.

Russia is not the only former colonial power to have complex relations with its former dominions in the wake of imperial retreat. However, even given its late start, it has not traveled as far along the path of postimperial normalization as countries like the United Kingdom, France, or Portugal had a quarter century after the end of empire. In part this is because these European countries, when they lost their overseas empires, suffered nothing like the loss of identity incurred by the breakup of Russia's "internal empire," and, in the case of the United Kingdom, its empire did not disappear overnight.[82] But it is also because Russia is a former imperial great power that has not yet accepted and internalized the important qualifier of "former."[83] Successful military adventurism both close to home and further afield prolongs this failure to readjust; for as long as interventions abroad, whether in Georgia, Crimea, or Syria, achieve the desired strategic effect at little cost, Russia will see little cause not to continue them.

However, the first military defeat would have far-reaching consequences. With its control of the information space at home, Russia can spin or explain away political reverses abroad, but not an unarguable military setback that calls into doubt either Russian military power itself or the ability to exercise it unchallenged. It follows that Russia can accept conflict where the stakes are as high as in Ukraine in 2014 or the risks as low as in Syria in 2015, but in other cases it would be wise to be cautious. To use the analogy of the United Kingdom again, Russia can enjoy any number of 1982 Falklands moments, but it cannot risk a single 1956 Suez moment without calling into question the entire basis of its aspiration to great-power status. Until that point comes, questioning whether Russia's assertive behavior against neighbors is right or wrong is, according to Ivan Kurilla, taboo: "Now most of the opposition figures want to refrain from discussing Crimea. The population were happy, so the Crimea question is postponed to after political reform when Russia is more democratic. . . . This is not a public discourse, not a discussion among even the opposition leaders."[84]

This approach constrains Russia's choices, since it is not acceptable to put forward policy options that give up on the goal of recognition as a major global player. It is axiomatic that Russia should be great.[85] The fact that this self-perception is not justifiable by any objective measures is irrelevant.[86] The day when Russia might view its imperial past as objectively as, say, Sweden, and build constructive relationships with its neighbors and former domains accordingly—or, in the words of Mark Galeotti, "when

Russia finally comes to terms with reality and learns to stop worrying and enjoy its second-rank status"[87]—seems at present fairly remote. Until that time, there is little in mainstream Russian political consciousness to curb Moscow's traditional restless instinct to expand the area over which it exerts control.

Excusing Russia

> Like it or not, we have to do a deal with the Russians which they see as protecting their interests.
> —SIR TONY BRENTON, *May 2017*[88]

Nevertheless, Russia has an admirable history of convincing some in the West that aggressive territorial expansion is in fact a defensive measure. This too is not a new phenomenon. When the Soviet Union was attacked by Germany in June 1941 it needed all the help and sympathy it could muster, but faced the handicap of widespread disapproval of its policy of overt aggression conducted against its neighbors in full collaboration with Hitler over the preceding two years. The simple explanation offered was that the USSR had seized Bessarabia, Northern Bukovina, half of Poland, the Baltic states, and parts of Finland only as a defensive measure against an anticipated attack from Germany, and the partnership in dividing Eastern Europe was in fact a far-sighted strategic preparation giving Russia defense in depth. Thereafter, even at the height of the Cold War, those who were willing to be convinced could comfort themselves with the notion that the Soviet acquisitions of 1939–40 "were all motivated by an almost desperate necessity for strengthening Russia's defenses against an anticipated attack sooner or later."[89]

This line of thinking affects the search for solutions to the present crisis over Ukraine. The argument runs that the West should respect Russia's interest in assuring itself of defense in depth beyond its borders, and consequently countries like Ukraine should endure subservience to the Kremlin for the sake of the greater good.[90] Denying the nations in between any say in their future is a key element of this approach: in the case of Ukraine, John Mearsheimer argues, "The United States and its allies should . . . aim to make it a neutral buffer between NATO and Russia, akin to Austria's position during the Cold War."[91] Mearsheimer is hardly alone: a neutral Ukraine is also the preferred solution for arch-realists like Zbigniew Brzezinski and Henry Kissinger.[92] Other analysts go further, seeking to impose neutrality on a wide range of countries, some of which are firmly established members of the Euro-Atlantic community or even of the EU. Michael O'Hanlon argues that "now is the time for Western nations to negotiate a new security architecture for neutral countries in eastern Europe to stabilize the region and reduce the risks of war with Russia"—graciously permitting that, under this new architecture, countries such as Sweden and Finland "could think of and describe themselves as Western states" if they wished.[93]

Both morality and practicality argue against this approach. To impose a foreign policy on a peaceful and unthreatening sovereign state in Europe would be an acceptable course of action to Russia but is hardly compatible with Western values. In addition, it ignores the potential disrupting factor of the population of the target country itself. Russia may say it wants to have its legitimate sphere of influence; but other countries may equally say they do not desire to come within it. As noted by Samuel Greene of the Russia Institute at King's College London: "Given Russia's demonstrated willingness to bring military force to bear, some may be tempted simply to cede the region, concluding that the costs of both supporting reform and containing Russia are too great for Europe to manage.... If the experience of the Euromaidan has taught policymakers anything, however, it should be that publics are ignored at our own peril."[94]

In practical terms, the history of Russian expansionism before, during, and after Soviet times argues that the resistance of the buffer states to Russian domination would be brief, and there would then once more be a line of confrontation between Russia and the West, once more bounding millions of free citizens who had previously chosen the West over Russia. Furthermore, even if the West were to surrender to moral bankruptcy and concede a sphere of influence to Russia, such a policy of appeasement has never served as a guarantee that more will not be demanded, since there are never specified limits to the extent of Russian ambition.

Even when Russian, or previously Soviet, action has provoked almost universal condemnation, the outrage has tended to be brief before the search for solutions to the latest crisis leads to strong pressure to disregard the incident and "move forward."[95] In 2008, Russia was censured for its conduct during the armed conflict with Georgia; but this was followed less than a year later by the U.S. "reset" and the return by Europe and NATO to "business as normal." The consequence can only have been to reduce the apparent risk to Russia of its subsequent seizure of Crimea and the beginning of an armed campaign in eastern Ukraine, since Moscow could reasonably have considered as part of its strategic calculations that these actions would similarly be swiftly forgiven and forgotten. But the 2009 U.S. reset is only one instance; there is no shortage of examples from the late twentieth century of Soviet military action against the peoples of Eastern Europe or further afield being followed by attempts to restore relations with Moscow.[96] The result, then as now, is invariably to encourage rather than deter Russian military adventurism.

In the case of Ukraine in particular, a range of Western academics and former officials have persistently argued that the West is as responsible as Russia for the crisis.[97] NATO enlargement is especially blamed for provoking Russia to defend its interests beyond its state borders. But this characterization of Russian security policy gives the entirely incorrect impression that Russian leaders lack any independent volition and that everything they do is simply a response to aggressive Western actions. In fact, Russia's tendency to behave aggressively toward its former Soviet neighbors long predates any steps by NATO to accept membership applications from Eastern Europe. The list of military interventions alone covers South Ossetia and Moldova (1992), Abkhazia (1993), and Tajikistan through the early 1990s, and when other forms of hostile state pressure are included, the roll call of former Soviet states that have fallen victim to Russian coercion is complete. In this context of persistent hostile action it has been described as "commendable . . . that Russian leaders made no attempt to foment violent unrest or full-fledged insurgency in Estonia or Latvia in the early 1990s"[98]—as though to do so would be normal and natural state behavior. In fact, during the 1990s Russia was perfectly capable of military intervention in its neighborhood without the excuse of NATO being anywhere nearby. In a similar way, a previous generation of revisionists blamed the onset of the Cold War on the United States rather than on Soviet expansionist ambitions, even though Moscow seized control in Eastern Europe without effective opposition during the period of Western postwar complacency and faith in good relations with the USSR.[99]

As part of the tendency to seek the roots of failure in the relationship between Russia and the West in the latter's capitals rather than in any fundamental contradiction, or in Russian behavior, Western experts as well as Russians have shown willingness to contort or invent facts in order to absolve Russia of guilt for offensive actions.[100] In this as in so much else, the present day is no different from previous centuries, when Astolphe de Custine noted how "foreigners who have described Russia have united with the Russians to deceive the world. Either Russia has as yet been described only by men whose position or character would not permit independence, or the most honest minds lose their freedom of judgment from the moment they enter Russia."[101] During the twentieth century, the repetition of the Soviet line came naturally to communist sympathizers, who enthusiastically promulgated propaganda every bit as blatantly false as the "fake news" disseminated by Moscow today.[102] The political motivation of furthering the aims of world communism has evaporated, but the mixture of those who repeat Russian disinformation out of cynicism and out of innocent and genuine conviction remains. In addition, as journalist David Satter argues, the tradition of sympathizers carrying Russia's messages to the West continues with the Valdai Discussion Club, where a select group of foreign academics and analysts are invited to mingle with senior Russian figures and hear Moscow's point of view at first hand: "Russian officials were unfailingly generous with their time and hospitality. . . . The participants, anxious not to offend their hosts for fear of not being invited back, engaged in self-censorship, as the Russian authorities knew they would. After the sessions, the participants in the 'club' returned to the West, where they often cited their firsthand contact with Russian leaders and parroted what they were told."[103]

This is an unfair generalization, as it ignores those who attend Valdai with their eyes open, as the best and only chance to observe the demeanor of the Russian leadership at close hand.[104] But in other cases it does undoubtedly work, lending weight and resonance to the arguments that Russia must be forgiven, excused, and tolerated, and—above all—that its aspiration to a sphere of unchallenged dominion in Europe is entirely defensive in nature. In 2016, the author was told by a prominent academic that he *knew* Russia had no aggressive designs on any other neighbors—because he had been told so by Putin and Lavrov while seated as a guest of honor in the front row at Valdai.

However unfashionable it may be in the West, realism as an approach to international relations is a guiding principle for Russia. As such, its application is an essential tool for viewing the world through Moscow's eyes, and assessing challenges and opportunities for Russia accordingly. The danger arises when realism is used as a euphemism for appeasement (or, in the case of the United States, isolationism). In short, understanding Russia should not tip over into excusing Russia.

THREE

Russia under Threat

Enmity by Default

[It is] in Russia's genes to be opposed, diametrically opposed, to the United States and Western democracies.

—FORMER U.S. DIRECTOR OF NATIONAL INTELLIGENCE JAMES CLAPPER, *June 2017*[1]

It is the first thing I always tell my subordinates: Europe hates us. Always has, and always will. It is in their genes.

—SENIOR RUSSIAN MILITARY OFFICER, *September 2016*[2]

Russia's recent foreign policy decisions have been characterized abroad as irrational and self-defeating. President Putin himself has been described by German chancellor Angela Merkel as inhabiting "a different world,"[3] and even some Russian commentators have suggested that he has departed to "a different reality."[4] Nevertheless, Russia's actions and reactions do follow a consistent internal logic. Most if not all of them in the last decade have a common foundation: restoring Russia's power, prestige, and influence in the world, and concurrently defending what Russia perceives to be its security needs, no matter how inexplicable that perception may be from outside the country. The necessary outcome of this aim is a need to constrain Western institutions in general and U.S. power in particular, including reducing the role of the United States in key regional security arrangements and the global security system as a whole. This includes reducing the perceived direct threat by the West to the Russian state and its ruling regime.

It is the nature of this threat perception that is especially hard for Western politicians and decision makers to comprehend and therefore adjust for. A defining feature of Russia's view of the world throughout history has been the assumption that foreign powers are plotting to invade—an extension of the presumption of hostile intent that guides everyday Russian personal and business interactions (see chapter 7). This assumption has, of course, occasionally been correct. Russia's repeated experience of devastating invasion has led to a profound sense of insecurity and has shaped national security perceptions to equate depth of territory held with security gained.

The preoccupation with simple physical security has been augmented by the persistent belief throughout its history that Russia's land borders constitute a critical vulnerability, and that the country must exert control far beyond them to protect itself. When Russia perceives itself as a besieged fortress, its lack of natural boundaries means this mental image resembles a besieged fortress with no walls. Edward Crankshaw, one of the first members of the British military mission to arrive in Moscow after the German invasion in 1941, graphically described the psychological effect:

> The vast bulk of Russia, the map so frightening to Western eyes, looks very different when you are sitting in the middle of it. Then you are conscious not of protective bulk but only of an extravagant and terrible length of highly vulnerable frontier.... To be in Moscow, as I was, when Hitler had sliced through that frontier and watch on the map the sinister black arrows marking the armoured spearheads of the German advance snaking ever closer, with no natural obstacles in their way, until they were actually beginning to curl round the city itself, was to understand something of the depth of the compulsion to push that frontier away, even if this made the land still harder to defend.[5]

The old quip that the only secure Russian border is one with a Russian soldier standing on both sides of it still provokes laughter, but it also represents a very real guiding principle for Russian national security preoccupations. The notion that border regions are by definition security challenges persists long after neighboring countries consider border issues to have been resolved. In another projection of Russia's own attitudes onto foreign states that are guided by entirely different motivations, leading Russian military thinkers cite fanciful territorial claims against Russia as a potential casus belli, concluding that "war can be triggered in this country's Western strategic area by, for example, territorial claims on Russia (its Kaliningrad and Pskov regions) by Western countries."[6] In short, a 2016 NATO study concludes, Russia sees "its neighbours not as potential Allies but as bridgeheads for potential foreign aggression, necessitating their subjugation or domination by whatever means available."[7]

As part of this, Russia sees its wealth—defined almost universally in terms of abundant natural resources or pure physical size—as a tempting prize for foreign powers to seize. Projection of Russian attitudes onto those powers in a form of mirroring makes it plausible for Russians to see their own country as presenting an attractive target for foreign intervention, with aims up to and including regime change, in order to gain control of these resources.[8] As expressed by former Russian envoy to NATO and now deputy prime minister Dmitriy Rogozin:

> Russia is an enormous country with a small population, we only have 140m people, it is not many, but it is the largest and richest country. Therefore we have to bear in mind that we should not have any illusions about our security. We need to be very physically strong and have brute physical force in order to protect our riches, because lots of people are trying to creep towards them."[9]

This perception was inevitably fueled by the U.S.-led invasion of Iraq in 2003 and the assumption that it was launched primarily to gain control of oil reserves. Four years later a Russian general explained to a NATO audience how his country's defensive preoccupations were driven by the realization that it is "dangerous to be gifted with natural resources when the US looks your way."[10]

Perceptions that Russia is under constant external threat are therefore internally consistent and are arguably evidence-based. But they also depend on a perception of Russia itself, and of foreign attitudes to it, that is wildly at odds with reality. Both the notion that Russia is an attractive target and the belief that there might be any desire to seize its resources have been fundamentally misguided for decades. Ronald Reagan noted in a private diary entry in 1983: "The Soviets are so defense minded, so paranoid about being attacked . . . no one here has any intention of doing anything like that. What the hell have they got that anyone would want?"[11] In fact, any real attack against Russia would be directly counterproductive for Western security interests. The former director of the FSB and now long-term secretary of Russia's Security Council, Nikolay Patrushev, explained in 2007 that Western intelligence agencies were "nurturing plans aimed at dismembering Russia."[12] This suggestion was startling to Western audiences: far from viewing instability in Russia as a desirable outcome, they saw it instead as a real and significant danger.[13]

Western analysts continue to debate whether this perception of external threat reflects a genuine belief among the Russian leadership or is a fabrication maintained for domestic political purposes. In fact, it can be neither or both. A substantial body of Western opinion holds that the portrayal of fictitious enemies is one of the few ways in which the Putin leadership maintains its support and legitimacy. In this respect, little has changed since Soviet times, when George Kennan observed: "A hostile international environment is the breath of life for [the] prevailing internal system in this country. . . . We are faced here with a tremendous vested interest dedicated to [the] proposition that Russia is a country walking a dangerous path among implacable enemies."[14]

But in the deepening state of confrontation between Russia and the West after 2014, the question of whether the perception of threat is real or invented becomes less and less significant. When Russia's public media output is focused so intently on preparing the population for conflict, and its armed forces and government are practicing so intensively for prevailing in it, the underlying drivers of this behavior become of more academic than practical interest; if there was ever a time when it was possible to adjust the trajectory of Russian leadership thinking on this issue, it has probably passed.

Underpinning this belief system is the unchanging assumption that other states are inherently adversarial, and consequently that world politics must be seen in terms of confrontation with a priori enemies.[15] During the Soviet period, an additional layer of suspicion was provided by recognition that communist rule needed to be defended despite its fundamental illegitimacy; the USSR was characterized by Crankshaw as "an imperial power run by men who got where they are by conspiracy and still think of the world in terms of a gigantic counter-conspiracy."[16] But Russian military and political leaders apply this assumption universally, even during periods such as the present day when the prospect of foreign attack is impossibly remote. Once world events are viewed through this distorting lens, the rationale of Russia's own actions in response comes into focus.

Like many other preconceptions driving Moscow's policy, the presumption of hostile intent by the West did not disappear during the period when the West considered relations were rosy. And this presumption was not solely imposed by the leadership. In 1999 Alexei Arbatov pointed out that "among a far wider range of Russians it is automatically assumed that the United States and its allies exploit Russia's weakness and abundant troubles to advance their own interests."[17] Predictions of impending conflict with the West long predate the post-2014 intensification of war rhetoric in Russian national media as a staple of alarmist commentary, as shown by this example from 2009:

> We do not want a war, but a war it will be. When? Presumably in 2010–2012. With whom? Presumably with everyone out there. Why? Because Russia will find itself in the possession of huge territory and colossal resources and absolutely unable to defend itself. Who are the foremost potential enemies? The United States and China. These two world powers aspire for global leadership, and each will need Russian riches to draw on in the forthcoming conflict.[18]

Today, polls suggest almost a quarter of Russians believe that "the country is surrounded by enemies," and two-thirds single out the United States as an enemy of Russia.[19]

The threat may also be delivered indirectly. Russia sees regional conflict as part of the overall confrontation between itself and the West; in this picture, Ukraine and other states on Russia's periphery are merely the theater of operations. This is the assumption that lies behind Putin's assertion that resistance to Russia in Ukraine is led by "a foreign legion, in this particular case, a NATO foreign legion, which is not pursuing Ukraine's national interests of course. They have completely different goals, related to achieving their geopolitical aim of containing Russia, and this is absolutely not in the Ukrainian people's national interests."[20] But the West is also described as plotting constantly to launch destabilization operations in Central Asia and hence target Russia's "soft underbelly."[21]

This assumption of impending conflict is reflected in Russia's strategic planning documentation. On December 31, 2015, the Russian Federation adopted a new National Security Strategy, a guiding document for how the Russian state protects itself, replacing the previous one published in 2009.[22] The new version sets a confident and assertive tone, still seeking to increase Russia's international influence and further challenge U.S. dominance in international affairs, but it is founded on the inevitability of war.[23] Provision for Russia's security is considered far more satisfactory than in previous iterations of the document, and Russia is considered to have the wherewithal to cope with both external and internal threats (although the internal ones are considered by default to be fomented by the West, led by the United States). Nevertheless, according to one detailed analysis, the Strategy reflects a worldview that exaggerates threats, underestimates the value of cooperation, treats confrontation as inevitable rather than contingent, and implies that the Kremlin will continue to rely predominantly on military power to assert itself and maintain its perceived privileged status.[24]

Regime Change and "Color Revolutions"

Unfortunately, our Western partners, having divided the USSR's geopolitical legacy, were certain of their own incontestable righteousness, having declared themselves the victors of the Cold War. They started to openly interfere in the sovereign affairs of countries and to export democracy in the same way as in its time the Soviet leadership tried to export the Socialist revolution to the whole world.

—VLADIMIR PUTIN, *October 2017*[25]

The nature of the perceived threat to Russia is not limited to military invasion. Throughout imperial Russian, Soviet Russian, and then post-Soviet Russian history, the West has in addition always been seen as a destabilizing social and cultural force that must be resisted.[26] This notion is hard to challenge, given fundamental Russian assumptions regarding relations between states: these assumptions determine that Western actions appear threatening to Moscow even when their intent is entirely innocent or defensive. Another recurring theme throughout the entire history of Russian official behavior is that, as a long-serving Russian correspondent for a British newspaper complained in 1906, "the foreigner, however well disposed, is inevitably suspected."[27] Seventy years earlier, Astolphe de Custine had similarly noted: "The diplomatic corps and Westerners in general have always been considered by this government, with its Byzantine spirit, and by Russia as a whole, as malevolent and jealous spies."[28]

More recent practical examples illustrate this suspicion. Any Western interest in the Arctic region—even scientific or academic, rather than military or commercial—is construed as an attempt to challenge or constrain Russia.[29] The EU's Eastern Partnership program too was perceived as a signal to Moscow that the West intended to exert influence in Russia's natural domain (see chapter 1). Actions that have nothing to do with Russia are seen as hostile because in Moscow, the notion that they could be conceived and planned without taking Russia into account is difficult to grasp, or, if grasped, is considered deeply insulting. In the absence of any rational—to Russia—explanation for EU interest in Russia's neighborhood, or U.S. interest in Ukraine, the only remaining explanation is hostile intent toward Russia—and Russia acts on this understanding.

Over the last thirty years, Soviet and Russian leaders have begun their tenure hoping for close cooperation with the West, then become disillusioned. This applies equally to Gorbachev, to Yeltsin, and to Putin. In Putin's view, "Our biggest mistake was that we trusted you too much. You interpreted our trust as weakness and you exploited that."[30] Yet the same process of disillusionment affects Western leaders, many of whom have entered office with the ambition of improving relations with Russia, only to see this ambition frustrated. On each side, this initial optimism is based on an assumption (or hope) that the other will understand and accommodate the opposing worldview and strategic priorities. But since the end of the Cold War this has not happened. Instead, relations between Russia and the West have resumed their cyclical nature, where high intentions founder on incompatible strategic priorities and a confrontation ensues, followed by a reset and then another deterioration. Notably, this cycle has considerably greater impact in Moscow than in European and North American capitals with their significantly more limited institutional memory.[31] One crucial outcome is a reinforcement of the already existing Russian suspicion that the West is not to be trusted and that its assurances of good-neighborliness are entirely false. And when the United States, the EU, and NATO protest that they do not have designs on Russia, this only deepens Russian suspicions that they are deceitful and practice double standards.

This perception of double standards extends to a presumed desire to destabilize Russia in order to topple its leadership, either by force or by stealth. The fear that the West is considering bringing about regime change in Russia appears deep-rooted among a broad sector of the Russian security elite—even though there is little doubt that uncontrolled or chaotic regime change in Russia would be directly contrary to Western interests.[32] Foreign Minister Sergey Lavrov has explained that "the West is making clear it does not want to force Russia to change policy but wants to secure regime change" by using sanctions to "destroy the economy and cause public protests."[33] This fear, too, is logical when viewed in the context of late Soviet history. Former Russian minister of the economy Yegor Gaidar traced the timeline of the collapse of the Soviet Union to September 13, 1985, when Saudi Arabia decided to increase oil production in order to abandon price protection.[34] The consequent collapse in oil prices fatally undermined the Soviet economy. In the context of economic challenges to Russia as a result of the less dramatic, but still significant, fall in oil prices from mid-2014 on, this connection cannot be far from the minds of Putin and his advisers.

An important underlying factor that drives alarm at the prospect of foreign intervention is the assessment that even if unsuccessful, intervention disrupts stable systems and creates dangerous disorder. Russian leadership statements consistently express fear of instability and "the accumulation of elements of chaos and anarchy in world affairs."[35] Alarm at the prospect of destabilization instigated from abroad is augmented and reinforced by Russia's collective, and Putin's personal, memory of catastrophic upheaval during the twentieth century. The state failures of 1917 and 1991 and recent memories of the political and economic disintegration of the early 1990s contribute to fears of external attacks seeking to compromise the stability of Russia's sovereignty. According to Lavrov, Russia's history has "enough revolutions" to provide a cautionary example because they always involve bloodshed and significant retardation of the country's development.[36] It has been argued that this fear of chaos strongly influences President Putin's attitudes "because for him, just like other Russian politicians of his generation, the central event of his life was the disintegration and collapse of the USSR."[37]

When this collapse is viewed through a conspiratorial lens and assumed to be the work of foreign powers plotting against Russia, it is easier to understand a wide range of current Russian measures that are based on suspicion of foreigners. One example is the gradually tightening restrictions on foreign travel, reminiscent of Soviet or indeed czarist times, in addition to specific measures intended to limit the contact of state officials with foreigners or foreign ideas by preventing them from traveling abroad.[38] This notion also lies behind the deep suspicion and hostility shown toward the persistent efforts by Western nations to foster democratic instincts in Russia and its neighbors, including by means of direct support of nongovernmental organizations (NGOs)—described by Putin as "jackals" and "foreign agents." But the strongest contributing factor in support of Russia's suspicion of Western intent comes in the form of the trend of "color revolutions"—a pattern of regime changes with the involvement, support, encouragement, or simply approval of Western powers.

"Color revolution" is an elastic concept. In Russian usage, it can be broad enough to include the changes of government in Georgia in 2003, Ukraine in 2004, and Kyrgyzstan in 2005, and attempts at the same in Uzbekistan in 2005, Belarus in 2006, and Armenia in 2008. Some Russian lists also include the removal of Slobodan Milošević in Serbia in 2000, the "Cedar Revolution" in Lebanon in 2005, and violent election protests in Moldova in 2009. Recent anti-Western media programming in Russia has reached further back into history in the search for examples, including pointing to the 1956 uprising in Hungary as the first color revolution.[39] This impressive list, in the Russian view, has one common denominator: the aim of illegal (but legitimized with Western support) replacement of unpopular leaders with regimes that were more amenable to the West, both because of their declared commitments to build liberal democratic states on the Western model and, in the European context, because of their aspiration for NATO membership and for economic links with the EU as an alternative to cooperation with Russia.

Instances of Western military intervention since Kosovo also fit the pattern, with the invasion of Iraq in 2003 and air operations in Libya in 2011 serving as examples of direct military force employed to remove regimes that had fallen into Western disfavor. Viewed from Moscow, and framed within the assumptions both of hostile intent by the West led by the United

States and of Russia's primary importance in world affairs, this consistent sequence of events leads quite logically to the conclusion that the West's habit of fostering and facilitating regime change by means of color revolutions, indiscriminately and with little regard for the consequences, may have Moscow as its eventual target.

A further assumption often asserted by Russian leaders is that popular protest movements in countries that eventually experience color revolutions cannot have arisen spontaneously but must have been financed and instigated from abroad. Suspicion of foreign orchestration came to the fore in Russia itself at the time of election protests in late 2011 and early 2012. During the protests President Putin said that he was offended at seeing protesters wearing white ribbons—a practice that, in his opinion, had been "developed abroad."[40] He also said that protesters had been "paid to participate," and that color revolutions were "tried and tested schemes for destabilizing a society."[41] In light of Russia's rich history of home-grown revolutions and regime changes, it may seem counterintuitive to assume at present that unrest and consequent regime change only happen when organized from abroad.[42] But the ambivalent way in which Russia marked the centenary of the October 1917 revolution must surely in part reflect the uncomfortable truth that this too, despite being celebrated in Russia for seventy years, was a color revolution funded and facilitated by a foreign adversary—in this case, Germany.[43]

Russia also cites foreign interference in the domestic political process in the 1990s—most prominently the reelection of Boris Yeltsin as president in 1996—as evidence of hostile foreign intent, and to some extent as a precedent for Russian attempts to influence the U.S. presidential election in 2016. But the accusations against the United States in this instance are also based on a false premise. Generously funded U.S. political consultants did contribute strongly to Yeltsin's campaign, but to a campaign to win support in a free vote rather than to ensure Yeltsin won despite the wishes of voters.[44] Russian commentators in effect confuse foreign help in *winning* an election in Russia in 1996 with foreign help in *subverting* an election in the United States twenty years later.

There is a strong continuity in Russia's perception of external and internal threats being intimately linked—justifiably, since the persistent nature of the Russian state and how it treats its subjects and empire means that foreign invaders of Russian dominions have often been greeted as liberators, most recently in 1941. This too spurs repressive measures against domestic political opposition. The challenge of supposed links between anticommunists within Bolshevik Russia and Whites and foreign forces from 1917 onward evolved into the menace of Soviet dissidents with foreign contacts and eventually, a hundred years later, into "foreign agents" funded from abroad. Consequently, a major leadership task after the election protests in 2011–12 was to alienate and discredit the domestic opposition by playing up its links to foreign dark forces, while at the same time ensuring that the United States was perceived even more strongly as an enemy in order to discourage contact with it. In all cases, tight domestic control is felt necessary to ensure stability and regime survival by limiting the scope for subversive foreign influence.

Ultimately the fear may not just be of the consequences of color revolutions for Russia as a country but also of the deeply personal consequences for its leadership. Regime change supported by the West has a tendency to end in the brutal murder of former leaders—sometimes live-streamed, as with the hanging of Saddam Hussein or the lynching of Muammar Qaddafi. As such, it replicates the pattern of regime succession in Russia not only in the twentieth century but well before it. Of the eight monarchs who ruled Russia between Peter the Great and the end of the eighteenth century, only two achieved the throne legally, but it did them little good as both were murdered, Peter III with the assistance of his wife and Paul with that of his son. Every one of the other six monarchs was brought to power by an armed coup d'état. This tradition continued into the twentieth century and to the end of the hereditary monarchy, with only one of Russia's last five emperors, Alexander III, dying of undisputed natural causes. As for the rest, Nicholas I was reputed to have committed suicide, Alexander II was assassinated, Nicholas II was murdered together with his family, and the true circumstances of the death of Alexander I remain obscure. Russian or Soviet leaders surviving the end of their tenure is a relatively recent phenomenon, aided by the negotiation between Boris Yeltsin and his successor Putin on immunity for Yeltsin and his family. It is not at all unnatural for the present Russian leaders to harbor a degree of concern that unless the (imagined) combination of Western and domestic threats is strongly contained, they themselves might also meet an unpleasant end.

The Arab Spring, Libya and Syria

This reminds me of a mediaeval call to crusade.
—VLADIMIR PUTIN, *commenting on Western plans for action against Libya, March 2011*[45]

Political upheaval across the Middle East and North Africa from 2011 onward firmly reinforced the Russian security leadership's assessment of the international situation. Putin later stated that Russia's initial reaction to the Arab Spring had been positive "because there were expectations of positive democratic changes." Russia's concerns arose later, as a result of the Western response to the uprisings—seen from Moscow as belligerent and interventionist—which Putin blamed for turning the Arab Spring into an "Islamist Autumn,"[46] or indeed an "Arab Winter."[47] In 2014 Putin described how "the people in those nations . . . were sick of tyranny and poverty, of their lack of prospects; but these feelings were taken advantage of cynically" in a series of "controlled revolutions" directed by the West.[48] At the same time, the rapid expansion of unrest caused concerns in Moscow that the wave of revolution and instability could spread to Russia's neighborhood, and in particular to the countries of Central Asia.[49]

In late 2013, a delegation from Russia's General Staff Academy visited the NATO Defense College in Rome, Italy. A primary theme of the briefings delivered was the negative outcomes of the Arab Spring and the manner in which the consequences of upheaval in the Middle East and North Africa were far worse than the political situations the upheavals had sought to address. Delegates provided a sobering list of predictions of highly damaging second-order effects, many of which—including confrontation with Islamic State and a spike in the Mediterranean migration crisis—proved entirely accurate. Further predictions included an increased likelihood of major war, not only as a result of the rise of political Islam and the uncontrolled spread of Libyan weapons throughout the region but also through a higher probability of assertive action against Israel and, eventually, the situation "when the Islamists gain enough strength to mount organized jihad against Europe."[50]

This provides additional context for the heightened perception of direct threat to Russia itself arising from events in an apparently remote region in

2011–13. One distinction drawn by some Russian academic analysis between the Arab Spring and the color revolutions in the former Soviet Union is that in the Middle East, change and popular uprisings were driven by internal social and economic problems, whereas in the post-Soviet states external interference played a much greater role than internal factors. But this view runs counter to the pervasive argument among Russian defense and security circles that political instability in the Middle East and Maghreb resulted from the plotting of the West, primarily the United States, as part of a campaign that posed a danger to Russia. Sergey Lavrov has commented repeatedly that the negative outcomes of the Arab Spring were a direct result of U.S. policy,[51] and at the height of the Arab Spring even then-president Dmitriy Medvedev echoed the view that Russia was vulnerable to the same kind of interference. In widely quoted comments from February 2011, he said: "Look at the situation that has unfolded in the Middle East and the Arab world. It is extremely bad. There are major difficulties ahead. . . . We need to look the truth in the eyes. This is the kind of scenario that they were preparing for us, and now they will be trying even harder to bring it about."[52]

The crucial turning point in Russia's attitude to the Arab Spring, and more broadly in its foreign policy as a whole, was Western actions in response to the civil war in Libya. Despite misgivings, Russia abstained from voting on UN Security Council Resolution 1973 in March 2011, in what was widely seen at the time as an unexpectedly helpful restraint.[53] In not using its veto, Russia briefly stepped away from its habitual stance against interference in internal affairs. This represented a significant shift in the normal Russian approach to international order and must have been preceded by intense discussion within the Russian political establishment. But subsequent events have convinced many in Moscow that it was an expensive mistake.[54]

The extraordinarily loose interpretation by Western powers of the resolution that Russia had allowed to be passed had a number of serious effects on Russian policy. Any trust in the West's good intentions that remained within Russia was undermined. It was made clear that strict limits had to be placed on cooperation with Western powers in order not to prejudice Russian interests. President Medvedev was publicly criticized by Putin and subsequently seen within hard-line Russian circles as a weaker leader who had attempted to compromise with the West and as a result, unsurprisingly, had been deceived instead.[55]

In Russia's perception, Libya represented not only the unconstitutional removal of a legitimate leader but also an alarming precedent as a model of revolution for implementation by the West elsewhere.[56] Following the descent of Libya into dangerous chaos—an entirely predictable development[57]—Russia noted a pattern consistent with the deterioration of the situation in Iraq following the U.S.-led invasion in 2003. Consequently, preventing a similar development of events in Syria in 2012–13 became an important Russian foreign policy task.[58]

In 2012, it appeared possible that the Syrian opposition would shortly achieve regime change.[59] When it did not, Western support to help it do so appeared imminent. Russia perceived this response as a demonstration of intent to topple another regime for the West's own purposes, with all the damaging and destabilizing consequences that would have entailed. The fact that President Obama had called the use of weapons of mass destruction in Syria a "red line," together with persistent messaging indicating a military response, left no one in Russia doubting that Syria would be attacked in September or October 2013.[60] But Russia's adroit manipulation of confrontation with Syria over the use of chemical weapons averted the possibility of imminent military action. Putin took a gamble in testing Russia's power and influence by standing up to the West, since Western intervention in Syria after strenuous opposition from Moscow would have destroyed all Russian political credibility. But instead, by facing down and containing the West, Russia gained legitimacy in some quarters as the protector of the status quo, sovereignty, and stability.

This action represented a major diplomatic and geopolitical turning point. It supported the Russian assessment that the United States could be manipulated back from the brink of military action or intervention. The powerful message sent to regimes around the world that were concerned about confrontation with the West was: "Russia is back and can help save you." Furthermore, the Russian leadership confirmed for itself that outmaneuvering the West was now possible. This contributed to the confidence with which, a year later, initial actions against Ukraine were undertaken—and subsequently, the seizure of Crimea validated the post-Georgia view that Russian direct military action could also be successful and lead to long-term strategic gain through presenting the world with a fait accompli. The following year this lesson was reinforced even more strongly for Russia by the results of its own intervention in Syria. Decisive military action had the effect of reversing U.S. and wider Western policy and arriving at plans for a political settlement that were entirely in accordance with Russia's desires.[61]

Overall, military action in 2014–16 taught Russia a highly dangerous lesson: that brisk and resolute deployment of military force can swiftly resolve intractable foreign policy challenges, with perceived strategic benefits out of proportion to any costs that may subsequently be incurred by sanctions or ostracism. This can only augment the likelihood that Russia might consider a similar response to perceived challenges along its western periphery. But it also clearly demonstrates the country's transformation under Putin's presidency. Bolstered by energy revenues channeled into rebuilding military power, Russia now feels sufficiently strong to use force to prevent international situations developing into perceived direct security threats to its key interests. Its situation is unrecognizable from the start of Putin's rule at the beginning of the previous decade.

Russia's Response

You and I are probably bad Christians: when you are slapped you should turn the other cheek. And I am not yet ready to do so on moral grounds. If we are slapped, we must retaliate, otherwise we will always be taken advantage of.

—VLADIMIR PUTIN, *December 2012*[62]

On becoming acting president at the end of 1999, Vladimir Putin inherited both a Russia and a world order in apparent disarray. The Foreign Policy Concept published in 2000 was written at a time of internal instability in Russia following the financial crash of 1998–99 and reflected unease in Moscow about NATO's Kosovo campaign. The *Concept* noted Russia's concerns about the nature of a unipolar world dominated by the United States—a world marked by "double standards," the use of force, and instability, a world in which Russia would need to protect its sovereign independence. Putin's foreign policy priority during his first two terms (1999–2008) was thus to restore both the Russian state and Russia's status in the world, with the ultimate aim of regaining recognition as a great power and the respect for Russia's interests that would come with this recognition. A central theme of policy during this period was a defensive stance: an effort to strengthen political and social unity in the face of an increasingly threatening international environment, recognizing Russian weakness and seeking to mitigate its consequences.[63]

Color revolutions and military interventions by the West in Kosovo, Iraq, and elsewhere continued to be seen in Moscow as a clear pattern of the erosion of the notion of state sovereignty as an absolute.[64] This was categorically unacceptable to Russia. In addition, a secondary effect of the 2003 Iraq invasion and its mismanaged consequences was to reinforce and confirm Russian suspicion of democracy itself in the broad sense, especially when "imposed from abroad." As described by Yevgeniy Satanovsky, president of the Institute of Middle Eastern Studies in Moscow, "The development of Iraq after Saddam Hussein's regime was overthrown cannot be considered a model of democracy; more than this, it is the worst possible advertisement for democracy."[65] Even earlier statements, including by Deputy Foreign Minister Grigoriy Karasin, had drawn a direct equivalence between democratization and destabilization with a subsequent "potential increase in extremism."[66] This too contributed to more recent campaigns to discredit the Russian liberal opposition among the general population and to the assumption that foreign efforts to encourage democratic movements or institutions are essentially hostile in intent. A Russian domestic response to these linked threats took the form of efforts to prevent attempts at foreign influence on Russian society and politics. This was visible in a number of domestic policy initiatives dating from 2000 onward, including not only ideological constructs such as "sovereign democracy"[67] but also legislation intended to strengthen domestic control.

During Putin's first two terms as president, both officials and analysts in Moscow shared a widespread belief that the international situation was becoming even more unstable and dangerous. Putin himself remarked in February 2008 that "today's world is not getting any simpler—on the contrary, it is ever more complicated and tough."[68] Foreign Minister Sergey Lavrov suggested in an end-of-year message in 2007 that in the following year, "unilateral moves by some countries may provoke global political breakdowns."[69] Commentators agreed that the international situation was deteriorating and marked by increasing disorder and instability—and was likely only to get worse.[70] But at the same time, Russia's official foreign policy review of 2007 called it a year of transition, after which Russia had the political will and accompanying resources to succeed in bringing about positive change.[71]

A speech by President Putin at the Munich Security Conference in February 2007 is widely seen as representing an important point in the evolution of relations between post-Soviet Russia and the West.[72] But it must be remembered that this was not because of any display of a new vector in Russian foreign policy. Instead, the speech marked the first time the West in general took notice of the mounting dissatisfaction and alarm emanating from Russia over the state of the international order, and over what Putin perceived as unilateral and irresponsible actions by the West, led by the United States.

In media representations of the time, this was one of the many iterations of the sudden resurgence of Cold War analogies since 1989.[73] But the widespread surprise at Putin's comments was not shared by the Russia-watching community. The themes he elaborated at the conference were familiar from Russian state discourse in previous years, and the forthrightness with which they were expressed had been gradually mounting over that period. It is likely that the 2007 speech received so much attention relative to previous expressions of the same concern because of its directness. After all, as Putin himself said, "This conference's structure allows me to avoid excessive politeness and the need to speak in roundabout, pleasant but empty diplomatic terms. This conference's format will allow me to say what I really think about international security problems."[74]

Putin had in fact been saying what he thought for some time; but in the West, if the message was received at all, it was not understood. The West had widely ignored Russian security thinking while the country was weak and could easily be overlooked, except as a potential source of dangerous instability itself in the event of state collapse. But the view from Moscow was very different. In 1995—when Russian defense capability was rapidly approaching its nadir—a study commissioned by the Russian Ministry of Defense found that the United States and its allies still represented the main threat to national security and recommended a return to a nuclear standoff and reoccupation of the Baltic states to counter "Western attempts to isolate and destroy Russia." Other recommendations included economic protectionism, a military-nuclear alliance with Iraq, Iran, and Libya, and the creation of a new union that would include Russia, Belarus, Kazakhstan, and Ukraine.[75] A decade later, shortly after Putin's Munich speech, this concern was undiminished: according to then chief of the General Staff Yuriy Baluyevsky, "Russia's transition to interaction with the West on the basis of forming common or close strategic interests has not strengthened the military security of our state. Russia should observe the immutable axiom that wars and armed conflicts will continue uninterrupted, because they are generated by the continuing rivalry between states."[76]

By contrast, Putin's third presidential term, starting in 2012, was marked not only by a heightened sense of urgency in facing foreign threats but also by a new sense of Russia's capability to take firm positive action to prevent them. Putin's perception of external challenge must surely have been exacerbated by the realization that the great majority of Western politicians and commentators treated his reappearance as bad news. But while the notion of the West as a looming threat is perennial, what was new in 2012 was both a more direct and immediate sense of this threat, whether imagined or not, and Russia's confidence and ability to actually do something about it.[77]

When the drafting of a new Military Doctrine was announced in 2014, it was specifically intended to reflect "the emergence of new challenges and threats to Russia's security manifested in the events of the 'Arab Spring,' in the armed conflict in Syria, and in the situation in and around Ukraine."[78] This was a response to the heightened perception of threat resulting from what Moscow saw as the increasing tempo of unrestrained and irresponsible interventions by the West with the intention of regime change, leaving chaos and disorder in their wake. Mismanagement of the aftermath of the Western invasion of Iraq in 2003 created conditions for the rise of the Islamic State. Western action in Libya in 2011 contributed to replacing a stable regime with an ungovernable space and a source of far-reaching instability and weapons proliferation. Western objectives in Syria in 2013–15 threatened to do the same. But in Russia itself, after a period in which the fundamental transformation of the military had left it weakened during a transitional phase, the early stages of Putin's third term saw clear demonstrations of military efficiency. In particular, these took the form of the "snap exercises" testing and demonstrating the capabilities of the reinvigorated armed forces.[79] These much-improved capabilities will have fed directly into the assessment that use of military force was the appropriate response to prevent the situation deteriorating further in Ukraine in early 2014 and in Syria in October 2015.

Another development that accelerated significantly after the beginning of Putin's third term was the increased degree of control over Russian civil society, and the firm implementation of suppressive measures and legislation that was either new, or already in place but not previously rigidly enforced. This new firm control was particularly marked in the treatment of NGOs, including but not limited to those receiving funding from abroad and now labeled "foreign agents," and also in the swift and dramatic clampdown in 2014–15 on the internet as a forum for free expression and access to information from overseas.

No matter how innocent their activities may appear to their sponsors overseas, foreign-backed NGOs are specifically highlighted in Russian security thinking as a means by which an external actor can deliver hostile effect within Russia, with objectives including "discrediting the current government agencies, eroding the prestige and public standing of the law enforcement agencies, particularly the armed forces, buying up the mass media and conducting information operations purportedly to protect democracy, and nominating delegates for local government elections, and infiltrating them into the elected government authorities."[80]

Meanwhile, the spread of the internet had been another important factor that accentuated the perception of threat among a leadership group whose members included many who had spent their formative years working in KGB counterintelligence. The internet represented a previously unavailable method by which hostile powers could directly reach Russian citizens. The Russian intelligence services have consistently and publicly stressed the potential for threats to national security arising from the internet ever since it first became available to ordinary Russians, and President Putin and his current and former colleagues share a deep mistrust, as well as apparent misunderstanding, of the nature and purpose of the internet.[81] According to FSB First Deputy Director Sergey Smirnov, speaking in early 2012: "New technologies are used by Western secret services to create and maintain a level of continual tension in society with serious intentions extending even to regime change."[82]

Russia's Information Security Doctrine published in 2016 thus showed a new focus on protecting citizens from information from abroad,[83] but here too the new policy is simply a return to Russia's historical default setting. Efforts to isolate Russians from foreign news have consistently been viewed as an essential part of ensuring national security. The czarist concern described by Astolphe de Custine that "the political system of Russia could not withstand twenty years of free communication with Western Europe"[84] survived from imperial times, was reinforced during the Soviet era, and has now reasserted itself after a brief quarter century of dangerous liberalism.

Lashing Out

Fifty years ago, I learnt one rule in the streets of Leningrad: if a fight is unavoidable, you have to hit first.
—VLADIMIR PUTIN, *October 2015*[85]

Through a Russian prism of threat assessment, unrelated events of the last fifteen years, including the invasion of Iraq in 2003, the Orange Revolution in Ukraine in 2004, and especially the Arab Spring, Western intervention in Libya, and election protests at home in 2011, can be combined through a consistent internal logic into a single trajectory. This trajectory leads to the conclusion that the West's habit of indiscriminately fostering and facilitating regime change by means of color revolutions may have Moscow as its eventual target. But the internal logic depends on a false premise: that the West harbors hostile intent toward the Kremlin itself in order to pillage Russia's resources.

The debate continues over whether this false premise reflects views genuinely held among Russia's leadership or is simply manufactured to provide a distraction from economic crisis at home and an excuse for expansionist adventurism abroad. The question is valid, but it has faded in importance as the narrative of conflict has become self-sustaining. In effect, President Putin's policy options have become constrained by an insistence on imminent danger.[86] Retreat from this narrative is impossible without a claim to some kind of strategic victory that averts the threat. The victory could be military or political, real or imaginary—but it must in some way show the West's retreat or humiliation.

The development of a strong military instrument for protecting Russia's interests abroad, and new repressive measures for protecting its leadership at home,[87] produce yet another of the permanent paradoxes of Russia. With countermeasures in place to address the two greatest (and interlinked) perceived challenges, President Putin would seem to be in a position of much greater security. And yet, since the start of his third term as president, even more academics and commentators outside Russia have been predicting the imminent collapse of the leadership structure (see chapter 10). This strong tendency can only be exacerbating what George Kennan called the "Kremlin's neurotic view of world affairs."[88] In this worldview, Western efforts to promote democracy and liberal markets are part of a pan-Western campaign to foster regime change in Moscow and serve only to plant fifth columnists in Russia in order to undermine it.[89]

In addition, there is a continuing debate among Russia-watching communities in the West as to whether Russia's actions are guided by a grand strategy or are purely opportunistic and tactical. One factor that is common to both these assessments is that Russia under President Putin will continue to be proactive, exploit opportunities where they are presented, and respond firmly to challenges and perceived threats where they arise. According to Sergey Karaganov, "Grand strategy in Russia has not changed since early czarist times. The need to maintain sovereignty and stability has been a permanent driver. This consists primarily of defence of the sovereign."[90] It follows that any action by the West that could promote still further the notion that the sovereign himself is under threat would be likely to provoke a damaging reaction by Moscow. Europe's next crisis should not be precipitated by the West unwittingly presenting a new opportunity or trigger through ignorance of the fundamental security perceptions that provoke the Russian security elite, and Putin himself, to action. There is no reason to suspect that Putin is not sincere when he states the value of a preemptive strike based on his childhood experiences in Leningrad.

This has obvious implications for the conduct of normal business with states around Russia's periphery. Interest by the United States, EU, and NATO in cooperation with Russia's neighbors is not anti-Russian—in the same way, for example, that cooperation with Portugal is not anti-Spanish. But it is undeniably prejudicial to Russian claims to spheres of interest. Viewed from Moscow, the distinction is academic. From Moscow's perspective, all three of these Western actors have a very clear agenda—even if it may not always have been clear to the actors themselves. This presumption of a giant and interlinked conspiracy was the mental framework in which Moscow could interpret a proposed economic agreement between Ukraine and the EU in 2014 as NATO preparing a grab for Sevastopol, thus precipitating the seizure of Crimea. It also has implications for states further afield. Interference in foreign elections, and the use of social media to stoke social divisions in North America and Europe, provide clear examples of Russia channeling its own neuroses about the offensive potential of the internet into hostile action against perceived adversaries, whether or not those adversaries recognize that they are in a state of conflict with Russia.

The United States and its NATO allies cannot change Russia's deep-rooted assumption about their aggressive intentions. In the twentieth century, George Kennan's assessment was that "suspicion in one degree or another is an integral part of [the] Soviet System, and will not yield entirely to any form of rational persuasion or assurance."[91] But this, like so much else, was not a feature of the Soviet system but of Russian attitudes and assumptions that are perennial. Neither is it a problem that results from President Putin being in power; instead, it is deeply ingrained in Russian thinking about security and Russia's position in the world, and it will persist long after Putin has departed.[92] In the meantime, every trivial error of action or message by the West is taken as evidence that Russia's assumption is correct. Even visual style can contribute to inadvertently reinforcing Russian impressions of hostile intent. Infographics released by NATO in 2017 to explain its new deployments in the Baltic states and the progress of missile defense plans were intended to highlight their strictly defensive nature. Instead, the arrangement of lines to text boxes on the map showed, with touching innocence, NATO troops and missiles converging on Moscow.[93] And during a conference on ballistic missile defense (BMD), an already highly neuralgic topic for Russia, a slide showing U.S. BMD plans presented by the director for international affairs of the U.S. Missile Defense Agency inadvertently mirrored the classic Cold War propaganda image of the USSR encircled by threatening foreign missiles.[94]

Whether the belief that Russia is under threat is sincere or not, the actions taken on its basis are the same. The West has consistently underestimated both the apparent conviction with which these views are held in Moscow, and the consequences of Russia acting to defend them. Russia is responding to these challenges, regardless of whether they are genuinely perceived or entirely fabricated, by taking steps to ensure its own security. Many of these steps resemble mobilization for war.[95] The result is that when engaging with Russia, the West is dealing with a power that regards its every move with deep suspicion and has readied the military potential to lash out at will. Whether this lashing out is believed to be in self-defense or not is immaterial for those in the path of the blows.

FOUR

Winning the Cold War

Russia's Defeat or Shared Victory?

Russia realized that it was not simply robbed, it was plundered.
—VLADIMIR PUTIN, *March 2014*[1]

Another important divergence of perception between Russia and the West that also resonates in Russian policy today is the question of how the Cold War ended—whether this was a defeat for the Soviet Union at the hands of the West or an instance of Russia voluntarily withdrawing from territory of its own accord.

Given Russia's consistent historical drive to expand its territory, it is not unnatural to perceive a withdrawal by Russia as a defeat. The previous occasion when Russia had retreated to within its own frontiers, and even ceded territory, was in 1918: a time when it was fatally weakened by war, revolution, and chaos and led by a small group that shortly before had seized control of the country in a coup and was temporarily prepared to sacrifice Russian national interest in favor of consolidating its grip on power. But whether through genuine conviction or an understandable urge to soothe severely bruised national pride, the comparable retreat at the end of the USSR seventy years later is portrayed in Russia as a constructive and responsible choice by Moscow. Russia came to see the redistribution of power in eastern Europe at the end of the Cold War as a process in which it had willingly acquiesced and cooperated, and disbanded both the "outer" and "inner" Soviet empires on its own rather than as a result of defeat or even of pressure to do so from the West.[2] In addition, the downfall of communism was perceived by some as an achievement by Russia rather than something that happened in spite of Russia.[3] This was in stark contrast to the perception in much of the rest of the world of a strategic defeat for a totalitarian power, which was then forced to withdraw from its occupied territories amid the collapse of its system of government.[4]

Even during the process, there was little overlap between Western and Russian interpretations of what was happening. To the West, this was a liberation of Russia, at which Russians should be rejoicing; consequently, the extent of national humiliation that came with the collapse of the Soviet Union and the end of centuries of Moscow's dominion over its immediate neighborhood was drastically underestimated or simply ignored.[5] To Russians, loss of status and territory also implied loss of security for the future, and the foundation for respecting and being proud of their own nation.[6] This grievance was fueled by the assumption in the West that Russia would now become a "normal" country, and that this naturally meant a country that was like the West and subscribed to its norms, values, and rules of behavior. The misguided notion that Russia was fundamentally a Western nation, but one that for the past seventy years had lost its way and was now rejoining the fold, led to an innocent but damaging arrogance. As a result, Russia's troubles in the 1990s compounded the misguided notion within the country that whatever the process of the end of the Cold War had been, Russia had as a result been treated like a defeated power, and that something comparable to the Treaty of Versailles had been imposed on it.[7]

Even before the end of the decade, the belief that Russia had voluntarily withdrawn from Europe and the Soviet republics led to criticism of its leaders at the time for not extracting some form of compensation from the West for doing so. According to this view, the rapprochement with the West was inadequately negotiated and poorly compensated. The withdrawal of the Soviet armed forces from Central Europe, acceptance of the unification of Germany, and relinquishing the "near abroad" were described as powerful bargaining chips that could have been traded for significant concessions to Moscow but instead were simply given away—a view that has grown stronger as memories of the reality of the period become more distant.[8] In light of the fundamental illegitimacy of the Soviet presence in Europe in the first place, this strongly resembles the persistent Russian habit of demanding compensation for doing the right thing, described in chapter 2 in the section "Cooperation and Disruption." But in addition, it ignores the substantial costs incurred by Western governments in managing aspects of the Soviet withdrawal and drawdown that Russia was at first unable, and later unwilling, to fund itself. For example, reunified Germany funded the relocation, retraining, and eventual building of housing for the Soviet garrisons stationed in the former German Democratic Republic, and the United States, United Kingdom, and Norway shouldered the costs of making safe Russia's abandoned nuclear submarines. All this, of course, came in the context of a massive influx of Western development, financial, and even humanitarian aid in the form of simple food shipments, now erased from the official Russian narrative as completely as Lend-Lease aid to the Soviet Union had been fifty years before.[9]

This lack of mutual understanding on how the Cold War ended has been conceptually formulated by Russia as a failure to conclude its formally negotiated settlement. According to this argument, "The existing volatile status quo in Europe cannot be taken as a legitimate 'order' per se. This lack of 'order' stems from the lack of a peace treaty to end the Cold War. This inconclusive moment ushered in a 'post-Yalta' period that saw the gradual destruction of the European/Eurasian political-security system."[10]

The argument that there was a possibility of a new and common security order in Europe that would have avoided the current heightened tensions between Russia and the West is a seductive one. But it founders on two key considerations. First, any potential there might have been for a post–Cold War settlement was compromised by a fundamental divergence of views on Russia's role in it. The basic choice was whether the Euro-Atlantic region extended to Russia, making Russia an insider and its security problems an integral part of European security, or whether the Euro-Atlantic region stopped short, in which case the two sides would inevitably in time become part of each other's security agenda. As seen from Moscow, "The central idea of a new arrangement in Europe . . . was the idea of an East-West convergence, instead of an absorption of the East by the West. In other words, Russia was willing to turn more 'European' provided that Europe would become more 'Russian'; Moscow and Brussels were expected to make reciprocal concessions and compromises."[11]

But in Brussels and other Western European capitals, there was no evident rationale for these concessions—still less in eastern Europe, which had only just escaped Russian domination and would have resisted fiercely any attempt to invite it back even in an attenuated form.

In addition, given the condition of Russia and an air of general optimism that conflict with it was a thing of the past, there was limited perception at the time of any reason why Russia would expect to be involved in the foreign policy decisions of countries beyond its borders.[12] But this is how Russia sees its desired settlement in Europe. President Putin and Foreign Minister Lavrov have pointed to precedents for constructive Russian involvement in European politics that led to periods of extended peace.[13] But the precedents they choose, the Congress of Vienna and the Yalta Conference agreements, are examples of victorious great powers—including Russia—agreeing among themselves to impose terms on smaller or defeated states. With or without Russia, this template is entirely incompatible with European notions of relations between states in the twenty-first century.

An additional complicating factor is Russia's claim that it received binding promises that NATO would not come any closer by enlarging to the east. Given the centrality of this issue to suggestions that Russia was deceived by an untrustworthy and expansionist NATO, it is not surprising that both sides of the argument have received extensive analysis supported by a mass of circumstantial, but not conclusive, evidence and recollections.[14] Even such central figures as Mikhail Gorbachev have provided material supporting both sides of the argument.[15] But for the current relationship it is the results, not the roots, of the controversy that matter: in short, NATO believed or decided it had not offered any guarantee to Russia that it would not accept new member states in Eastern Europe, but Russia believed or decided it had.

Either way, in deciding to accept applications to NATO from Eastern Europe, the United States and its European allies made a choice based on values rather than on a full and proper assessment of the implications. It was recognized in Russia, even if not in NATO, that the fact of membership meant the easternmost NATO allies would expect to be defended against the only meaningful conventional threat they would ever face—namely, Russia. This in turn meant that unless NATO's guarantees were to be entirely hollow, it would undertake military planning and force deployments against Russia in much closer proximity to it, or indeed on its borders. Assurances as to the defensive nature of the alliance were fatally undermined in Russian eyes by its intervention in the former Yugoslavia in 1999, after which there was little prospect that further NATO enlargement could be undertaken in any way that would ultimately prove palatable to Moscow. And yet the alternative to NATO enlargement could have been worse. In light of Russia's willingness to launch military interventions against its neighbors, a refusal to accept new members up to and including the Baltic states in 2004 could have increased the potential for conflict in Europe, since the applicant states would then have been in the same situation as Georgia and Ukraine—friends of the West but not protected by it, and consequently softer targets for Russia in the event of a crisis.

The first steps toward enlargement of NATO, against the background of a period of such deeply mismatched assumptions and expectations about the nature of the relationship, reinforced Russia's suspicions of Western intentions. NATO enlargement was not an automatic or inevitable process: many within the alliance saw no obvious advantage in extension and recognized that offering security guarantees that could not be honored was highly dangerous.[16] It was predicted, accurately, that the result of NATO enlargement would be to "inflame the nationalistic, anti-Western and militarist tendencies in Russian opinion: to have an adverse effect on the development of Russian democracy; to restore the atmosphere of the cold war to East-West relations, and to impel Russian foreign policy in directions decidedly not to our liking. . . . They would see their prestige (always uppermost in the Russian mind) and their security interests as adversely affected."[17]

But NATO enlargement should not be considered the key or even the only driver of the crisis in the relationship. The need for enlargement, and Russia's reaction to it, are both symptoms of more fundamental dysfunction and incompatibility. Crucially, Russia's turn against the West preceded NATO enlargement, and was driven at least as much by concerns about status and overall Western intentions as by genuine military threat perceptions.[18] All of these were inflamed by Russia's experience of the ten years between the fall of the Berlin Wall and President Putin's arrival in power.

The 1990s

I want to ask you for forgiveness, because many of our hopes have not come true, because what we thought would be easy turned out to be painfully difficult.

—BORIS YELTSIN, *resignation speech, December 1999*[19]

The beginning of the 1990s saw a simple assumption that, left to its own devices and unconstrained by a repressive communist regime, Russia would be transformed by default into a liberal democracy. This expectation was held on both sides—in the West through willful ignorance or oversight of Russian history, and in Russia through an incomplete understanding of what the process would involve. A widespread perception in the West was that it would be sufficient to renounce the Soviet system by changing the flag, introducing a market economy, rewriting the constitution, and holding democratic elections, while ignoring far deeper institutional, structural, and psychological obstacles to development. In Russia, according to the polls of the time, "The ideal future of Russia was seen as the state with market economy, democratic institutions and human rights. But these moods reflected the desire for a quick change rather than inherent worth and understating [understanding] of democratic principles. Democracy, for the majority of Russians was not a goal, but rather a synonym of western prosperity."[20]

Confusing the two was common. At this time, Nobel Prize–winning author Svetlana Alexievich "was with everybody else running around the square shouting 'Freedom! Freedom!,' even if we didn't have any idea what that meant. And when freedom showed up, and Yeltsin quickly transformed into Tsar Boris, and the oligarchs into his boyars, we understood soon enough that all we really wanted was a better life."[21] Similarly, when the prominent journalist Vladislav Listyev spoke in 1990 of totalitarianism being embedded in Russian genes because of "several generations that have never known democracy," he was understating the case—in fact, Russia has never known democracy in the Western sense at all. But the utopian vision of a future Russia laid out by Listyev also included simpler aspirations, such as people "being able to go to a shop and buy what they need."[22]

The disappointments of the 1990s went far beyond a failure to achieve a dream of democracy, and the gradual realization that what had happened instead was state capture by a kleptocracy and the deliberate conversion by the communist apparatus of its monopoly on political power into vast personal financial power for its individual members or appointees.[23] Banking crises, nonpayment of salaries, hyperinflation, and the economic collapse of 1998 all became associated in the popular consciousness with the attempt at democratization. The vast amount of money that poured into Russia from the West in the form of loans and direct aid was either disregarded or described as a tool to "enslave Russia financially"—or to deliberately cripple it when large amounts of loan financing were withdrawn in August 1998 following Russia's domestic default and moratorium on repaying foreign loans. That loans and finance did not constitute an all-embracing bailout of Soviet industry also created incomprehension and resentment. This result was inevitable owing to the widespread initial assumption in Russia that foreigners would invest funds in modernizing all sectors of the economy, including industries that were uncompetitive or had already lost their internal markets with the end of the planned economy.[24] Other indices of a functioning society and a competent state were deteriorating rapidly too. Mortality rates rose sharply as the result of a daunting range of contributing factors, of which murder, violence, and disorder were only a part.[25] To take just one example, airline safety in the USSR was already notoriously poor, but accident statistics for air passenger transport increased no less than tenfold in the period from 1992 to 1996.[26]

Resentment and disillusion with both foreign partnerships and domestic reform caused many Russians to see themselves as victims of unfair treatment by other international actors, who they thought had taken advantage of Russia's weakness and treated it as a defeated country.[27] Other grievances included a perception that the West had imposed its own standards and interfered in domestic politics, and the largely justified complaint that during the 1990s Russia stood alone against Islamist terrorism while the West, failing fully to recognize the threat until 9/11, offered only criticism of Russia's methods of subduing the North Caucasus, with no comprehension of the broader challenge. In effect, as stated in later years by President Putin, a hostile West was perceived to be not only exploiting its temporary advantage but deliberately keeping Russia weak.[28] It is this narrative that the present leadership exploits, both to warn of the dangers of Western influence and to discourage calls for another attempt at liberalization and democratization.

The United States had made the conscious decision at the end of the Cold War, in keeping with its consistent foreign policy, that both its values and its interests lay with promoting democracy and human rights throughout the world, including in eastern Europe. The rest of the West followed suit. Moscow saw some actions resulting from this stance, such as the Kosovo operation and the invasion of Iraq, as threatening or at the least alarming, but in addition they had been undertaken with no reference to Russia, which had simply not been a factor in decision making. Moscow perceived that fact alone as deeply insulting. But as explained by former senior State Department official Philip Gordon, the alternative would have been entirely impractical:

> If the relationship with Russia were the predominant or only focus of U.S. foreign policy, it could have taken the view that it's none of Washington's business who governs in the Baltic states, Poland, the Balkans, all other things. That would have been an option, if good relations with Russia were the sole goal. I don't think that is consistent with our interests and values, nor do I think it would have actually led to a better relationship with Russia.[29]

Nevertheless, at the end of the Cold War, Western leaders had made the deliberate decision to incorporate Russia into existing economic and political structures in order to cement peace. The transformation of the Group of Seven leading industrialized nations (G-7) into the Group of Eight, including Russia, was not merited by Russia's economic power at the time; and the decision to recognize Russia as the successor state to the Soviet Union in the United Nations, including as a permanent member of the Security Council, was by no means automatic. These and other institutional devices were geared to easing the pain of Russia's transition and the loss of its international status. Russia's response was, however, ambivalent; the generosity of this outreach and inclusion led Moscow to suspect it was being flattered to deceive, and superficially consulted only to legitimize policies decided elsewhere.[30] Full integration with the Euro-Atlantic community was never in prospect, in part because Russia declined to accept U.S. leadership. Driven by its sense of exceptionalism and the enduring notion—despite appearances at the time—that it was a global power, Russia rejected partnership with the West if it meant absorption into the West.[31] It also rapidly became clear that its ambitious goal of partnership on its own terms was entirely unrealistic.[32]

Russia was in fact considered a threat to its neighbors and the West during the 1990s, but only because of the risk of economic collapse, a breakdown in political and administrative order, or a slide into general lawlessness.[33] Each of these was a real and significant danger, compounded by the likelihood of disputes with newly independent states over territory or borders. Major territorial readjustments at the dissolution of the Soviet Union were in fact avoided, despite being considered. Russian ambassador to the United States Vladimir Lukin argued in early 1992 that if the plan for open borders within the CIS failed, referendums should be held to adjust those borders to reflect better the actual settlement patterns of ethnic Russians. Lukin cited eastern Ukraine as one region where this approach should be adopted.[34] Clashes did claim lives during the process of detaching the former Soviet republics from Russia, including in the Baltic states, but overall, compared with the catastrophic results of dissolutions of other compound states such as Yugoslavia in the 1990s or India in 1947, the end of the USSR was strikingly peaceful.

Outside Russia too, during the same period there were fears of ethnic strife and the revival of old conflicts and border disputes across eastern Europe, with the potential for half the continent to sink into a seething mass of Yugoslav-style wars. Active diplomacy by Western countries made sure this did not happen, and NATO and EU membership eventually cemented peace in place. The reasonable assumption that Russia would not want to be surrounded by a belt of unstable neighbors, weak states, and potential crises led to a belief that Russia should be content with this arrangement—and yet in the longer term, as demonstrated in Ukraine, Russia preferred crisis and instability to the alternative of being a direct neighbor of NATO or the EU.

At the end of a deeply damaging and traumatic decade, Vladimir Putin became leader of a country with no effective power, whether economic or military, and set the goal of restoring to Russia not only this power but also the influence and status it conferred. The response to his much-quoted comment in 2005 calling the end of the Soviet Union the greatest geopolitical catastrophe of the twentieth century is indicative of the huge gulf in understanding that persisted between Russia and the West about what happened during that decade. Outside Russia, Putin's comment caused horror and incomprehension. Within Russia, with the economy yet to be rescued by the rising energy prices of the mid-2000s, it met widespread recognition and gave rise to a sense of affirmation.

By the end of Putin's second term and his subsequent tour as prime minister, some progress toward his aims could be detected. An assessment in 2008 noted the transition of Russian foreign policy from a defensive approach founded on weakness to a more confident stance, accompanied by the beginning of attempts to renegotiate the results of the post–Cold War period.[35] Boosted by energy revenues and driven by a focused and determined leader, Russia had already left behind its period of weakness and chaos and begun the trajectory toward a new assertiveness. And together with the goal of restoring Russia to what was considered its rightful status abroad came a rejection of the political chaos of the 1990s and a return to a far more traditional approach to internal governance.

PART II

Russia's Internal System

FIVE

Ruling Russia

The Firm Hand

The miracle is that Russia has a government at all. The country is both too big and too Russian for it to have been governable by Western methods.

—SASHA KENNAWAY, *December 1999*[1]

Russia's traditional form of governance has been consistent through almost the entirety of its history. It is only since the end of the Soviet Union that modifications have begun to the pattern of autocratic rule with a small and restricted upper class and a negligible middle class, shored up by an anonymous oppressed and exploited mass.[2]

From the earliest stages of its existence, Russia was faced with the necessity of harnessing all its meager resources for defense, war, and colonization, on a geographic scale beyond what was conceivable in Europe. Despotic government, building on the Mongol legacy of absolutism, presented a means of coping with a more or less perpetual state of emergency and external conflict. In addition, the basic Mongol principles of unqualified submission to the state and the compulsory and permanent state service of all individuals and classes of society had permeated the Muscovite social structure and were subsequently preserved by centuries of Russian rulers unwilling, or in some cases unable, to implement change.[3] Together, these related influences contributed to a presumption that the country was in effect owned by its rulers, who could do as they pleased with it: the grand princes inherited from the Khans a perverse form of legitimacy, supplanting them as conquerors of their own subjects.[4] The inclination to run the country for personal profit persists today, since the social development of Russia has never quite overcome the understanding that those in power—from the most junior traffic policeman to the ruler of the country—have an automatic right to self-enrichment.[5]

The result was a political system that not only differed fundamentally from that of Western Europe from its very beginnings but also diverged further through failing to develop over time. The default to a strong state directed by a single autocrat is just one manifestation of Russia's historical and cultural experience as essentially distinct from that of Western nations.[6] In fact, what in the West was regarded as arbitrary authoritarianism was considered in Russia an elemental necessity, a precondition for functioning governance.[7] Political analyst Andrey Sushentsov asks, rhetorically, if there is any other way that "a government can rule a continent-sized country with around 50% of territory in the permanent frost, with very low population density, complicated geography and neighborhood while providing the same level of government service, medicine, education, security, transport and other services to the people in a territorial body 11 time zones long?"[8]

The Russian philosopher and sociologist Aleksandr Akhiezer suggests that acceptance of this state of affairs derives not only from practical considerations but also from societal development failing through suppression or innate incapacity, meaning that even today, "Russia is populated by an archaic people with a peasant consciousness, who have no need of a state, only of a czar and a few of his minions."[9] While this description may be extreme, current political developments in Russia do not contradict it.[10] Since arriving in power at the turn of the twenty-first century, Vladimir Putin has steadily acted to eliminate independent centers of power. One by one, institutions capable of providing an alternative to unitary power were subordinated, starting with the media, followed by business, and ending with parliament and the courts. The result is a society in which the regime, personified in the ruler, in the traditional Russian style has become the only wielder of true power.

But the ruler has always needed ways of ensuring that this power was exercised as he wished. In the past, reliable control over the vast dominions required trust, not in order to delegate decision making but to ensure that decisions made centrally were ruthlessly implemented. Putin too is therefore within the mainstream of Russian practice in appointing to key positions the individuals he has known the longest. Many of Putin's allies who served with him in the KGB or worked with him in 1990s St. Petersburg, or both, remain closely associated with him today, whether in government or business positions, or moving smoothly between the two. One result of this reliance on known associates is that the boundaries are further blurred between enacting domestic and even international state policy, on the one hand, and preserving the financial and other interests of the leadership elite on the other.[11] More recently, the Russian instinct and conditioned preference for centralized control have found expression in the use of technology not to decentralize but to further concentrate decision making and monitor implementation.[12] This tendency is taken to extremes in the National Defense Control Center in Moscow, set up in part to centralize oversight of Russian military activities wherever in the world they take place. By contrast, when a senior Russian delegation made an official visit to the NATO command bunker at Mons in Belgium in January 2012, it suspected it had been deceived, since—with most decision making delegated to operational commanders—it saw no evidence of direct command and control of all NATO's deployed operations being exercised from there.

President Putin's tendency to rely on personalized relationships also has implications for dealings with foreign partners, especially when combined with a failure to appreciate that Western leaders do not enjoy the same degree of freedom to make and enact decisions.[13]

> [Putin's] closest alliances with the West have all gone the same way. Whether it was Jacques Chirac in France, Silvio Berlusconi in Italy or Gerhard Schröder in Germany, each was built on a personal rapport with an incoming head of state, always another man, usually also a blowhard. Each collapsed when that leader was confronted by the limitations of democracy: term limits, a free press, an independent legislature, an unhappy electorate, or any of the other checks and balances built into their constitutions. But with each new attempt at a friendship with the West, Putin seemed to hope that his counterparts could override these curbs on their authority the same way Putin has done in Russia.[14]

Veteran Russia-watcher Fiona Hill, at the time of writing serving as senior director for European and Russian affairs on the U.S. National Security Council, suggests that "Putin does not have deep insight into the way our societies work, nor does he care to obtain it."[15] But the lack of insight into how Western democracies and societies work is not restricted to Putin. Many others, especially senior officials, assume that the West functions much like Russia, with the judiciary and media following instructions from the state and the democratic institutions existing largely for show.[16] This gulf in comprehension will only grow wider as Russia's self-imposed isolation deepens.

In the light of Russia's history and their own personal experiences, these senior officials share with their leader a number of assumptions and rules, sometimes explicit and sometimes unspoken, that frame Russia's political system today. Exeter University's David Lewis summarizes these as the following:

- a view of political order that is essentially Hobbesian, promoting a strong state and hierarchical political elite as a bulwark against chaos, and subordinating all other actors to the political regime;

- a profound suspicion of western influence, combined with a constant search for international respect, status and acceptance;

- a view—shared with Machiavelli—of the masses, as 'ungrateful, fickle, false, cowardly, covetous', prone to manipulation by western intelligence agencies or unscrupulous opposition leaders;

- a commitment to the mantras of economic growth and structural reform, and full integration into a global financial elite, while refusing to allow a genuine market economy to develop at home.[17]

Regardless of how the views of Russia's population may be developing, its leadership elite shows every sign of considering the tradition of autocracy inherited from czarist and Soviet times to be the only answer to the challenge of ruling Russia. As a consequence, the challenge Russia presents to the outside world is often construed as being embodied in one man: Vladimir Putin.

Russia and Its President

Do we have a Putin problem or a Russia problem?
—HEARD AT POLICY SEMINARS DISCUSSING
RUSSIA; REPEATED AD NAUSEAM.

This question, routinely asked of Russia analysts in the West, goes to the heart of long-term planning for better management of the relationship. It betrays a persistent but misguided hope that the West's difficulties with Russia are temporary and are caused only by the personal wickedness or delusion of Vladimir Putin. It also contributes to a body of literature on the drivers of Russia's foreign policy centering on the person of Putin himself, and sometimes understating the extent to which his actions abroad follow a traditional and consistent Russian pattern.[18] Instead of being an aberration in Russian history, Putin has in fact been following its mainstream, and embodying and implementing many of the persistent Russian approaches to both domestic and interstate relations described in this book.[19]

The belief that renewed Russian assertiveness is entirely generated by the will of its current president is due to an accident of timing. Russian intentions and security concerns have not changed. What has changed, and drastically, during Putin's leadership is Russia's capability to address them. Russia began to review its perception of its own strengths in the mid-2000s as it benefited from a sudden influx of revenue thanks to higher oil prices, which transformed a struggling economy and led to consistent budget surpluses. Russia's armed forces immediately felt the difference, as funds started to flow into the cash-starved defense sector as a priority.[20] Another result was that in the middle of the last decade, Moscow intensified its pattern of employing a wide range of coercive tools in not always successful attempts to maintain influence and leverage over its Western neighbors.[21] These efforts reflected Russia's growing self-confidence built on its newfound energy wealth, and hence its ability to absorb any negative economic impact from unfriendly actions against the West.[22] High-profile incidents during this period included gas cutoffs for Ukraine in 2006, the crude sociocyber offensive against Estonia in May 2007, and ultimately the use of military force against Georgia in 2008. In each case, the results validated this approach for Putin: the Georgian conflict in particular demonstrated the validity of the use of armed force as a foreign policy tool, bringing swift and effective results with only limited and temporary economic and reputational costs to bear.

Each new instance of Russia demonstrating hostility to its neighbours or the West in general caused renewed surprise and consternation to those Western governments whose limited attention span and institutional memory prevented them from realizing that all such cases were features of a persistent trend. In fact, a review by a U.S. academic in 2012, early in President Putin's third presidency, found that "except for the need to respond to new circumstances, no important shift has been found in the direction of Russian foreign policy, with reassertion of Great Power status abroad and continuity and stability at home remaining principal objectives."[23] This underlines the point that Russia does not consist of one man, and the problems apparently presented by Putin are actually problems inherent in dealing with Russia as a country. Putin is not alone in thinking the way he does, especially among the elite clique at whose head he stands; consequently, there is a strong likelihood that any successor is likely to have similar views and a similar attitude to both domestic and foreign policy.[24] Current challenges will persist after Putin because the policies he has implemented and overseen represent a reversion to the norm in Russian thinking about security policy and relations with the outside world.

In the meantime, the focus on Putin as the personification of the challenge to the West has generated a minor industry constructing images of Putin or seeking to explain the inner workings of his court.[25] According to author and *Economist* editor Arkadiy Ostrovsky, "'Write 3,000 words on what Putin really thinks' is a regular tasker for journalists."[26] Inevitably the assessments that result have a tendency to confidently state the absolutely unknowable. In this respect, in the absence of any real means of understanding "what Putin really thinks," Putinology resembles speculation from previous decades about the inner workings of the Soviet regime. Kremlinology during the Cold War gave rise to much informed and sober assessment based on the limited information available, but also to a proliferation of evidence-free flights of fancy. Writing in 1956, Edward Crankshaw described the latter approach as constructing "a variety of engaging and plausible theories, circumstantial to a degree, any one of which may be true, each one of which is likely to be wrong. . . . It serves no useful purpose, unless to familiarize the reader with the names of the leaders. . . . On the other hand, it very certainly distracts the eye from the fundamental issues."[27]

Sixty years later the British scholar Andrew Monaghan described Putinology in strikingly similar terms, noting that it "reflects the undoubted centrality of Putin to the current Russian political landscape. But it increasingly distorts our understanding of Russian political life and, by relying on dubious sources, speculation and assertion, generates much additional noise that distracts and obstructs our understanding of how Russia works."[28]

This kind of speculation is only encouraged by Russia's culture of opacity. Russia does not—yet—suffer from the same degree of obsessive secrecy regarding even the most trivial details of the workings of the state that was embraced as a norm by the Soviets,[29] but attempting to reach informed conclusions about what is going on by using the same metrics as for liberal democracies is worse than futile. As a consequence, Crankshaw's description of the Soviet Union's behavior in 1984 is also instantly recognizable in the Russia of today: the country

> has only itself to blame if we conclude the worst on every possible occasion, since the leadership devotes so much energy to concealing not only from the outer world but also from its own people and, indeed, itself the truth about its simplest activities behind a smoke-screen of mystification (a national inheritance) and by the propagation of systematic or institutionalised lies. . . . One can understand the historical causes of this nonsensical way of carrying on and yet still stand amazed and flummoxed by its more bizarre manifestations.[30]

Polls and Legitimacy

> It doesn't matter if he's a billionaire, it doesn't matter if he has five wives, he is what Russia needs now.
> —SENIOR RUSSIAN MILITARY OFFICER
> DESCRIBING PRESIDENT PUTIN, *April 2016*[31]

One such manifestation is the manner in which all of this is, on the surface, accepted by the great majority of Russia's citizens. President Putin's public opinion ratings fluctuate, but within a relatively narrow band: his popularity is both far greater than any politician in a Western liberal democracy could ever aspire to and beyond comparison with those of his predecessor, Yeltsin. This can be confusing for Western observers, especially when in their eyes things in Russia are not going well and the leadership, whether because of accusations of corruption or falling living standards resulting from low energy prices, ought to be unpopular.

A number of reasons can be identified for this apparent oddity.[32] One is the regime's track record of success in making sure that public opinion is not aware of any viable alternatives to President Putin, who effectively stands alone on the political scene. Western commentators tempted into a superficial assessment of his popularity among Russian citizens tend to overlook the point that this has never been tested in a free and fair election against credible opponents. Another reason is the survival, subtly and unsubtly encouraged by the regime, of an idea unchanged since the embodiment of Russia in the czar: identification of the ruler with the country. Hence "public opinion data do not accurately reflect people's opinions about the government because of the massive impact of propaganda and the difficulty in formulating proper questions as a result of this propaganda. For example, when Russians are asked, 'do you support Putin?' they hear, 'do you love Russia?' because of the way the media portray the president as the embodiment of the nation."[33]

This phenomenon is one that has persisted for centuries through far greater hardships inflicted by the state than those facing Russians today:

> In spite of the constant barbarities which the Russians suffered under the autocracy and its tax-farmers, the lack of a general system of justice, the power of the nobles which fed the growth of serfdom, and the quasi-impossibility of redress or defence or avoidance of injustice (other than by flight), the nation had, by the early sixteenth century . . . a strange pride in their absolute sovereign whether he was well-disposed towards them or not.[34]

It is also remarkably resilient to suggestions or proof of the ruling elite's venality, corruption, and bad faith. Society's recognition of the regime's unjust nature does not affect poll ratings, or even willingness to vote for it.[35] Polls showed the majority of Russians agreed with opposition campaigner Aleksey Navalny that One Russia was the party "of crooks and thieves"—

but would still vote for it.[36] A general low level of interest in participating in the political process helps in this regard: "In Russia, the prevailing culture is one of 'spectator' participation, in which the individual plays the role of a passive observer of all that transpires within the country. The role of this passive observer is relegated to the ceremonial approval of the existing authority during elections."[37]

But in addition, personal enrichment by leadership figures, while not publicly condoned, is at least expected at all levels of society, and, as long as the leader is effective, it does not attract the same censure it would in the West. In this respect Putin also benefits personally from the notion of the "bad boyars"—that it is Russia's government that is to blame for any societal woes and the ruler, be it the czar, Stalin, or Putin, is both kindly and infallible.[38] In czarist times, "It was axiomatic with the peasants that the Czar loved them as God loved his children and if he only knew their plight he would straighten out all their troubles. They therefore hated all officials who barred the way between themselves and the throne."[39] Later, during communist repressions, the pitiful letters addressed personally to Stalin and assuming that he would wish to correct injustices betrayed the same syndrome. Today, Western correspondents in Moscow note a resurgence of the same belief system among ordinary Russians.[40]

It follows that what discredits Putin in Western eyes does not necessarily do so among Russians. But this does not affect the assumption in the West that Russia's leadership is constantly seeking ways of legitimizing the regime—of validating its tenure by providing its subjects with a reason not to rise in revolt.

Russia has necessarily had to resort to an ideology to provide a rationale for a system of government whose foundations in legitimacy were suspect. For the communist regime, if you could not rule by the will of God, as the czars had done, then ruling by an appropriately adjusted historical imperative was the next best thing and provided adequate excuses for a whole range of appalling regime behavior at home and abroad. Today the notion of regime legitimation provides counterarguments to the idea that President Putin's foreign policy aspirations have remained unchanged, and are only now being implemented thanks to renewed Russian strength. According to this counterargument, Russian foreign policy choices should be interpreted primarily as reflecting domestic security priorities, and actions abroad should be understood as contributing to maintaining control at home. In this view, increased military assertiveness results not from the simple availability of reinvigorated military capability but from "a gradual process of sweeping away prior taboos on the use of force in the worldview of the Putin regime."[41] In other words, the leadership relies on the fact that while individual Russians might view almost every element of official social and economic policy with strong disfavor, this is compensated for by consciousness of the rising prestige of Russia abroad.[42]

A further development of this theory is that, in response to multiple challenges, the Russian leadership has moved to a crisis mode that resorts to exceptional measures in both foreign and domestic policy. In this mode, as President Putin is no longer able to provide Russians with increasing standards of living, protecting them from an outside threat becomes his system's main source of legitimacy. The peak in oil prices during Putin's first two terms in office not only boosted Russians' pride in their country's rediscovered assertiveness but also caused Putin himself to be associated in many people's minds with the strong growth of the Russian economy and an improvement in personal living standards during this period. But when Putin returned to office in 2012, economic improvement was a thing of the past, as the price of oil had dropped, and there were worrying signs of popular discontent in the form of the election protests.[43] The result was a turn to aggressive nationalism and a continuing search for military victories.[44]

However, it still follows from this argument that an atmosphere of crisis and imminent threat from abroad is not a phase Russia is going through but rather a permanent feature that, barring energy windfalls, the regime relies on to maintain its popularity and power. It also follows that Russian leaders create insecurity abroad in proportion to their own insecurity at home: if the ruling class conducts foreign policy as a means of preserving its wealth and power in Russia, then the aggressiveness of this foreign policy must grow in proportion to the perception of threat to the political and economic survival of this class.[45]

This survival is by no means under immediate threat. But if this line of argument is correct, in the absence of any systemic overhaul of the Russian economy to provide a sound basis for renewed growth that is not hostage to energy prices, assertive behavior abroad is likely to continue regardless of the West's reaction to it. Even substantial concessions to Russia designed to dispel all possible perceptions of threat to Moscow would not remove this key driver of Russian military adventurism.

Once again, there is little in this that is new. Belonging to a strong Russia provided a distraction from deficiencies of the social system or the economy at home long before the Putin presidency.[46] In Soviet times, as recalled by Lev Gudkov, Russians "considered themselves subjects of the most militarily powerful and territorially vast empire (we used to be feared and respected by everyone), which was a way to compensate for their poverty and pitiful everyday life pervaded by the realization of being dependent on their superiors and the chronic state of helpless, humiliation, and inability to stand up for their rights and interests."[47]

Yet for all the discussion both in Russia and abroad of how Putin legitimates his rule, one fundamental point always remains unstated, and it is a critical point for understanding how Russia differs from the West. It is simply that when describing most other European countries, analysts and commentators do not need to engage in this discussion of the legitimacy of power—because it is unquestionably legitimate to start with.

Isolation and Secrecy

> The Russian troika is now hauled by three old nags, xenophobia, fear and intimidation, hurtling back to a discredited past.
> —ANGUS ROXBURGH, *June 2017*[48]

The understanding that the Russian form of governance and social system is an anomaly has prompted Russian leaders throughout history to seek to minimize contact between their subjects and the outside world. At the outset of the Cold War, George Kennan explained that "Russian rulers have invariably sensed that their rule was . . . unable to stand comparison or contact with political systems of Western countries. For this reason they have always feared foreign penetration, feared direct contact between Western world and their own, feared what would happen if Russians learned truth about world without or if foreigners learned truth about world within."[49]

Once again, this approach, while commonly associated with the Soviet regime, is in fact a centuries-old feature of life in Russia. In the 1660s it was noted that "to continue them in this lowness of spirit, and to keep them from seeing the liberty which other nations about them enjoy, the Muscovites are, upon pain of death, prohibited to go out of the Countrey."[50] Almost two centuries later the Marquis de Custine betrayed a rare moment of sympathy for Russia's rulers: "The more I see of Russia, the more I agree with the Emperor when he forbids Russians to travel and makes access to his own country difficult for foreigners. The political system of Russia could not withstand twenty years of free communication with Western Europe."[51]

The largest and most potentially threatening exposure of Soviet citizens to the West came at the end of World War II. As Soviet troops discovered to their surprise that Germany and the countries of Eastern Europe had not only enjoyed a vastly superior standard of living to their own but also a substantially greater degree of personal freedom, there was a threat that they could bring back dangerous and subversive notions of liberalism and change when they returned home. This was not an unreasonable fear: in the previous century, Russian officers who had seen Europe and especially France during the Napoleonic Wars formed the core of the Decembrist movement that later mounted a brief challenge to the monarchy. Consequently, all those who had been prisoners of the Germans, or even temporarily out of Soviet control, were regarded as possible traitors and disappeared into the Gulag, or were swiftly murdered as soon as they were back in Soviet hands, in many cases delivered there by British and American forces in one of the most shameful capitulations to Stalin of the postwar period.

This was, of course, only a proportion of the Soviet citizens who had by now been abroad; but it would have been impractical to imprison or execute the entire Red Army. In any case, the fears may have been at least partly misplaced. The first instinctive reaction to Europe by many Soviet soldiers seems to have been not to envy European material benefits and seek improvements at home, but to destroy them in order to bring Europe down to the level of Russia.[52] More than forty years later, during the armed conflict with Georgia in 2008, Russian troops displayed very similar reactions to realizing that the soldiers of their adversary enjoyed a much higher standard of living and material comfort: namely, not just looting but wanton destruction and indiscriminate defecation.[53]

Today, Russian citizens have enjoyed almost complete freedom to travel abroad for nearly three decades. But contrary to perceptions in other countries, the number of Russians who travel is still relatively limited: 72 percent do not have a current passport allowing foreign travel, and 59 percent have never been beyond the borders of the former USSR.[54] Nevertheless, tighter restrictions on who can leave the country are being introduced, including a ban on foreign travel imposed on an impressively wide range of state employees.[55] In 2018 the list of countries to which Interior Ministry employees—including, for example, policemen—could travel outside the former Soviet Union was cut to just three: Vietnam, Cuba, and China, echoing the list of "fraternal socialist countries" from the Cold War.[56]

This leaves the problem of Russians who are permanently outside Russia, whether as emigrés or because they had settled in another republic of the Soviet Union. For these, Russia has developed a comprehensive "compatriots policy," designed in part to serve as a "cultural firewall beyond Russia's borders."[57] Russian cultural researcher Mikhail Suslov points out that "the uneasy relationship between Russia and its nationals abroad has historical roots as well. . . . Russian settlers who dared to step outside the realm of the tsar found themselves in a legal, political and ideological limbo of sorts: they were at once both traitors who escaped state oppression, as well as the avant-garde of the state, its outpost and line of defense against external threats."[58]

This duality persists today. Measures such as the law on dual citizenship and the registration of holders of foreign passports contribute to fear, uncertainty, and doubt among Russians abroad,[59] while at the same time diasporas serve as a tool of foreign policy as Russia seeks to leverage them against the host nation.[60] But Suslov continues that the "confrontational instrumentalization" of Russians abroad is compromised by the number of those compatriots who have deliberately made their lives in the West. "The importance of 'global Russians' is downplayed," he notes, "and there are even attempts to alienate them and reinterpret [them] as 'traitors' of Russia, whereas compatriots in the 'near abroad' are seen as [an] integral part of Russia proper, temporarily separated from it by the evil will of Russia's Western enemies."

These "global Russians" are those who left voluntarily because they could do without Russia and saw their future elsewhere. As a result, the prominent, talented, or wealthy feature disproportionately in this group; there are more Russian-speaking Nobel Prize winners living permanently abroad than inside Russia, joined by composers and musicians, leading IT and software developers, and a significant proportion of oligarchs who have not found an accommodation with the current leadership.[61] This disproportion is reminiscent of the overrepresentation of the intelligentsia in a former wave of emigration, when Jews were permitted to leave the USSR for Israel—leading to the joke about Israel requesting that as it had now received more than enough orchestra conductors, could the Soviet Union please send some bus conductors instead. The departure of a self-selecting subset of motivated individuals deprives Russia of an important portion of its intellectual and entrepreneurial elite. But Russia suffering this self-inflicted cost is not a new phenomenon. In previous centuries, a significant proportion of Russians showing this level of personal initiative and defiance of the regime would instead have been imprisoned, exiled, or murdered by the state.

In addition to preventing its subjects from meeting foreigners, Russia has repeatedly isolated itself from foreign influence by preventing the flow of information that could carry foreign ideas. In previous centuries, this took the form of closing down private printing presses and periodically banning the import or possession of books from abroad. Domestic information too was subject to censorship of varying degrees of severity; detailed regulations for czarist censors "laid down the principle that it was the business of the government to direct public opinion along lines suited to the needs of the moment."[62] The same principle was applied during Soviet times, with varying consistency: during occasional "thaws" in the postwar period, the regime deliberately encouraged a spirit of free enquiry. However, it invariably did not like the results.[63] Material to be printed in the national press was vetted ahead of publication, but provincial papers were checked retrospectively. This meant that the provincial press, when available, was highly valuable to Cold War researchers and analysts gleaning whatever information they could about events and conditions in the Soviet Union. In today's Russia there are indications that provincial media might once again be more independent-minded and less inclined to follow central media instructions.[64]

Nevertheless, the instinct toward suppression of information is still strong. President Putin's response to media coverage of widespread theft and corruption in Russia is not to instigate or step up measures against corruption but to encourage media managers to "filter" these reports.[65] The continuing tightening of control over media in Russia has led to the creation of Meduza, the first media outlet to be established by emigrés since Soviet times.[66] As such, it has restarted a long tradition according to which, even before Soviet times, "most Russian journalists who were not mere hirelings, writing in support of the bureaucracy, had been obliged to work underground, or to write abroad and trust to the ruses of war for a circulation in their own country."[67]

For much of the post-Soviet period the internet represented a channel of communication that, while monitored, was largely outside the control of the authorities. This began to change radically in 2013, with the start of a general tightening of control over activity online, including the stepping up of monitoring and surveillance measures.[68] Not just the Russian state but the Russian Orthodox Church as well had grown alarmed at the content available through the internet and the manner of its distribution.[69] The absence of formal censorship in Russia does not prevent the authorities from taking steps to control the flow of information in advance of specific events.[70] And a proposed ban on some uses of internet telephony, intrinsically harder to monitor than other forms of voice or data communication, may limit still further the options for Russians to have conversations where the state is not a silent third party.[71]

The more conservative of Russia's security agencies construe free and unrestricted communications with the outside world as a significant security challenge. Even in 1972 it was noted that the task of ensuring political conformity was vastly more difficult than a generation earlier because potential free thinkers were "in regular contact with each other and, worse still, with the outside world."[72] But any Soviet citizen who wanted to access news from abroad could do so quietly at home with a short-wave radio without anybody necessarily being aware of it. Now the equivalent tool is the internet; but to use it without the authorities being aware is impossible because of the automatic capturing and recording of online activity. While it is not illegal to access foreign news, consciousness that doing so anonymously is impossible must, if considered, have a chilling effect.[73]

The official policy of isolation, both physically and through control of information, may help Russia address perceived security threats, but it is undoubtedly damaging in other areas. One such area is the economy. A system that isolates its population will inevitably place constraints on its growth in a global environment in which openness, innovation, and education are increasingly fundamental components of economic competency. Another area, inevitably, to suffer is good relations and clear communications with the West. Regardless of the number of Russians living abroad, by retreating into itself Russia will only deepen its habitual misunderstanding of the outside world.

SIX

The Individual and the State

People and Property

To enter Russia, you must deposit your free will along with your passport at the frontier.
—ASTOLPHE DE CUSTINE, *1839*[1]

As soon as a Russian steps off the plane outside Russia, he suddenly acquires rights.
—DAVID SATTER, *2013*[2]

One of the most persistent features of Russian life that distinguishes it most starkly from the European tradition is the balance of interests between the state and its subjects.

In Europe, especially those parts of it with the longest traditions of civil liberties and democracy, this balance is based on commonly accepted principles of reciprocity of rights and responsibilities. Russia has never experienced this balance; instead, civil society as understood in the West did not take shape, and the main principle of social organization was collectivity (*sobornost'*), founded on the subordination of individualism to the interests of the group.[3] Instead of a cooperative reciprocity, the relationship between individual and state in Russia has at times resembled a battle of wills in which the tendency to treat the individual as raw material for the realization of the state's ambitions is countered by the tendency of the individual to seek to outwit the state wherever possible.[4] It is largely for this reason that this book refers to Russians as subjects, rather than citizens, of Russia.

Political analyst Tatiana Stanovaya notes that "70 years of Soviet power and the exclusive dominance of the state, the habit of strong paternalism and conformism and collectivism, have all led to the state maintaining primacy over the interests of ordinary people."[5] But once again, to look to the Soviet past for the roots of distinctive features of Russianness is to not look far enough. Communalism was not an invention of the Soviet era but an innate characteristic of Russian society. For generations, collective will took priority over individual needs and rights in Russia, and mutual dependence was a unifying factor.[6] The Russian state was the ultimate expression of this unity and benefited from its acceptance as normal and natural. As Stuart Ramsay Tompkins observed, not just under communism but throughout previous centuries,

> the great mass of Russians never faltered in their attachment to the basic concepts laid down by the Muscovite tsars that Russia's world mission and their own role as "gatherers of the Russian land" required that all institutions, church and school, should be but instruments in furthering this grand design. The individual Russian, if he were to share in this great world destiny, must subordinate his private interests to those of the state.[7]

In fact, throughout the centuries the ideas of legality and liberty, of the rule of law and the rights of the individual, have been largely outside the bounds of Russian experience.[8] Writing in 1850, Aleksandr Herzen saw the contrast with Europe as stark: "Unquestioning recognition of the individual is one of the great human principles in European life. . . . With us the individual has always been crushed, absorbed, he has never even tried to emerge. Free speech with us has always been considered insolence, independence subversion; man was engulfed in the State, dissolved in the community."[9]

Dissolution of self into the community was not just a matter of enforcing commonly accepted values and rules of behavior; at times it was the only available way of meeting basic needs. During the Soviet period, living accommodation, a place in kindergarten for children, health care, access to goods in short supply, and more were for the most part obtained through attachment to the collective. Work collectives took responsibility for both benefits bestowed and sanctions imposed on individuals.[10] The manner in which the individual was traditionally beholden to the group is a significant factor in perceptions from the twentieth century and earlier that Russia was deficient in "many of the ideas and ideals which are basic in the formation of the Western character: the respect for the individual and the concept of the State as his servant . . . the ethical heritage . . . the traditions of individual initiative and independence."[11]

This balance of interests is shifting still further under the influence of Russia's current sense of emergency, with an intensification of state efforts to suppress independent political initiative or activism.[12] Beyond a liberal-minded minority, these efforts do not engender widespread public opposition: the period after the seizure of Crimea saw a strong increase in the number of Russian poll respondents agreeing that the state should be made stronger and that it was appropriate for individual rights to be restricted in the interest of the state under certain circumstances.[13]

The unreliability of property rights in Russia is another phenomenon often associated with the post-Soviet period of robber capitalism. But here too, Russia is continuing an age-old tradition. Where the entire nation was in some respects considered the personal property of the ruler, assets were granted to individuals to manage rather than to possess in their own right; this conditionality was replicated down through Muscovy's social structures, with "no man accounting that which he hath to be sure his own."[14] Thus, according to Andrei Piontkovsky, in this respect the current system of managing Russia's major assets

> is not state capitalism . . . but a much more archaic system of rule, traditional in Russia. The most trusted supporters of the sovereigns of Muscovy were granted fiefdoms together with the villeins who lived on them. Today, ten or fifteen petty clerks, who used to work with Major Putin in the Dresden residency or at the St Petersburg Mayoralty, are granted oil, gas and arms fiefdoms together with the villeins who pump out the oil or forge the weapons.[15]

But as ownership is conditional, even the top oligarchs do not "own" the assets; they may manage them and be their beneficiaries, but it is the leadership that has granted the right to do so and at any point can revoke that right, passing the assets on to someone else.[16] As a rule, Russia's large corporations and their notional owners accept this concept without challenging it. The most prominent exception to this generalized acceptance was Mikhail Khodorkovsky. At the beginning of Putin's presidency Khodorkovsky not only sought to gain political influence. He also implied that he intended to challenge the nature of business in Russia by agitating against corruption and for a transparent, competitive, law-abiding business environment similar to that of the West, based on formal and legal principles rather than on informal and largely arbitrary understandings. Since doing so would have undermined the entire foundation of power in Russia, it is hardly surprising that he had to be reined in and his assets, in the form of the Yukos oil company, expropriated and redistributed. In this respect, Khodorkovsky was disciplined for violating the rules not of the state but of the collective.

In addition to ownership of property, Russia's history of ownership of people must be considered a significant influence on relations between the state and its subjects, and also on interpersonal relationships in Russia today. Echoes of feudalism remained long after serfdom was abolished in 1861, assisted by Russia's subjugation of its own people—what historian Alexander Etkind calls the process of internal colonization.[17] In Soviet times, employees of collective farms were once again bound to their workplace, not being issued even internal passports allowing travel. The treatment of individuals as property returned in almost institutionalized form in the post-Soviet Russian armed forces. At the end of the twentieth century the hiring out of Russian soldier labor for commercial purposes was, if not officially acceptable, then certainly by no means unexpected. Almost absolute authority over a large pool of unskilled labor was one of the few means of improving some officers' material condition during the extended period when salaries were hopelessly insufficient, and in addition were paid irregularly or not at all—to the extent that the concept of actually living on a junior officer's salary became an obvious nonsense. Soldier rental covered a huge range of different degrees and experiences, from industrial-scale manpower supply to commercial enterprises down to conscripts engaged as unpaid personal servants for officers or their families. While in many cases the experience for the soldiers may have been fairly benign (some unofficial workplaces were clearly far preferable to life in barracks), other forms of extracurricular assignment were distinctly unsafe or unsavory.[18]

Collective assumptions about the value of individuals also come to the fore when Russia fights wars. Russia is traditionally considered careless with the lives of its soldiery and callous about those of the civilian populations among which it fights. To Western eyes, the campaigns in Chechnya abound with examples of senseless inhumanity by the Russian forces (with the equally brutal behavior of their adversaries often overlooked). But the eventual condition of Chechnya—terrorized but stable—compared with the region's role throughout the first half of the 1990s as a center of lawlessness that spread terror throughout southern Russia presents a case study confirming Russia's rational assessment that the end justifies the means. It also provides context for Russia's operations in Syria, where both the final objective and the means used to get there are repellent to Western sensitivities but entirely logical to Russian commanders and leaders.

U.S. ambassador to the United Nations Nikki Haley may ask of Syria, "How many more children have to die before Russia cares?,"[19] but the question misses the point. The idea that Russia lacks consideration for collateral damage and civilian casualties is based on a false premise; both of these are essential elements of Russian policy, aimed at terrorizing the enemy and its civilian support base into submission as rapidly as possible so as to end the fighting and restore or impose order. When Russia considers the results of Western interventions in Afghanistan, Iraq, and Libya, it can even argue that its approach is the more moral one, since crushing the will to resist swiftly delivers peace and stability rather than prolonged chaos and destabilization. Western countries may assume that the restriction of personal liberties entailed in submitting to authoritarian regimes is an unacceptable price to pay for peace. But for Russia, in keeping with traditional assumptions about the role of the individual, this is a far less significant factor than ending the fighting and restoring a stable and functioning society.

This does not mean that Russia sets no value on human life, whether it is the life of the adversary, or of civilians, or of its own soldiery. But this value has a different weight relative to other considerations of fighting and winning wars. In the West, casualty aversion is one of the key factors driving advances in military technology intended to protect vulnerable soldiers from harm or allow them to operate at a greater distance from it. In the Russian military tradition, this was not a consideration, and soldiers have time and again been treated as more expendable than machines or weapons.[20]

This attitude may now be changing. Under the influence of social and especially demographic change, Russia has dramatically adjusted the way it treats conscripts, and is showing signs of viewing them as a valued and finite resource rather than—as throughout its previous history—the cheapest of all military commodities.[21] One expression of this shift is a new willingness to develop technology, for example combat robots, intended specifically to reduce casualties.[22] But even here, while Western militaries instinctively shy away from removing humans from the decision chain because of the risk of collateral damage and civilian casualties,[23] this is not a concern for Russia. It is considered normal to entrust operations to these combat systems with the capability of independently identifying and engaging targets without human intervention.[24]

Powerlessness in the face of the state has traditionally given rise to a further aspect of Russian society that both Russians and foreigners find distasteful: the tendency to exert power by any other means available, primarily at the expense of fellow subjects. This propensity to abuse any slight advantage or preferential position has been observed from the earliest stages of the formation of Russian society. As described by the English ambassador to Moscow, Giles Fletcher, in the sixteenth century:

> For as themselves are very hardly and cruelly dealth withal by their chief Magistrates, and other superiors, so are they cruel one against another, specially over their inferiors, and such as are under them. So that the basest and wretchedest that stoopeth and croucheth like a dogge to the Gentleman, and licketh up the dust that lieth at his feete, is an intolerable tyrant, where he hath the advantage.[25]

Two and a half centuries later, the same pattern held strong:

> A man raised ever so little above the level of the mob, immediately acquires the right—even more, he contracts the obligation to maltreat other men to whom he is charged to transmit the blows that he himself receives from above; he is free to seek some recompense in the ills he inflicts for those to which he submits. Thus the spirit of iniquity descends from rank to rank into the very foundations of this unfortunate society.[26]

Abusing positions of power was also encouraged by economic necessity, with or without the additional complications of systemic corruption: even in the late nineteenth century the question was asked: "What is one to do if, under present social conditions, everyone who does not exploit someone else is doomed almost to die of hunger?"[27] The result in living memory was a distinctive feature of everyday life in Soviet Russia: shop workers, ticket office clerks, and legions of bureaucrats exploiting every petty power their position gave them to improve their sense of self-worth or their income at the expense of supplicants. While social change and the influence of a relatively liberalized economy have substantially attenuated this syndrome in the private sector since the end of communism, official impunity has meant change is slower within the apparatus of state.[28]

As in other areas, the combination of these attitudes and assumptions has direct implications for engaging with Russia as a state. Some of the most obvious implications are for Western policy based on human rights and democratization, which is fatally compromised if it does not take into account the distinction between theory and practice in Russia. Formally, the Russian constitution proclaims the protection of human rights. But in practice and in ideological statements made or endorsed by political leaders, it is clear that the Russian tradition is the supremacy of the commune, not the individual. One direct result of this different conception is misunderstandings between Russia and the EU. Samuel Greene, director of the King's College London Russia Institute, explains that this is not a result of any shortage of effort to engage in the relationship between Brussels and Moscow; rather, the cause lies in Europe's failure to understand Russia. Many of what Brussels perceived as benefits of engagement for Russia were "predicated on the increasingly untenable premise that Russian elites were beholden to their electorate. . . . The traditional approach to conditionality—offering 'carrots' such as economic integration or visa-free travel to publics in return for policy cooperation by their governments—does not work when governments are not accountable to their citizens."[29]

Furthermore, an approach based on individual rights risks being interpreted as hostile not only by the regime but by its subjects too. According to Vladimir Ivanov of the EastWest Institute, Western criticism of Russia's authoritarian leanings is "considered by Russians to be an ideological and psychological attempt to impose Western values against the will of the Russian people, and against traditional Russian values—and so a threat to Russia's national identity."[30]

Overall, the nature of everyday relations between individuals in Russia has constituted a persistent psychological barrier to meaningful social change. Well-intentioned initiatives for educational reform in the 1990s foundered on the realization that Russian schools could not promote values and behaviors that were not prevalent in society.[31] In similar fashion, attempts to make military service in Russia in the 1990s a less brutal, crime-ridden, and dangerous experience were undermined by conscripts simply replicating behavior experienced in civilian life.[32] Less directly, the restless urge to domination and exertion of power that is engendered within Russian society finds echoes in Russia's assumptions about the nature of relations between states.[33] Put simply, understanding how Russia treats other countries becomes easier as one understands how Russians treat one another.

Law and Justice

Russia has never been a country that has lived under the rule of law. It was and is ruled by Man. Indeed the will and whim of a single autocrat determined the life of individuals.
—SASHA KENNAWAY, *November 1996*[34]

The 1990s in Russia are often referred to as "lawless," but widespread illegality was as much a consequence of a superabundance of law as of its being inconsistently applied.

Under Yeltsin, the uneasy legacy of laws still in place from the Soviet period and the deadlock between president and parliaments led to uncontrollable proliferation of competing laws (*zakony*), decrees (*ukazy*), decisions (*postanovleniya*), and instructions (*rasporiazheniya*). The result was multiple layers of often mutually contradictory legislation and regulations from a bewildering number of sources. This was especially the case in the relatively new field of business and tax law, where every government agency from the president, ministries and Federal Assembly down to a regional tax office or custom house would issue its own regulations or its own specific interpretations of rules from higher authority. The resulting chaos contributed to a chronic inability to collect taxes for the state or regional budgets, and persisted until Putin became president. As part of his broad-based campaign to put Russia's affairs in order, he oversaw a drastic reduction in corporate tax rates combined with real efforts to systematize tax rules, as a generally successful incentive for companies and individuals to actually pay their tax. Contrary to a common external perception, this period in fact saw substantial reinforcement of the rule of law in many fields in Russia. According to Vladimir Ivanov,

> The situation improved significantly when Putin came to power. He established some order in how the law is applied in the regions. There was a massive practice of abuse of human rights in the regions, because everybody acted independently and there was no level playing field in the law. Putin made a great effort to impose order, and in my view this helped a lot to establish a formal basis for the protection of human rights.[35]

This "imposition of order" extended to the Putin presidency's first arriving at a working relationship with the State Duma, and then marginalizing it as a competitive center of power. The Duma's new role as primarily a conveyor belt for legislation conceived and commissioned by the presidential administration meant that a working process for getting fundamental legislation in place was finally established, with messy debate and disputation reduced to a minimum.

But the effect of legal confusion during the 1990s had been to highlight, rather than create, a situation in which the vast majority of Russians existed by default in breach of the law.

Maurice Baring wrote of Russia in 1910 that "as a general rule the local administrative officials by the manner of their interpretation, are completely successful in sacrificing the spirit to the letter of the law. . . . It must be remembered that not only what is on the lists of prohibited things is regarded as a crime, but also what is not on the unwritten lists of things that are allowed."[36] Laws that were both broad and at times vague created a juridical environment where most human activities could if necessary be framed as illegal. Alena Ledeneva describes how the system worked through the rest of the twentieth century:

> While everybody is under the threat of punishment, the actual punishment is "suspended" but can be enforced at any time. The principle of "suspended punishment," whereby a certain freedom and flexibility did exist but could be restricted at any moment, worked well in the Soviet system.

It became routine practice for the authorities to switch to the written code only "when necessary." A similar tendency became evident in the 1990s, notably for the same reasons: the formal rules were impossible to follow and it was not feasible to prosecute everyone.[37]

Selective application of restrictive legislation is summarized in the perennial aphorism that "the severity of Russia's laws is alleviated by the fact they may not necessarily be applied."

David Satter suggests that since this system is almost universal, and means that almost every citizen is vulnerable to facing criminal charges, the only way to avoid prosecution is to demonstrate loyalty to the authorities.[38] But even liberal behavior and criticism of the authorities have at times been permitted in Russia within commonly understood boundaries.[39] Under normal circumstances it is generally clear what standards of behavior will be acceptable and what will invite legal sanction.[40] It is when these boundaries change, sometimes without warning, that Russian subjects are caught out and discover that commonly accepted activities will now be treated as cause for criminal conviction. One high-profile casualty of this shifting of rules of the game is the theater and film director Kirill Serebrennikov, prosecuted for embezzlement in 2017. The "unabashedly modernist and anticlerical" Serebrennikov routinely touched on subjects of sensitivity to the authorities, but worked in an industry that needed to "find ways to circumvent the law simply to get the work done. And it works until some of the director's enemies within the state system decide to punish them, or the state itself decides it is no longer interested in supporting certain projects. Pulling the plug is easy because everyone is a potential fraud or embezzler."[41]

As described in more detail in chapter 9 in the section "Repression Lite," actual murder by the Russian state is now the exception rather than the rule. But arbitrary and unexpected arrest and detention persist as hazards for Russians, whether innocent or guilty.[42] As Russian minister of justice Aleksandr Konovalov noted in 2008, "In developed countries . . . a man knows very well what he can be severely punished for, and when [by contrast] he can proceed calmly and confidently because he is acting within his rights."[43] For Russia, this remains an aspiration. One of the most widely disseminated videos from anticorruption protests in Moscow in June 2017 showed a bystander in a "Russia" baseball cap criticizing opposition demonstrators at length—before he too was grabbed from behind at random by the police and hauled away.[44]

These arbitrary aspects of justice are another feature of Russian life that has remained remarkably persistent through history. As described in 1906, any unsuspecting Russian who had fallen foul of the police

> may then be brought up for trial before a Judge and sentenced to two years', five years', or ten years' imprisonment or exile, according to the state of the judge's political opinions or digestion.... But the Russian suspect has two advantages still: he may be thrown out of prison as unexpectedly as he was thrown in, and with as little reason given.... It is very seldom, however, that the most convincing defence makes the least difference to the sentence, for that has been decided beforehand.[45]

Justice administered by supposedly independent courts but in fact delivered in accordance with political instructions is another long-standing Russian tradition. In the sixteenth century it was observed that Russians "have no written law.... Their only law is their Speaking Law, that is, the pleasure of their Prince, and of his magistrates and officers."[46] The "speaking law" has an echo today in the form of *telefonnoye pravo*, or "telephone law," which refers among other things to the practice of directing judges to pass specific verdicts and sentences.[47] Away from high-profile cases, the results of *telefonnoye pravo* and directed verdicts can be detected, for example, in judges delivering identically worded sentences in separate cases.[48]

Once again, this is no new phenomenon in post-Soviet times; examples abound throughout the czarist and communist periods of the law being applied flexibly, thereby allowing individuals to be dealt with in a manner that is seen as appropriate rather than necessarily juridically correct. A new criminal code of the Soviet Union introduced in 1958 abolished retrospective legislation. But this was not seen as an obstacle to a 1961 law specifying the death penalty for currency speculation being applied to individuals who had already been convicted and sentenced to jail terms under the previous law, since replacing their imprisonment with death sentences was felt to be right and just.[49] Sasha Kennaway recounts a similar case from Russia in the same period: "The police were upset, especially since one of the [severed] heads belonged to the local police chief.... I asked what happened to the killer. He was shot in spite of the legal code which prescribed life imprisonment for such murders. It was such an awful crime that an exception was made for him, said my companion. It did not occur to him that he was condoning an act by the state that flouted its own law."[50] Since such practices attract Western criticism, Lev Gudkov suggests that one consequence of Russia's most recent alienation has been "enormous relief upon discarding the burdensome normative obligations associated with the West."[51]

These are specific features of the long-established Russian principle that laws are for the governed, not for the government or the state. Russia's leadership is content to rule by law without accepting the rule of law. On the one hand, all individuals and groups must be held to the laws of the country. On the other hand, the country itself determines the law and hence is not obliged to observe it; although if it becomes absolutely necessary, the law can be changed to legitimize state behavior.[52] The Russian public as a whole appears content with this arrangement and routinely accepts unlawful actions by leadership figures.[53] This in turn creates an environment where officials such as judges can flaunt their wealth with impunity even when no explanation is presented for it other than unrestrained corruption.[54]

Less privileged Russians have needed to find a way of working around the law rather than within it. One response is reliance on informal networks and relationships to collude against the system: the incoherence of formal rules compels almost all Russians, willingly or not, to violate them and to operate under agreements and rules of behavior that are introduced and negotiated outside formal institutions.[55] These rules make use of noncontractual but binding relationships such as kinship, friendships, and other trust-centered relationships to get things done (or, in Soviet times and the early 1990s, to access scarce resources).[56] With the end of communism it was informal structures that shaped the development of post-Soviet Russia and led to the capture first of large sectors of the economy, and later of the political system as a whole, by a class of instant capitalists—among whom KGB officers and veterans featured prominently. As a tightly knit fraternity with unmatched access to inside information, personal contacts, slush funds of hard currency, and other mechanisms to get things done both in Russia and abroad, these formed a ready-made network ideally poised to take advantages of the opportunities presented by the early development of an approximately free market in Russia.[57] Thirty years later, despite adjustments to the procedures, ethics, and formalities of corruption both before and after the end of the Soviet Union, "informal practices" remain integral to making business work.[58] Dynastic marriages and appointing sons and daughters to positions of trust in family firms are examples of informal mechanisms compensating for the absence of formal guarantees of succession.

It is when formality is imposed, for example during legal disputes in London between arch-oligarchs, that it becomes instantly clear how incompatible rigid legal frameworks are with what journalist Peter Pomerantsev calls "the liquid mass of networks, corruption, and evasion—elusive yet instantly recognizable to members—that orders Russia."[59] And yet it is when Russian practices collide with the outside world that understanding Russian notions of legality and justice becomes most important. This does not just apply in business dealings, where a fundamental rule of investing in Russia is to ensure protection of the investment from abuse of legal process. In international relations too, it is critical for responding appropriately to Russia's routine calls for international law to be observed: just as it does with domestic law, Russia sees this as a tool for achieving effect rather than an institution to be respected in its own right. Here too, Russia's practice is driven by a presumption of distinctiveness from the West, and yet more examples arise of apparently common terminology masking vast differences in understanding. Official rhetoric regarding international law demonstrates that concepts like "peacekeepers," "genocide," and occasionally "international law" itself carry an entirely different meaning in Russia than their literal translation would suggest.[60] Consequently the semblance of common interest with Russia can, as so often, mask fundamental disagreements.

To understand the roots of these disagreements requires an understanding of the distinctive framework of morals and morality, right and wrong, that Russia has inherited from its unique history and social structure. This is explored in the next part of the book.

PART III

Russia's Inheritance

SEVEN

Russia's Moral Framework

Religion, Totems, and Ideology

The state and my faith are united. They can't be separated. The values of the church and the state coincide.
—ARCHPRIEST IOANN GARMASH, *July 2017*[1]

The role of the church and religion in Russian society and politics is complex and can express itself in unexpected ways. Another Russian self-perception that is often incomprehensible from abroad is as a center of true Christian values, a "third Rome." Notions like these give rise to foreign policy statements that are otherwise baffling, such as (in late April 2016) foreign minister Sergey Lavrov rejecting a return to "business as usual" with Europe because Russia was too Christian: normal dealings with the West would imply Russia becoming more like Europe, "but that runs counter to the fundaments of our culture, which is based on the Orthodox religion, on Christianity."[2] The statement may be glib and its premise unsustainable, but there is little doubt it chimes with mainstream opinion in Russia.

The Russian Orthodox Church regards itself as indistinguishable from the state, and fills a role of state facilitator that is entirely alien to Western notions; in effect, its traditional role has been in support of secular authority, while the Church of Rome and its offshoots have primarily been an alternative or even competitive source of power. In Russia the Orthodox Church exists to give its blessing, quite literally, to state enterprises, including some that in Western eyes might seem distinctly un-Christian.[3] Yet at the same time, Russian churchgoers refer to there being two churches—the formal, official apparatus, which is indistinguishable from the state, and the church as a religious institution, less prestigious but more relevant to personal faith.

Russia is also home to distinctive overlapping philosophical traditions in the national narrative, many of which also bear on foreign policy. Examples from previous centuries include the "Russian Idea," the intellectual notion that the essence of the Russian nation could be characterized by certain timeless features, including messianic, Orthodox spirituality and a sense of community.[4] The philosophy most often linked to Russian state aspirations at present is Eurasianism, commonly associated with popular hirsute ideologue Aleksandr Dugin; but throughout history, up to and including current political applications, each of these themes and traditions has been readily harnessed to the state interest of an expansionist Russia. The alternative reality created by Russian state media today is the continuation of a long tradition in which Russia's intellectual leaders have detached their country from Western rationality and its preoccupation with truth based on logic and have pursued different, mystical goals and a separate, metaphysical and highly subjective notion of truth.[5]

At the same time, much of this separate truth has been arrived at through seeking a way of rationalizing or excusing the fact that, for centuries, life for the great majority of Russians has been consistently miserable. Historical descriptions of Russian attitudes emphasize the search for ways to avoid personal responsibility for a person's condition and surroundings by seeking external phenomena to thank for good fortune or blame for bad luck, instead of taking steps to bring about an improvement. Even today there is a strong belief in the role of fate, magic, or divine intervention in positive outcomes and in the role of foreign conspiracy in negative ones.[6]

But this is only one expression of a Russian need for a unifying belief system. During the Soviet era, communism sporadically suppressed Christianity but comfortably adopted its symbolism to replace it in Russian life. Marxist-Leninist ideology had its bearded prophet, Karl Marx, and his ideologically baptized messiah, Lenin. Those who fought and died for the liberation of the proletariat from capitalism provided the heroes, saints, and martyrs. The initial sacred book was *Das Kapital*, supplemented by an enormous volume of canonical and apocryphal writings.[7] Another aspect of the coherence between church and state that only partially resurfaced in communist times was the semidivine nature of the ruler. In imperial times, in some sectors of society (especially remote and rural ones) the czar was sacrosanct and so elevated as to be more or less indistinguishable from God, a perception encouraged by the church to protect the ruler.[8] The "personality cult" of Stalin, while all-pervasive, approached deification without actually reaching it, although letters to Stalin took on the role of prayers to God. Some of the excesses of the Stalin cult have faint echoes in the current adulation of President Putin, especially in the religious overtones of phrases like "Putin is our all."[9]

With the end of the USSR, the simultaneous disappearance of communism as a guiding philosophy that united Russians and of Russian power and influence in the world left an ideological vacuum, which was filled in the early 1990s by such extraordinary phenomena as the *"ekstrasens"* craze.[10] Cults and mysticism flourished. For over two years, listeners to Mayak, a major national radio station, woke to the eerie, robotic preaching of Shoko Asahara, the leader of the Japanese Aum Shinrikyo death cult—eerie and robotic because Asahara, a non-Russian speaker, had recorded a large number of individual Russian words, which were then cut and spliced into sermons by his followers.[11]

This ideological gap was not properly filled until after the arrival in power of President Putin and the renewed emphasis on the notion of Russia as a great state. As part of this, current Russian state historiography takes on quasi-religious characteristics. The Great Patriotic War in particular is achieving the status of a second state religion, protected by law; Russian initiatives against the "falsification of history" and laws against the "rehabilitation of Nazism" (which cover almost any objective retelling of the role of the Soviet Union in 1939–40) have assumed the role of czarist antiblasphemy legislation and Soviet measures to protect the Communist Party from criticism. Even the language of historical discourse now includes religious references: discussions questioning the canonical version of history risk being branded "blasphemous" and "sacrilegious."[12]

At the same time, the church's position as a state authority is being reinforced by the revival of official sanctions for offences related to religion. Much of the criticism over the harsh sentences handed down to members of the punk band Pussy Riot for "hooliganism inspired by religious hatred" after their 2012 protest at the altar screen of a Moscow cathedral implied that this was a uniquely Russian reaction, glossing over the fact that their actions would have been considered unconditionally offensive in any church, or indeed any place of worship, anywhere in the world.[13] But other prosecutions that have been brought for far less intrusive actions "insulting the religious feelings of the faithful" (under Article 148 of the Russian Criminal Code) look strikingly like an antiblasphemy campaign.[14] While not incurring anything approaching the harsh punishments handed down by the czarist courts for heresy, impiety, or sacrilege, or by Soviet courts or tribunals for the slightest criticism of the Communist Party or its leaders, they still represent a further constriction of the acceptable bounds of behavior in Russia.

The Threat of Western Decadence

> The European Union and its Member States consider as one of their priorities the dissemination of their neo-liberal values as a universal lifestyle for all other members of the international community.
> —RUSSIAN FOREIGN MINISTRY REPORT ON
> HUMAN RIGHTS IN THE EU, 2013[15]

"Traditional values" are an object of Russian national policy and are defined in the National Security Strategy.[16] Many of these values stand in direct contradiction to societal trends in the West. Growing alarm over the pernicious influence of European decadence in the previous decade[17] was summarized by President Putin's argument in 2013 that relativism had led Euro-Atlantic countries into a "moral crisis . . . implementing policies that equate large families with same-sex partnerships, belief in God with belief in Satan."[18] Before and since then, European efforts to promote Western values have tended to consolidate Russia's concerns. The fact that the director of the European Values think tank in Prague and head of its "Kremlin Watch" initiative features in injudicious videos from his younger days on websites dedicated to homosexual pornography[19] is not relevant to his aptitude for the post—but it will nonetheless confirm Russia's worst suspicions about those values. German chancellor Angela Merkel commented that "Putin believes that we're decadent, we're gay, we have women with beards.... That it's a strong Russia of real men versus the decadent West."[20]

Attitudes to sexual diversity provide a specific source of alienation from the West, leading to its rejection by Russia.[21] In January 2014, immediately before the seizure of Crimea, Russia presented its annual report on human rights in the EU, protesting strenuously at the "aggressive promotion of sexual minorities' rights" and stating that "attempts have been made to enforce on other countries an alien view of homosexuality and same-sex marriages as a norm of life and some kind of a natural social phenomenon that deserves support at the state level."[22] Shortly afterward the European Parliament confirmed that Moscow was indeed correct in this assessment, by issuing a post-EU-Russia summit resolution heavily emphasizing human rights, especially those of sexual minorities, and calling for legislative change in Russia.[23] In fact, before it was overshadowed by more immediate concerns, such as the flight of President Viktor Yanukovych and the outbreak of hostilities in Ukraine's East, the challenge posed by sexual diversity to traditional values constituted a substantial element of the perceived threat of Europeanization approaching Russia through Ukraine.[24]

The officially encouraged reemergence of an instinctive and traditional conservatism in Russia may in large part be a backlash against the excesses of the 1990s, when for a time it seemed all values were suspended in Russia's larger cities. But appearances of real liberalization in Russia after the end of communism were somewhat deceptive, since superficial or urban adoption of European values obscured persistent and even deeper attachment to traditional ones, allowing them to resurface in later post-Soviet times.[25] The current decade in particular has seen a hardening of attitudes, especially in the provinces and among older Russians, toward the West and toward nonconformist cultures within Russia itself.[26]

This particular gap between Russia and the West is growing wider. Even if President Putin's comment that representatives of sexual minorities visiting Russia "can feel free and not restrained, but leave children alone please"[27] does indeed indicate a confusion between homosexuality and paedophilia, it reflects assumptions that were prevalent in Western Europe only a couple of generations ago. But as a key element in value systems that continue to diverge, attitudes toward sexuality and the family, sometimes summarized as Christian values, constitute an increasingly important factor in Russia's international isolation.

These widely differing cultural contexts give rise to more trivial misunderstandings over sex and sexuality as well. When not conducting official duties, President Putin routinely and publicly engages in manly pursuits, with or without a shirt. This alternately amuses and bemuses Western audiences, since the emphasis on masculinity appears over the top and verging on the camp. Such behavior is so out of kilter with Western norms that liberal commentators struggle to explain its appeal, and search for deeper meanings: to gender studies professionals, this "use of gender norms [is] part of a legitimation strategy employed by regimes in power and by their political opponents."[28] Put more simply, in a country where acceptance of gender stereotypes is widespread and considered normal, and furthermore the need for a strong leader is generally recognized, there is nothing untoward about reassuring demonstrations by that leader that he is a man's man.

While it may indeed be based on the genuine convictions of a wide range of Russia's leaders and subjects, the "conservative revolution in official cultural policy" has also been harnessed for political ends both at home and abroad.[29] Domestically, it is used to emphasize the threat from the West and Russia's status as a nation apart: conservatism is presented to Russians in a way that stresses their difference from and superiority to others.[30] Abroad, Russia seeks, with some success, to assume the leadership of those in the West who strive to resist the imposition of liberal values.[31] This is not the first time Russia has led similar efforts: after the turmoil of the Napoleonic Wars, it brought together the Holy Alliance of the Russian and Austrian emperors and the Kingdom of Prussia in part to resist alarming trends of democratization, liberalism, and secularism.

In combination, these trends often effectively obscure more fundamental ways in which values taken for granted in the West differ from reality in Russia. In the West the aspiration, and quite often the fact, is that individuals have rights, governments are accountable, small countries are sovereign, and contracts are sacred—none of which apply in Russia and some of which are positively threatening in Russia's view of the world. As a result, the Russian leadership's focus on moral decadence as a key rationale for avoiding values contamination from the West is once again an entirely rational measure for self-protection.

Truth and Untruth . . .

There seem to be three characteristics distinguishing Russia from Europe (or from the rest of Europe), all tied closely to the primacy of the state: a higher regard for raw power, a lower regard for truth telling, and, perhaps consequently, pervasive distrust.
—ROMAN SKASKIW, *March 2016*[32]

During the 2014 seizure of Crimea, the West was startled and bewildered by how comfortably President Putin and other senior Russian figures were making public statements that were self-evidently untrue. The approach was so remote from what had been considered normal Western practice that politicians and news media were unsure how to respond. Since that time, ubiquitous Russian campaigns of disinformation, most recently characterized as "fake news," have prompted renewed study of how Russia uses and abuses falsehoods for a wide variety of aims. This renewed scrutiny has led to the important realization that, contrary to traditional Western assumptions, when deployed by Russia lies need not be even remotely believable in order to achieve their desired effect.[33] Nevertheless, the West does not always fully understand the power and effectiveness of Russian willingness to tell a lie that both the speaker and the listener know is a lie, and this misperception contributes to the West's inability to find real countermeasures to Russian disinformation.[34] This section therefore attempts to unpick Russian attitudes to truth and untruth, both conscious and instinctive, in order to provide context and understanding for their use both as a tool of foreign and security policy and in everyday domestic contexts.

According to one Russian sociological study, "The Western legal notion (enshrined in the democratic system) that lies are a fundamental violation of human rights is not inherent to how Russians think about lies. Instead, Russians [consider] referential content of the situation, the motivations and intentions of the liar, and his or her background knowledge of the situation."[35]

In other words, truth is conditional, not absolute. This is reflected in the choice of words available in Russian to describe what in English would be called "truth." The first translation that comes to mind is usually *pravda*, but an alternative, *istina*, is also available, and the differences between the two are helpful for understanding the distinctive Russian approach to truth and untruth.

Pravda denotes a conformity with accepted versions of facts or events. *Istina* denotes a truth beyond the known facts of the world. *Pravda* may accord with ethical, moral, or legal standards of correctness. But *istina* refers to metaphysical, unchanging truths about life, existence, and the universe. It exists independently of, and can be considered superior to, worldly notions such as justice, ethics, and morality. There can be degrees of *pravda*, such as *polupravda* (half-truth) or *nepravda* (untruth). What constitutes *pravda* may be subject to debate. But there can be no quantification of degrees of *istina*.[36] In a Russian thesaurus, *pravda* corresponds to fair or realistic, while *istina* corresponds to real, actual, or genuine.[37] Or, put more simply, "*Pravda* is a tactical truth, and *istina* is actual truth."[38] The net effect is that when assessing whether statements by Russian leaders or citizens are true or not, they can be measured by two entirely separate criteria. In effect, a statement can be considered "true" in Russia because it is *pravda* but found to be untrue in the West because it is not *istina*.

Tellingly, the Russian words for untruths also do not correspond neatly to the Western philosophical tradition of dividing assertions cleanly into just two categories, true and false. The English word "lie," in particular, does not convey the wide range of modalities of Russian deception, each described by a specific Russian term that defies accurate and complete rendering into English.[39] When reviewing an early draft of this book, a Russian academic suggested avoiding the word "lie" altogether, as its emotive nature in English was not appropriate for describing a shared conspiracy in avoiding the truth as a survival mechanism. One alternative formulation put forward was "collective construction of a functional mythology." This gives important context to the instinct to lie out of loyalty, on behalf of a country or a system that otherwise is indefensible. Traveling in Russia in the 1960s, Laurens van der Post was initially startled at the inhabitants' propensity to repeat obvious fictions with great conviction—but eventually concluded that "officials, I believe, deceived me, perhaps out of duty, patriotism, or fear, all of which I could understand. They were small men caught up in a system and forced to make a machine work which was basically of the wrong design."[40]

Domestically, deception is an established, acknowledged, and in part accepted component of political culture. It causes no surprise at all when promises made to the Russian people by their leaders, even when not strictly untrue, eventually turn out to be meaningless.[41] But this dissembling works in both directions. In the general air of mistrust and deceit, Russians at all levels of society can respond to being lied to by the authorities by returning the favor. In the Soviet era, the word *tufta* indicated a particular kind of conspiracy to fulfill the plan and deceive the state by submitting entirely fictitious output or production figures. More recently, President Putin specified in 2010 that live video from high-priority construction projects should be fed directly to his desk.[42] The assumption that this was necessary for productive work to take place suggests that the cycle of systemic dysfunctionality caused by mutual deception is alive and well.[43]

In an article advising on the conduct of political negotiations, U.S. academic Kimberly Marten points out in addition that "Russians value '*khitrost*' (cunning or wiliness)."[44] In some respects this is unsurprising, given their history: an especial facility at deception was a survival mechanism, whether faced with the Mongol, the tax collector, the landowner, the recruiting sergeant, the Cossack, the gendarme, the commissar, or anyone else who constituted higher authority and posed a very real threat to life and livelihood. As a result, according to the Marquis de Custine, "The thing that dominates [Russians'] character and the conduct of their entire life is cunning. No one has the right to reproach them for this most natural consequence of their situation."[45]

The traditional advantages of cunning find expression in Russian folk and fairy tales. In the modern, sanitized versions of such tales in the West, as a general principle, good, truth, honesty, and decency prevail. Many Russian tales, by contrast, still center on the principle of *kto kogo perekhitrit*—he who prevails will be he who can be more cunning, sly, and devious than the adversary—with the implicit assumption that the adversary too is aiming to be cunning, sly, and devious. Considering this kind of implicit psychological framework can give context for helping to understand why, in the present day, open-handed offers of friendship and support from the West are met with suspicion.[46] It also provides the background for what is often perceived as the fundamental duplicity of Russia's stated goals in international relations, where subversion or outright invasion is ordinarily accompanied by protestations of goodwill and the desire for peace. As described at the time of the Crimean War, "All the nations that have aspired to universal domination have declared their designs loudly and openly. The first nation that has not admitted its goal is the Russian people. . . . This is what allows them easily and with the least danger to be the most aggressive."[47] More than a century later the diagnosis was the same: "Russia is successful because she can be friendly and subversive at the same time. She is like the friend who, while spending a pleasant weekend at a country-house, loses no opportunity to convince the staff to do away with their host."[48]

A common counter to the accusation that Russia's leaders engage in habitual mendacity is that "all politicians lie." Even if this is taken as true, it overlooks the difference between lies of temporary expediency and lies as a fixed principle of government. With the striking exception of the Donald Trump administration in the United States, Western politicians lie as an exception, and in the hope that people will believe them (the Western assumption is that lying, and getting away with it, requires being plausible). Russian politicians and officials lie by default, not necessarily with the expectation or even the hope that they will be believed.

Untruths also serve as a demonstration of power. When both sides know that what has been said is a lie but the weaker side is powerless to challenge it, this provides an ideal mechanism for the everyday petty power politics of Russian life described in chapter 6. But the same principle holds good for the international stage. For example, when President Putin told other world leaders to their face in November 2014 that Russian troops were not present in eastern Ukraine, he revealed their impotence to influence Russian behavior.[49]

Two further examples should serve to illustrate how this tendency expresses itself in Russia today, in both foreign relations and domestic politics. Abroad, recognition of Russia's distant and recent history as an aggressor leads to the deployment of lie as counterfact. The often repeated claim that "Russia has never invaded anyone or started a conflict, only ever acted in self defense," is highly effective at stopping debate on the nature of Russian power in its tracks or diverting it into painstaking elaboration of the wide selection of instances from this century and the previous one that demonstrate this claim to be fatuous. At home, the video referred to in chapter 6 of a regime supporter being unexpectedly snatched by police at opposition demonstrations in June 2017 contains a classic example of the lie as justification of the unjustifiable. Observing the arrest immediately before his own, the "Russia" baseball cap wearer says, "He just said he would blow something up"—a spontaneous invention for the benefit of the authorities, designed to justify their actions.[50]

. . . and Doublethink

> The great majority . . . cultivate in themselves utter ignorance as an essential condition of survival in contemporary Russia.
>
> —VLADIMIR PASTUKHOV, *December 2014*[51]

The realization that untruth and deception are a fixed principle of life in Russia is sometimes supposed to derive from the Soviet past.[52] But just as in many other instances, the roots of this behavior go far deeper than the twentieth century. The immediate post-Soviet period, with a relative flourishing of independent media, was a rare anomaly in Russian history. At other times, in conditions of total or near-total information control, it has always been straightforward for Russia's rulers not only to propagate an official fiction but also to require its faithful and unquestioning acceptance. The result is that truth is not a constant but is constantly reinvented. In 1839, de Custine observed that Russia "remakes facts; it wages war on evidence and triumphs in the battle . . . for evidence has no defender in this country, no more than justice, when they embarrass the State."[53] This strikes an immediate chord today with Western researchers seeking to identify and counter the constant and constantly changing stream of disinformation from Moscow.

In former, more repressive times, "doublethink" in the form of willing self-deception in order to subscribe to these official myths was yet another essential survival mechanism.[54] One important component of this suspension of disbelief in the Soviet era was referred to as the conflict between the television and the refrigerator, that is, between the official portrayal of life in the USSR being comfortable and pleasant, and people's day-to-day experiences of having an empty fridge—if indeed they possessed one in the first place. This phenomenon is now resurgent as a result of the state media's creation of an alternative reality when describing events both within and outside the country.[55] Although Russia today is far from the standards of repression of Soviet rule, the requirement for doublethink (as originally defined by George Orwell based on his experiences of communist propaganda) has already returned. It is once again the case that hypocrisy and contradictions should not be pointed out in public. Officials question official narratives at the risk of losing their jobs—even official historians discussing history.[56] A similar doublethink extends to ubiquitous Russian corruption, condemned as iniquitous but embraced as the way to get things done.[57] Above all, the echoes of repression are discernible in ordinary Russians pretending to maintain faith in leadership benevolence and promises in spite of all available evidence that they are false.

A degree of mental agility is required to follow Russia's shifting and often evidence-free official state narratives. Recent polls on the history of World War II, for example, show a dramatic shift in Russian public attitudes and an embracing of Soviet-era myths. But according to Russian domestic policy researcher Andrey Kolesnikov, these "attitudes are not evidence of a nation regressing in its ability to understand facts, but of one adapting to changing circumstances."[58] The subordination of common sense to political or ideological imperatives, long thought to be a vanished feature of the Soviet past, has resurfaced. It has led among other things to the Moscow City Council adopting measures to constrain the spread of HIV not on the basis of medical advice but in accordance with a report by the Russian Institute for Strategic Studies (RISI) that focused instead on HIV as a by-product of the Western information war against Russia and a conspiracy by condom manufacturers.[59]

The control of thought has at all times been assumed by the authorities to be a necessary function of government in Russia.[60] Consequently, private or nonconformist thought is often of necessity driven into hiding or exile. As a result, while all cultures have differences between "public" and "private" selves, in Russia the divergence can be extreme.[61] De Custine's harsh verdict on Russia quoted earlier, that "whoever has well examined that country will be content to live anywhere else," was echoed almost exactly 100 years later by another Frenchman, André Gide: "As it always happens that we recognize the value of certain advantages only after we have lost them, there is nothing like a stay in the USSR . . . to help us appreciate the inappreciable liberty of thought we still enjoy in France."[62] But the path of least resistance remains to accept and embrace state narratives and the virtual reality created by television, replete with officially promoted facts about both Russia and the West that not only have no basis in reality but are swiftly and easily verifiable as fictions.[63] According to Ivan Kolpakov, editor in chief of the Russian emigré news site Meduza, "The most complicated thing is that some part of the audience understands that it's a fake reality but they are consuming it nevertheless. . . . They choose it."[64] In historian Catherine Merridale's phrase, this is "building lives by keeping to the agreed script."[65]

The requirement for political conformity also governs some aspects of academic work, especially in the fields of politics and international relations, where Russia's theoretical perspectives have largely been shaped by political rather than academic considerations. In particular, academia has been instrumentalized to legitimize and conceptualize policy preferences.[66] Political analyst Maria Lipman notes that historical research is especially affected, where "all kinds of 'historical' versions and interpretations [are] driven by servility with no regard whatsoever for established facts or academic authority."[67]

Equal and opposite to the unimportance of plausibility when telling lies is the unimportance of relying on established facts when telling the truth. Once again, this is no new phenomenon. In the sixteenth century Giles Fletcher noted that "the Russe neither believes anything that an other man speaks, nor speaks anything himself worthy to be believed."[68] Revolutionary turned conservative philosopher Lev Tikhomirov, writing in the late nineteenth century, complained that "in Russia little attention is paid to facts as they are."[69] In the same year a British author echoed the complaint: "They lack that reverence for facts that lies at the root of the Anglo-Saxon character. A Russian can no more bow to a fact, acknowledging it as final and decisive, than he can to a personal appreciation or to a mere opinion founded upon insufficient or no grounds; he is ever ready to act in open defiance of it."[70] Today, Russia is reverting to type as a country where not only the expression of opinion but even the recital of established facts can be forbidden.[71]

Even accepted facts do not stand alone but may be diluted or obscured by unrelated preconceptions. This is one way in which incomprehension at Russian statements is augmented by the manner in which they are communicated, which is often incompatible with Western assumptions. Elena Fell, a Russian academic who has also worked at British universities, has developed a particular facility for comparing the communication styles of the two societies—including the differing understandings of truth, facts, and rationality. She notes that cross-cultural communication, "important in business situations and essential in diplomacy," is fatally compromised by the fact that "Russians and Westerners access, process and communicate information in different ways." This is because "Western traditions prescribe paying mindful attention to detail. . . . Russians, on the other hand, practise the opposite approach." Specifically, "Russians tend to mentally condense reality into a series of substantial, meaningful elements and disregard what they consider trivial. Thus, a significant portion of reality remains verbally unacknowledged."[72] Conversely, "Russians may be uneasy about Westerners' insistence on paying attention to details . . . and their preference for unnecessary rationalisation."[73]

Scholar of strategy and military culture Dima Adamsky agrees:

> The products of this [Russian] cultural environment predominantly express themselves in indirect, cyclical, understated, and vague language in text and speech, relying on the listener's or reader's ability to grasp the meaning from the context. Form, ceremony, and the expression of respect are emphasized at the expense of content; nonverbal signals might be more important than words. In negotiations the message is permitted to evolve without referring to the problem directly.[74]

Elena Fell concludes that this "approach to reality is . . . an entrenched feature of the Russian character that was purposefully taught, encouraged and nurtured during the course of the 20th century and beyond."[75] But it also means that habits of communication may cause Western listeners to conclude their Russian interlocutors are being evasive or dishonest, even in circumstances where they are in fact being open, truthful, and—as they see it—direct.[76]

Finally, Russia also projects the requirement for doublethink abroad, demanding collusion in a variety of shared myths about the country's role in the world. Whether the purpose is for comfort in the notion that Russia is a greater power or for political control makes little difference to the result, which is a significant constraint on Russia's ability to form normal relationships with its neighbors or the West in general.[77] Nowhere is this clearer than in Russia's treatment of its own history, discussed in the next chapter.

EIGHT

History Matters

The Longer Perspective

> When studying Russian history, it is not surprising to find threads, both fine and coarse, which are woven without a break throughout the fabric of the Russian chronicle.
> —JAMES FOOTE, *1972*[1]

There is a continuing fashion for drawing historical parallels between the state of relations with today's Russia and periods from the Soviet and imperial Russian past. Comparisons are made not only with the Cold War but also with the beginning of World War I, the aftermath of the Crimean War, the late 1930s, the Stolypin period, and many other episodes. In fact, it is hard to think of a period of Russian history since approximately the late eighteenth century that has not been referred to in some venue or another as setting a precedent for what is happening today.

All these comparisons have some validity, and all have their flaws. But the fact that it is possible to draw so many indicates that there are consistent themes throughout Russian history, and that Russian social and geographic reality induces Russia's leaders to act in consistent ways when faced with challenges. What this means is that, contrary to popular belief, under certain circumstances Russian leadership actions are entirely predictable. Nevertheless, inability or unwillingness by the West to consider context and history and the lack of institutional memory repeatedly lead to problems in the relationship. And Russia is rediscovered anew each time these problems arise, even though they return consistently and derive from the same underlying factors.[2]

A clear example is the notion that Russian assertiveness in 2014 onward was a new policy departure. It was not: the intent behind it had remained consistent but had been disregarded by major Western powers because Russia had been incapable of implementing it for two decades during one of its intermittent phases of relative weakness.[3] In fact, Russia's history is above all repetitive, following the same convulsive historical cycle of revolutionary transformation, breakdown, consolidation, and stagnation.[4] From Peter the Great to Vladimir Putin, circumstances have changed, but the rhythm has remained extraordinarily consistent.[5]

The continuity of Russian history was maintained through the twentieth century. Rather than constituting a break from Russian tradition, the Soviet regime co-opted, preserved, suspended, or renamed permanent features of Russian life. As well as replacing religion domestically, communism found itself well suited to filling other traditional Russian roles. Under the czars, Russia's messianic mission and global aspirations had been represented by the Orthodox Church and later by pan-Slavism; the new vehicle under Soviet rule was "international communism." Russia replaced the czarist oppressive bureaucracy, secret police, and instruments of repression with Soviet equivalents.[6] In short, even at the height of the Cold War, for all that the USSR proclaimed itself to be building a new and unprecedented society, Westerners who were able to view Russia at first hand concluded that the Soviet regime was, in essence, a traditional Russian autocracy that conformed to basic Russian cultural patterns.[7]

Other aspects of the Soviet state replicated their czarist predecessors too, since, as Edward Crankshaw has written, in Russia "it takes an explosion on the scale of the 1917 Revolution to bring about any effective change. Even then, when the dust has settled, it is soon discovered (thankfully?) that ancient customs have not died."[8] The result was that during the twentieth century,

> For the vast majority of the Russian people, communist Russia, as all Russias before, still remains Mother Russia. Moreover, they or their fathers never knew better. There is little to choose from their point or view be-

tween the Tsars and the despotic rule of Stalin. The same secret political police operated then and it operates now. The same official, seated behind a writing desk, pushed him about then and pushes him now. There was a privileged class then; there is one now. Only the names have changed.[9]

In other words, as Laurens van der Post put it in 1965, "The Revolution, for all its claims to the contrary, has not abolished the past: at the most it has suspended it."[10]

President Putin appears to agree. He has referred to revolutions in Russia as "a rupture in history" that should be disregarded in order to understand the country's historical development as a nation. As stated in Putin's December 12, 2012, presidential address to the Federal Assembly, even though the upheavals of 1917 and 1991 constituted "a devastating blow to the nation's cultural and spiritual code . . . the breakdown of traditions and historical unity, and demoralization of society," they should be disregarded when the history of Russia is considered as an unbroken thousand-year narrative.[11] When viewing Russia from abroad, it is easy to underestimate the sense of historical continuity, which reaches much further back than Russia's latest incarnations in the twentieth and twenty-first centuries. As a result of this continuity, political scientists question the extent to which the national identity of contemporary Russian citizens differs from that of their Soviet predecessors or the subjects of the Russian Empire.[12]

Protecting History

Like every other country in the world, she is the prisoner of her own history, traditions, preconceptions, immemorial fears. Perhaps more than any other country, because Russia's history has been so special to her, her traditions so ingrown, her preconceptions so deliberately exalted into articles of faith.

—EDWARD CRANKSHAW, *1977*[13]

At the same time, how Russians understand their own history, and the ways in which that understanding differs from what is commonly believed in other countries (or, on occasion, from established fact), are important components of how Russia conducts itself as a state.

The way history is managed has real implications for post-Soviet Russia's policy and its neighbors' security. As Edward Keenan noted as early as 1994:

> The reexamination of a characteristic cluster of Russian national myths, most of which have become international scholarly myths, is no idle pursuit. . . . How Russians and others have come to believe these myths [is] directly relevant to how we can expect Russians to behave as international actors. . . . There is no telling, at this stage, which of the various available histories of their international behavior will be the one they prefer to refer to in making and justifying crucial decisions in the near term.[14]

This choice of various available histories derived from a consistent Russian practice over centuries of revising or reinventing history at will, and then demanding universal acceptance of the new version. As so often happens, a feature of Russian life that is commonly associated with Soviet times is in fact much older: Russia's reputation as a country with an unpredictable past long predates 1917. The tendency for evidence-free reinvention was summarized by Astolphe de Custine:

> The facts—the raw material of every report—are usually counted for nothing [in Russia] where the past, the future, and the present are at the disposition of the master. . . . The memory of what happened yesterday is the property of the czar; he alters the annals of the country according to his own good pleasure and dispenses, each day, to his people the historical truths which accord with the fiction of the moment.[15]

Today, as throughout history, it is within the power of the Russian leadership to redefine the past arbitrarily.[16] The result has been the development of a history of Russia that is negotiable and malleable for the authorities, but unchallengeable for everybody else[17]—the dangers of uncontrolled examination of Russia's history by the younger generation in particular appear well recognized.[18] But the need to protect the currently approved version of history extends far beyond education or academic debate and into the realm of national security. Among "threats to national security in the sphere of culture," Russia's most recent National Security Strategy lists "attempts to falsify Russian and world history."[19] And its Military Doctrine counts "subversive information activities . . . aimed at undermining historical, spiritual and patriotic traditions related to the defense of the Motherland" as a "main internal military risk."[20] Russia wishes to ensure its historical narratives are unchallenged, but by doing so it only underlines how so many of them do not stand up to objective scrutiny because they are based on fiction, distortion, or omission. If the version of Russia's history proclaimed by the state were instead based in fact, it would not need this kind of protection from challenge and debate.

A central element of Russia's protection of its version of history is concealment—whether obscuring inconvenient facts or suppressing research uncovering fabrications. The politicization of history presents particular hazards to professional historians in Russia, up to and including senior state officials.[21] As part of a broader trend of policy and legislation ensuring that the Soviet mythology is not challenged, Director of the State Archives Sergei Mironenko was sacked for pointing out that a famous heroic episode from World War II was in fact largely fictitious. But even after the Soviet war story of "Panfilov's 28 men" dying heroically in the defense of Moscow was shown to have been invented, this did not prevent it receiving official endorsement from President Putin.[22]

Even before Soviet times, where suitable Russian history did not exist, it had to be invented. Myths and false claims devised to legitimate the regime are hardly unique to Russia; what is unusual is the persistency with which they are still applied in modern times. The notion that the rulers of Moscow that emerged from Mongol domination were in any real way the successors to the state of Kievan Rus' that had vanished centuries earlier does not stand up to even brief scrutiny, and yet it is a version of history staunchly defended by Russia now, especially in the context of its current confrontation with Ukraine.[23]

This is a more palatable version of national origins than the alternative, that instead of a legitimate heritage, Moscow rose to prominence thanks to a sequence of twelve princes who all saw the advantage of keeping on good terms with the Mongols by prompt delivery of the tribute they demanded, while using the relative stability this servitude afforded to extend the territory they controlled by any means available.[24] Through adept management both of enduring conflict and chaos and of their own image, they later "stood forth as the 'princes of all Russia' and as 'the gatherers of the Russian lands'. These titles, which they assumed, show an astounding flair for the skilful manipulation of public opinion that drew the veil over their earlier rascality and surrounded them with a halo of national heroes which they hardly merited."[25]

Today protection of the official version of Russian history is important as a rallying point for domestic cohesion, especially when the leadership may perceive a need to bolster the citizenry's loyalty and commitment. In looking to the past, Moscow is seeking elements that could unite its subjects under Putin.[26] References to history provide two key rationales to justify this unity: Russia as a besieged fortress needs a strong commander, and anyone questioning this leadership or the power of the commander—for instance, by accusing him of corruption or questioning the legitimacy of the regime—is by doing so attacking the country itself.[27]

Within this context, it is the history of the twentieth century that is of critical importance to Moscow. But Russia seeks to promote the Soviet version of this history not only at home but even beyond its borders. Its concern to promulgate a version of history that describes its own role favorably, and the incorporation of this concern into security policy, becomes a foreign policy issue when denial of the Soviet past also leads to Russian attempts to suppress history in Ukraine and formerly occupied states such as Estonia, Latvia, and Lithuania.[28]

Poland is a particular target of Russian campaigns in this respect. Although it was by no means the only country to be occupied by the Soviet Union twice during World War II, as well as by Nazi Germany, it poses a direct challenge to Russia's account of that war by the simple fact that it was simultaneously invaded by both of those powers in cooperation in 1939—and thus reference to this fact is now a criminal offense in Russia.[29] Hence Russia consistently threatens Poland for dissenting from the Soviet version of the history of World War II,[30] and Russian officials provide increasingly fanciful and insulting explanations for that country's appalling fate during the war—including blaming Poland for starting the war in the first place by not allowing Russia to invade it.[31]

Ukraine too presents a serious challenge to the Russian narrative of events during the Soviet period. The Holodomor famine induced by murderous Stalinist policies, and the roots of national resistance movements in Ukraine during and after World War II, are entirely incompatible with Russia's presentation of events during the same period.[32] But even more fundamentally, Ukraine's post-2014 implicit rejection of the idea that Russians and Ukrainians are one people undercuts Russia's idea of what constitutes the Russian nation and civilization, and where its roots lie.

For as long as Russia's population is once more presented with unashamedly Soviet explanations of twentieth-century history, a common understanding with the West of history and Russia's role in it will grow ever more remote.[33] This divergence will make differences with neighbors and partners further afield even with respect to shared recent history more, not less, difficult to resolve. The only alternative is perhaps even more damaging, and that is general acceptance of the Russian version. Even though the portrayal of events of the twentieth century, in particular by present-day Russian policymakers, is so remote from the evidential basis that it needs to be protected by Russian law and national security policy, it remains contagious among Western historians inclined to view history as a competition of narratives rather than a search for accuracy. This contagion is particularly damaging when combined with a view of Russia as inheriting the imperial rights and interests of the Soviet Union—a view that automatically deprecates the rights of those countries formerly occupied or dominated by the USSR.[34]

Soviet and pre-Soviet history continues to provide a useful framework of legitimation for the actions of Russia's leadership to themselves and their subjects. The liberalization of history during the 1990s, presenting Russians with deeply unpleasant truths about their immediate and more distant pasts, could have been a pivotal moment in the country's development as a state. Other nations in similar circumstances have seized the opportunity.[35] But instead, new historical awareness produced an opposite reaction. Even while many of Russia's archives were accessible to an unprecedented degree, it was predicted accurately that "most Russians will be more likely than they have been in recent decades officially to embrace the traditional myths . . . and to consider them justifications for political positions and actions."[36] Nobel Prize–winner Svetlana Alexievich suggests that Russia was unable to cope with the shaking of fundamental beliefs that came with revelations about the Soviet past because "we didn't have what was needed . . . the moral strength, the understanding, the intellectual elite, so many things."[37] At present, despite responses from the state that have evolved from indifference to intense harassment, dedicated individuals are still chronicling the victims of Soviet repressions.[38] But Russia's measures in response to the exposure of Soviet crimes have reverted to the Soviet Union's own practice of creating doubt and confusion by establishing counternarratives that are sufficiently similar to distract from the original atrocity.[39]

Facing up to and coming to terms with Russia's twentieth-century history would have been an indispensable condition for joining the twenty-first century as a country among others, rather than as one that stands apart because it retains the psychological detritus of a totalitarian superpower.[40] Other nations too, especially those that suffered invasion and occupation at the hands of the Soviet Union, might reasonably consider that a key step toward Russia leaving its Soviet past behind would be to actually remember it, and allow a faithful version of it to be acknowledged by its leaders and taught in its schools. But Russia looked at its own history during the 1990s and did not like what it saw, and at present there is no sign that a similar liberalization will be allowed to trouble its conscience in the foreseeable future. The country has experienced its crisis of national identity and has overcome it by ignoring it. As a result, if Russia is to change, the roots of that change must lie elsewhere than in consideration of history.

PART IV

Prospects for Change

NINE

Opposition, Protests, and Discontent

Political Expression

I decided to explain to the children how democracy works. So I let them vote for what we would have for dinner. They all voted for ice cream. But we live in Russia, so they had borsch.
—RUSSIAN JOKE OF UNCERTAIN ANTIQUITY[1]

The extent and significance of both public protest and the organized political opposition in Russia are commonly overstated in the West.

The majority of widespread protest events in Russia in the current century have been linked not to calls for political change but to single issues that affected material well-being, such as monetization of benefits in 2005 or the truck driver protests that peaked in 2016.[2] Against this background, political protests over the results of elections in 2011–12 mobilized an unexpected number of supporters, appearing to take not only the Kremlin but also initially the protest organizers by surprise. While the protests were never likely to be widespread, numerous, or durable enough to actually present the leadership with serious and immediate concern for its future, they did cause a reconsideration of the approach that should be taken to political dissent.

Among the political concessions made after the 2011–12 protests was a relaxation of electoral legislation, including the return of elections for regional governors—even if these were accompanied by perennial evidence of election rigging.³ But the protests also triggered an acceleration of repressive measures, including enhanced surveillance and control of internet usage in order to curb activism.⁴ At the same time, major steps have been taken to ensure that dissatisfaction as expressed in popular unrest cannot mount a serious challenge to the regime. The creation of the National Guard, with its wide-ranging remit and its reporting chain directly to the president, provides a new and powerful tool for suppressing dissent.⁵ The Guard, estimated to comprise more than 350,000 personnel, was formed by amalgamating a number of paramilitary organizations intended to maintain internal order.⁶ But this is not an internal security force as it would be understood in Western Europe: its available equipment, including armored vehicles, machine guns, Shmel rocket flame-throwers, and GM-94 pump-action grenade launchers, implies an assumption that it may be called on to inflict mass casualties.⁷ Even though the prospect of serious and widespread unrest seems at present remote, if repressive violence is needed in the short term to quell dissent, the regime has now established the tool to apply it.

Russia's opposition has often been more popular in the West than in Russia because its message of protest is welcomed by Western academics, politicians, and media but has limited appeal to many voters at home. In addition, a blend of idealism and optimism can lead Western depictions of opposition movements and protests to be vastly oversimplified. In particular, they fall victim to the mistaken assumption that just because some people are opposing or protesting against Vladimir Putin, this makes them liberals, espousing Western values and in tune with Western notions of democratic development. When assessing just how palatable to the West any alternative to President Putin would really be, it is helpful to consider the precedent of Aleksandr Solzhenitsyn. Lauded as a dissident while still living in the Soviet Union, Solzhenitsyn startled his supporters after his expulsion with his deeply nationalist view of how Russia should develop, and his condemnation of Western values.⁸ Those who uncritically endorse any figures that stand in opposition to Putin risk once again being caught unawares once their actual intent and goals are closely examined.

The prospects for any genuinely Western-leaning liberal opposition movement are constrained not only by the Kremlin but also by domestic attitudes. If you ask Russians whether they believe they live in a democracy, the answer naturally depends on which Russians you ask. Liberal intellectuals will say no, and only indefatigable optimists will say that there is any prospect of doing so in the future.[9] Others of an older generation will say no, and will be very grateful for the fact because democracy implies all of the worst features of Western decadence and is inextricably linked with traumatic memories of the 1990s. Somewhere in between is a sector of the population that will say yes, Russia is a democracy—but what exactly this means would only be detected by further careful questioning as to exactly how these Russians understand the word.

In this way, similarly to other examples of political terminology, the fact that a term has been translated into Russian does not mean that it retains anything like its original meaning. But as memories of the 1990s and the association between attempts at democratization and economic chaos recede, the negative associations that come with the word democracy are fading too. With the transition of the political system in Russia through a number of different adjectives (sovereign democracy, managed democracy, and now "decorative democracy"), the perceived danger of reckless adoption of democracy with none of the traditional attenuating factors of Russian autocracy has lessened. As a result, there may now be many more Russians who would be willing to say that they live in a democracy because it is perceived to be the right thing to say, rather than because they aspire to exerting genuine influence on the country's political direction.

In fact, despite foreign attention to protests and opposition figures, interest in official politics among ordinary Russians appears still to be declining. The essence of decorative democracy in Russia is that the façade of independent institutions such as the electoral system, the Duma and Federation Council, the court system, and the media has been preserved, but the primary purpose of these institutions is now to implement the instructions of the central leadership. The resulting perception that elections have little practical impact on life in Russia has led to a vicious cycle of political disengagement. In some ways this is a return to the Russian norm after a time during the pre-Putin period when it appeared, briefly, that mass participation in democracy might be meaningful. For Russians before the end of the Soviet Union, "The deeper part of their history which had become the national state of mind as well as their present system made it impossible in the short term to impose their will on their leaders."[10] Today, alienation from politics and from the authorities remains one of the key characteristics of mass political consciousness. Combined with an assumption of lingering paternalistic dependence on the state, this exacerbates widespread political apathy and the perception that there is little point or purpose in challenging the existing order of things.[11] In polls ahead of the State Duma elections in 2016, over half of respondents said their family and social circles did not discuss the elections at all—and of those who did, one-third said they had witnessed discussions but did not participate in them themselves. Well over half said they had no interest at all in the current activity of the State Duma.[12] Another poll at the same time found that almost three quarters of Russians were "sure that they have no influence on the situation in the country," and (perhaps as a result) 64 percent felt no responsibility for it.[13]

The prevalence of this attitude may well be entirely comfortable for the current leadership, since it will mean fewer people taking an interest in what that leadership says or does domestically, which in turn means less effort required to manage domestic opinion. As long as those who do turn out for elections vote as directed, or control of the voting process is maintained so that the count can be adjusted as required, no authoritarian regime is likely to be upset by its subjects displaying apathy at election time.[14] But those who do not turn out to vote may be disengaged rather than apathetic; in other words, they may well be concerned over the state of the country but may not see elections as in any way relevant to addressing those concerns.[15] The outcome of some regional elections in September 2017 suggests that if these voters can be convinced of the relevance of electoral politics by being given a real choice between candidates on substantive issues, they could swiftly reengage in the process.

But this is unlikely in the short term to have a political effect at the national level. The economic hardships of 2014–16 caused discontent among Russians, but little or none of it was directed against Putin. At the time of writing, with the economy improving (even if slowly), there is no plausible challenge to his hold on power. This is especially the case since no currently prominent political figures in Russia are likely to be interested in disrupting the system for fear of suffering painful consequences and the loss of the privileged position they currently enjoy. But even though it is highly unlikely the opposition could at present mount a serious challenge to the ruling elite led by President Putin, that is no reason to allow it to gain momentum and become a serious destabilizing threat later. Consequently, the state works hard to suppress or subvert any indication of plausible opposition developing.

Repression Lite

> If the contemporary Russian system does not fit expectations of a Western-style democracy, this does not yet make this system a Soviet or neo-Soviet one.
> —ANDREI TSYGANKOV, *August 2015*[16]

In this new political environment, the most prominent opposition figures and their supporters are targeted using both official and unofficial repressive measures.[17] Instances of prosecution for expressing views critical of the state, while nowhere near as pervasive as during Soviet times, are rapidly on the rise. At times these prosecutions can be impervious to irony. In November 2017 a court in St. Petersburg sentenced a man to two years in prison because, in an internet post written from jail, where he was already serving a previous sentence, he called the Russian government a "repressive regime."[18] As well as heightened judicial intolerance, measures of control and repression from the late Soviet period have been revived, including punitive psychiatric treatment,[19] a fashion for informers,[20] and campaigns of denunciation of authors and their work in state media.[21] Collective condemnation of dissenters is encouraged by orchestrated hate arranged through television.[22] Echoes of the Soviet campaigns against internal dissent and "enemies of the people" are frequent, including President Putin's warning of "action by a fifth column, a disparate bunch of national traitors."[23]

The Kremlin can act against opposition forces with little domestic disapproval or without censure, within an overall climate of much-reduced tolerance for public expressions of opposition to authority. While a few prominent figures such as Aleksei Navalny seem intent on continuing opposition despite varying forms of discouragement, other less well-known activists, especially those working in Russia's regions and away from major cities, are more susceptible to threat and coercion.[24] This too includes a return to traditional Soviet means of administrative punishment, such as excluding family members from their university studies—with the additional implication that they then immediately become subject to conscription.[25]

In parallel with this, the same period has seen greatly increased powers and capabilities for monitoring the online and other private correspondence and conversations of citizens. But this state policy does not appear to encounter any serious public resistance other than from a small number of well-informed and technically literate activists. This may be a result of the official warnings of the dangers of disorder, with President Putin intimating that if protests are not curbed, they could lead to chaos and disaster along the lines of the Arab Spring.[26] According to political analyst Tatiana Stanovaya, those with long memories may be

> so frightened of a return of the 1990s crisis and disorder that most Russians prefer, just as in Hobbes, to renounce many of their rights for the sake of security and prosperity. To be sure, this preference is encouraged by the state itself, which for years has made capital on the fears of the 1990s, but all the same it is based on its own historical and social socioeconomic roots.[27]

But criticism of Russia for being illiberal needs to be placed in context. Russia in 2018 is showing a strong trend toward authoritarianism, but it is still a far less restrictive society than at any time during its Soviet or pre-Soviet history. One telling statistic is the number of deaths at the hands of the regime. The entirely justified outrage over murders or attempted murders of individuals who have angered the Russian state or its rulers obscures a critical point: that for the first time in Russian history, such murders are the exception, not the rule.

The wave of apartment bombings in Russia at the very beginning of President Putin's rule are widely considered to have been ordered by the state as part of the consolidation of his power. David Satter, author of an angry but well-argued book on the apartment bombings and other instances of murder alleged to have been instigated by the Russian state, suggests that "murdering hundreds of randomly chosen civilians . . . is fully consistent with the kind of country that Russia, in the wake of communism, has become."[28] But this is to ignore the much longer tradition in Soviet and imperial Russia of treating the lives of subjects as insignificant when weighed against any conceivable, or even inconceivable, plot, conspiracy, or challenge to the authorities, and casually obliterating them. Russia has from its very beginning embraced savage violence and brutality, torture, assassination, purges, and pogroms as means of keeping order; the deaths through execution and deportation of millions under Stalin were well within the mainstream of Russian practice over centuries, just on an industrial scale.[29]

By contrast, after almost two decades of the Putin era, ordinary citizens no longer need fear unexpected and arbitrary death at the hands of the authorities, since Russia has entered an unprecedented period of not engaging in casual mass murder of its subjects as a response to real or imagined security threats. This takes a certain amount of mental adjustment by seasoned observers. In April 2017, a bomb attack in the St. Petersburg metro killed fifteen people and injured many more. In the immediate aftermath and before a clear picture of the attack had emerged, informed analysts both in Russia and abroad speculated that it had been staged by the authorities. This presumption was based on precedent: the Russian state had not only the means, motive, and opportunity to do so but also a history that clearly demonstrated its lack of compunction in causing civilian casualties, including among its own population, for even the slightest foreign policy advantage or to secure its position against the most ephemeral threats.

Nevertheless, at the time of writing it appears that to be murdered by the Russian state today, you have to represent a particularly prominent or effective form of opposition or to cost the elite a particularly large amount of money. These two categories cover two very distinct groups of individuals.[30] According to opposition politician Vladimir Kara-Murza, repeatedly the target of poisoning attempts, there is a "clear line between just saying things that are against the regime, and it's a totally different thing to go after their own personal interests, after their pockets."[31] The latter consistently proves fatal. High-profile corruption cases from the 2000s, such as Hermitage Capital Management in 2008 and Three Whales (*Tri kita*) in 2003, tend to result in multiple fatalities, some of them years later, as key players and witnesses are gradually eliminated. Many of these murders take place beyond Russia's borders, including in the United Kingdom,[32] the United States,[33] and elsewhere.[34]

Murders outside Russia also include a specific category where assassination is intended not only to punish or silence the individual but also to send a message to the country where he or she has taken up residence. Murders on commercial grounds often make some attempt at concealment, simulating accident or suicide. By contrast, the two most prominent attacks on former Russian intelligence officers residing in the United Kingdom, Aleksandr Litvinenko in 2006 and Sergei Skripal in 2018, were demonstrative in nature. By using exotic and highly lethal substances that placed large numbers of other individuals at risk of contamination—polonium and Novichok nerve agent, respectively—Russia clearly indicated its disregard for relations with the United Kingdom and for its population. The case of Sergei Skripal, however, may have given Moscow pause for thought; the unified response of international condemnation, including severe curtailing of diplomatic posts, was unexpectedly firm. If Russia feels its assessment that it could carry out attacks of this kind abroad with only limited consequences was a miscalculation, they may become even more rare in the short term.

Within Russia itself, the shooting of opposition leader Boris Nemtsov in February 2015 also appears exceptional. Accusations against President Putin of ordering Nemtsov's murder will persist for as long as the Russian criminal justice system remains unable to carry out one of its core functions and identify, or perhaps disclose, who commissioned this and other high-profile killings. But the Putin leadership has long had alternative means of dealing with far more realistic challengers. In 2004 Ivan Rybkin was a candidate in the Russian presidential elections. He accused Putin of corruption and disappeared shortly before the voting. Two weeks later he reappeared in a disoriented state, claiming that he had been drugged and subjected to degrading treatment—and then withdrew his candidacy. But again, compared with Russia's historical norms, these incidents are strikingly rare. Russian commentator Andrei Piontkovsky appears to have been accurate in his prediction that "at the beginning of the twenty-first century, the change of elites will probably be far less bloody than in the first half of the twentieth century. Only a few individuals will rot in prison or mysteriously disappear, perhaps a few dozen. The majority of those wishing to emigrate will be afforded the opportunity to do so."[35]

Protest and the Internet

> The national intellectual, social and practical infrastructure for a new kind of Russia is being built.
> —MARK GALEOTTI, *July 2017*[36]

Where the will to engage in politics or protest is present, the harnessing of communications technology has emerged as a key enabling factor, both within the electoral system and for single-issue activism. The mobilizing power of the internet and social media had been noted even before the wave of election protests in 2011–12;[37] now, among the youngest generations that have reached the age to vote or protest since that time, unhindered mass peer-to-peer communications offer a fundamentally new means not only of raising and sharing political consciousness but also of organizing to do something about it. By the time of the September 2017 elections, the influence of these technologies had become universal, including the use of crowdsourcing to negotiate the exceedingly onerous procedures for registering as a political candidate (designed primarily to discourage would-be politicians).[38] Away from the ballot box, the internet is also exceptionally useful in the aftermath of protests, not only for tweeting from inside the back of a police van but also, more practically, for using iPhone apps to let everybody know you have been arrested and working out at which police station you are most likely to be found.[39]

A distinguishing feature of the primary users of these technologies is their youth, and it is this that also sets them apart from the general trend of political apathy described above. The fact that young people are the main social base for Aleksei Navalny's political activism is linked with the fact that Navalny is practically the only politician, opposition or otherwise, who constantly and effectively interacts with his supporters—not only at electoral meetings but especially online through his blog and "Navalny Live" YouTube channel. One of Navalny's key mobilizing messages that resonates with this audience is that young people in Russia need not be second-class citizens but are entitled to the same demands and interests as those in the West; as Navalny puts it, "You are normal people." Among his followers, the confidence of youth does combine with a belief that life in Russia could, or perhaps even should, be better.[40] But this can also produce counterintuitive results. According to polling in May 2017, under-twenty-fives combine an attachment to foreign travel and a desire to see Russia develop into a place "like the developed countries of the West," on the one hand, with, on the other, approval of President Putin and a tendency to "tell their parents that it would be better if life in Russia was like it was in the USSR."[41]

Nevertheless, the availability and use of technologies for freely accessing and exchanging information and opinions, in combination with growing awareness and exposure to life, conditions, and opportunities outside Russia, are shifting attitudes among a definable sector of the population, primarily but not exclusively from the younger generations. In some ways this resembles the reemergence of a mildly dissident intelligentsia:

> There is a minority in Russia [that is] well educated, inventive, active and somewhat successful. I mean so called "creative class." They are businessmen, scientists, engineers, artists, journalists, teachers, doctors, other intelligents in the good sense and a part (alas only part) of ordinary Russians—workers, farmers. There exists quite understandable conflict between the nature of so called "creative class" and existing medieval style of ruling with official agitprop, endemic corruption, high scale theft, power of oligarchs. . . . The conflict that I try to describe will not vanish and later or sooner (I hope rather sooner) will result in profound changes in political situation in Russia.[42]

Protests in the summer of 2017 over plans for widespread urban regeneration in Moscow exemplified a number of the key themes discussed here. The announcement of the intent to demolish thousands of five-storey apartment blocks dating back to the Khrushchev era and to resettle the inhabitants in new developments was made without any evident consideration that those inhabitants might have an opinion on the idea—still less that they might mount coordinated opposition. According to policy analyst and former journalist Aleksandr Baunov:

> Evidently, the city authorities had convinced themselves that the residents of these blocks were mostly poor and elderly, and loyal consumers of state television, who would meekly obey the order to move from one apartment to another. In fact, many khrushchyovkites belong to a classic European urban middle class. Indeed, many of them have mortgages, having bought

the apartments and spent money renovating them. . . . To these people, the new government rehousing program looks like an act of outright confiscation.[43]

When Muscovites mobilized to oppose the plans, this revealed a nascent form of civil society—based around a property-owning middle class more extensive than at any time in previous Russian history—that had found a common interest and was willing and able to self-organize to defend it.[44] The extensive use of online communication and coordination tools highlighted the role of information and communications technologies in facilitating this dissent.[45]

Regardless of the eventual outcome of the renovation protests, together with youth electoral activism they demonstrate the potential for freely available communications technologies to transform political engagement in Russia. Nevertheless, as with all indicators of potential social development in Russia, caution is required. The Russian experience over decades and centuries suggests that when one considers prospects for fundamental change, optimism is dangerous, and has until now generally been misplaced.

TEN

Change from Within

Optimism . . .

> Western hopes were always too high and disappointments too deep. We don't want hopes to be too high this time.
> —IVAN KURILLA, *August 2017*[1]

Among analysts of Russia, the most consistently reliable predictions of future developments tend to come from the most pessimistic and cynical observers. There is some debate in this circle as to whether they become this way through a lifetime of exposure to Russia, or whether in order to assess Russia successfully it helps to be naturally inclined to cynicism and pessimism.

Predictions about Russia in the academic and journalistic communities, by contrast, have a tendency to be hostage to optimism and wishful thinking. Importantly, this often evidence-free analysis spills over into the public policy community, with significant negative implications for managing the relationship with Russia.[2] Ideas from the last decade that enjoyed brief popularity despite being entirely wrong include the "Putin-Medvedev split"—an assumption of conflict between the hidebound, reactionary Vladimir Putin and the supposedly forward-thinking, progressive modernizer Dmitriy Medvedev. Another example is the surprisingly durable notion that street demonstrations against election results in 2011–12 meant the end of Putin's power. Initially, this suggestion was largely based on misinterpretation and overstatement of the size and impact of these protests; in fact, manifestations of popular discontent and protest in Russia are routinely described as "unprecedented," even though their size and scope have been gradually declining since the 1990s. But this last idea was a symptom of a persistent search for evidence to support a widespread but largely unjustified hope that the Putin era is drawing to a close.

Russian and foreign academics, analysts, and experts who find the current leadership of Russia distasteful often express their optimism in the form of repeated predictions of the imminent demise of the regime. Even well-informed and intelligent observers can be seduced by this notion; a typical example was the confident prediction in mid-2016 that "the current trajectory of the Russian regime is unstable and without dramatic change it will crumble within the next year. . . . The Russian regime has only two ways out of its coming crisis. It can either reconcile with the West or change leader."[3] And when the predicted collapse fails to materialize, its prophesiers appear undeterred and seek fresh rationales to support their hopes. This expectation of downfall is so widespread that it can at times resemble a consensus. In 2012, it was quite reasonable to write that "very few analysts would subscribe to the view that [Putin] will be able to serve even one presidential term without major disorder in his system of governance"[4]—since this indeed appeared the majority view among influential writers on Russia. A related argument is that the Putinist system itself is unsustainable.[5] Assessments of the durability of Putin's rule became even more pessimistic during his third term, with a number of respected academics routinely predicting "the collapse of the regime or its radical transformation accompanied by leadership change."[6] And yet the concern that any elections, "tightly managed as they are, might . . . unleash an avalanche of heretofore hidden mass discontent" has until now not been vindicated.[7]

Groundless optimism, maintained in the face of consistent contrary evidence and consequent repeated disappointment, gives rise to "common analytical sins and questionable assumptions that bedevil the field of Russia analysis."[8] It also leads to recurrent resets, as the United States and the West succumb to the triumph of hope over experience and believe that a fresh start in relations with Russia will make everything work out this time. Yet the trend is the reverse. The result of each cycle of reset followed by disappointment is a deeper crisis each time. A study published in 2011 described in detail the several repetitions of this cycle since the end of the Cold War, and on the basis of that analysis predicted there would shortly be a return to confrontation, which duly materialized in the crisis over Ukraine.[9] On each occasion Western politicians appear to be caught unawares. In part, this results from the absence of institutional memory, and the inability while distracted or overwhelmed by events to undertake a sober assessment of the relationship with Russia. In combination with the seduction of optimism, this also leads to a tendency to seek the roots of failure in the relationship in Western capitals rather than in any fundamental contradiction between the two sides or in Russia's own behavior.[10] But failing to understand the basic incompatibilities between the Russian and the Western views of the world makes repeated disappointment almost inevitable.

Already at the dawn of the Putin era, the perennial optimism of former U.S. ambassador to Moscow Michael McFaul led him to argue against those who said that Russia was "lost to the West."[11] But the belief that Russia was in transition to democracy and acceptance of Western values remained startlingly persistent during the subsequent decade and a half before the crisis over Ukraine.[12] According to David Satter, this failure to recognize reality "crippled Western policy toward Russia, rendering it naive and ineffectual. From the moment Putin took power, the West maintained an image of Russia that bore no relation to reality."[13] This allowed the adoption of successive rationales for the hope that Russia would join the West, as one by one they were proved baseless: first, "hope that external factors such as the economic crisis in 2008 would undermine resistance, even oblige it to join the West," then "hopes that first Putin, then Medvedev would lead liberal change," then "hope of internal change in which a new, post-Soviet and more Western-oriented generation would emerge to replace them."[14]

In the context of this prolonged sense of inevitability about Russia rejoining the West, crises and disputes were often seen as temporary, transient hitches, and those Russia analysts who urged caution in dealing with Moscow were deprecated as proponents of outdated Cold War stereotypes. It was not until 2014 brought a crisis sufficiently deep to be impossible to ignore that political leaders in some—not all—European states belatedly recognized that "for too long the EU's relationship with Russia has been based on the optimistic premise that Russia has been on a trajectory towards becoming a democratic 'European' country."[15]

For some, this premise has now been replaced by a long-term strategy of waiting until Russia itself starts to redefine its own understanding of what constitutes a great power in a globalized world.[16] But there are few indications that this redefinition is impending. Western commentators can claim that some Russians are now convinced of their country's need for change in the form of modernization, rule of law, and constructive relations with the West.[17] But the expectation of liberalization is often based on the assumption of a general and broad-based desire for democratization among the Russian population, despite the negative associations of democracy with the trauma of the 1990s referred to in chapter 4.[18] As already noted, this assumption is sustained by the disproportionate weight assigned to liberal voices in commentary on Russia: Ivan Kurilla says of his own caste that "liberal intellectuals criticize the Russian government for being insufficiently democratic, but this is just a portion of a part of the Russian population, so it [gives] a biased and simplified picture of Russia."[19]

. . . and Disappointment

It is strange how repetitive we find the story of Russia.
—JAMES FOOTE, 1972[20]

The regular confounding of undue optimism also results from the cyclical nature of Russian history. In both domestic affairs and relations with the West, promising periods of liberalization are invariably followed by a repressive or confrontational reaction.[21]

Internally, the reaction is to experiments with liberalism that go too far and unleash processes perceived as destabilizing to the regime. Alexander II, remembered primarily as the czar who oversaw emancipation of the serfs, also introduced a vast range of other reforms affecting the army, the church, commerce, and banking. He relaxed censorship, reined in the secret police, and lifted the ban on travel and the restrictions on students. Naturally, Alexander III responded by reversing this dangerous liberalism. Other czars too devoted considerable efforts to undoing all the policies of the preceding sovereign. In the twentieth century, periodic easing of state repression caused both Russians and foreigners repeatedly to ask themselves whether the time for change had finally arrived.[22] But they also triggered disturbing social upheaval, as in the period following the death of Stalin, giving rise to a disorienting blend of optimism and fear.[23] U.S. academic Kathleen E. Smith argues that in the light of these and other examples, "Vladimir Putin has demonstrated that one can draw cautionary lessons from moments of liberation and liberalization."[24] The 1990s in particular underscored that, for Russia, stability can only be ensured by constraining freedom.

This too contributes to the inevitable brevity of periods of rapprochement with the West, where high hopes during periods of liberalization give way to dismay at the realization of Moscow's true ambitions, in a process repeated time and again.[25] The exception that proved the rule came during World War II, when the governments of the Western Allies at times wilfully provided their populations with an entirely misleading picture of Soviet Russia in order to justify alliance with it to defeat Nazi Germany. The suspension of disbelief that this required delayed Western realization of Moscow's underlying hostility until it was proved beyond doubt by its treatment of Eastern Europe at the outset of the Cold War. But this too was seen at the time by perceptive Russia-watchers as just another iteration of a consistent pattern. Writing in 1947, Edward Crankshaw noted how the distinctive feature of the relationship with Russia is the "monotonous and gloomy regularity with which the birth and recurrent rebirth of goodwill . . . has been succeeded by the resurrection of suspicion, hardening quickly into hostility open or concealed."[26]

In addition, the occasional outbreaks of relative liberalism in Russia feed the impression that the authoritarian reaction is a temporary aberration. The resulting hope for a change of regime consistently overlooks the important point that in Russia, as elsewhere, change is not always for the better. During Soviet times, this gave rise to a similar irrepressible optimism with each change of leader, "greeted with public expressions of hope in Western countries that changes for the better may be on the way. But the lesson of the inevitable disappointment that follows, sooner or later, is never learnt."[27]

Even the end of the Soviet Union was not the first occasion when complete collapse of the Russian regime gave rise to widespread assumptions that the country would now become Westernized and "free." Blaming Russia's appalling treatment of its subjects on communism overlooks the fact that long before the Bolshevik revolution, it was already the norm (as described by Russia correspondent Henry Nevinson in 1906) that "day by day the noblest and most thoughtful men and women of Russia are shot, imprisoned, or dragged away to the oblivion of Siberia."[28] With the czarist regime widely seen as a despotic tyranny, surviving only through rigid constraints on the freedom of thought of the educated classes and by the whips and sabres of the Cossacks for the peasantry, it was hard to conceive how revolution could in fact make things even worse. This meant that on the forced abdication of Nicholas II in 1917, alongside alarm at the implicit challenge to monarchies elsewhere, "the Western Allies, the United States and free countries everywhere applauded: Russia had at last cast off her chains. . . . Russia was presumably going to have liberal institutions at long last and enter the family of civilized nations."[29] But despite this welcoming of change, based on the assumption that democracy might finally be reaching Russia, the Provisional Government's progressive plans for early competitive elections, rights reforms, and a forward-thinking constitution were crushed eight months later by the Bolshevik coup. The result was over seventy years of communist rule, with worse excesses of mass repression and state murder than had been seen since the darkest days of Russia's early history.[30]

The fact that hopes for positive change in Russia remain consistently unjustified does not mean they may not eventually be fulfilled. The period of the Carter administration in the United States saw a similar belief trend that "the Soviet system was in deep trouble and all the West needed to do was to sit back and wait for it to collapse."[31] And so, eventually, it did—although it took much longer than envisaged. But the particular lesson of the end of the Soviet Union, just as with the end of imperial Russia before it, is that those who look forward to regime change in Russia should be careful what they wish for. Even within the current system, former Kremlin adviser Gleb Pavlovskiy warns that doubts over the succession to Putin may make Russia "more prone to instability than the late Soviet Union was with its orderly queue of successors in the Politburo."[32]

There is also, of course, still hope for a real rapprochement and collaborative relationship between Russia and the West, including political liberalization. Ivan Kurilla warns: "I would be cautious in saying that Russia will quickly become a Western democracy but we will inevitably come to a new cycle of reform sooner or later, and this will get us into a better position than now."[33] But the list of preconditions liberals attach to this hope is ambitious. In the words of fellow Russian academic Pavel Luzin:

First of all Russia needs internal reform. Many of the current political and economic institutions need to be changed or just eliminated. Clear, comprehensible and durable rules of the game need to be established. It is important that property rights must be guaranteed, a constitutional mechanism for rotation of power must be established, and real rather than fake federalism and local government must be established within Russia. Russia must create an open society and economy."[34]

In other words, Russia needs to be a fundamentally different country from the one we see today.

Social Change

One of the most depressing aspects of Russian history is the total absence of the peaceful processes of evolution.
—LAURENS VAN DER POST, *1965*[35]

Hope for substantial societal change in Russia was long pinned on the development of a middle class that would come to comprehend and defend its own interests. Perhaps surprisingly, this was also considered possible during the Soviet Union. In 1962 it was assessed that "an educated, prosperous, and powerful Russian community, which is more and more a middleclass or bourgeois community, despite the absence of private property, must inevitably relax political intolerance and party-line orthodoxy and move toward greater freedom of speech, press, and assembly and greater public participation in public policy-making. And this is happening. It has been happening now for several years."[36] But, as always, the "relaxation of intolerance" of the early 1960s failed to achieve permanence.

The end of communism naturally brought greater hopes for the emergence of a middle class. But the failure to develop strong property rights has undermined this optimism. According to Tatiana Stanovaya, "In order to become like the West, Russia would have to develop a broad class of property owners, and civil society which is not financially dependent on the state. That would require entirely different socio-economic conditions. And where these would arise from is unclear."[37] One possible answer is given by Sergey Utkin of the Center for Situation Analysis at the Russian Academy of Sciences, who notes that "the current generation is the first in a long time that can leave property to its children. This will change attitudes."[38] Another, as described in chapter 9, comes in the unexpected wave of political mobilization based on the mass discontent of Muscovites over the planned demolitions of their *khrushchevki* apartment blocks.

A separate, longer-term aspect of societal change that has long been expected to create liberal Western attitudes in Russia has been the simple succession of generations. In the early 1990s, within the context of Russia being expected to gravitate naturally toward the West, it was thought that two or perhaps three generations of distance from the Soviet past would substantially transform Russia by default toward liberalism. In fact, in some respects the opposite is true: distance has instead produced a false nostalgia for communist times, and political inclinations have been subjected to other, more powerful factors than the soft attraction of the West.

This is, of course, a generalization. Within each post-Soviet generation there will be differences in outlook generated by differences in social class, geography, ethnicity, income, and other variables. Perhaps to a greater extent than in European countries, the formative experiences of members of each generation vary widely depending on where they live. With internet access strongly dependent on mobile connectivity, and internet penetration in rural areas impressive but patchy, the sector of the youngest generation that is unprivileged, poorly educated, rural, and relatively isolated may well continue to place greater reliance on state media as a primary source of information about Russia and the world—and consequently may retain substantially different attitudes from those of their urban, internet-connected coevals.[39]

Even among educated urbanites, dramatic change in material circumstances may not in itself lead to a departure from traditional Russian or Soviet attitudes.[40] Nevertheless, it is possible to subdivide the late Soviet and post-Soviet generations with surprising precision according to the specific periods of Russian history during which their formative experiences occurred. Just as with the very distinct generations that were born in the years between 1941 and the death of Stalin in 1953, the striking differences between these experiences have created discrete societal groups. Political scientist Vladimir Pastukhov draws the dividing lines by year of birth as follows: 1970–1985 (the "disappointed generation"),

1985–2000 (the "lost generation"), and after 2000 (the "generation of the future," so called because its attitudes and behavior are so different from those of its predecessors).[41] Each of these generations is worth examining in turn.

The Disappointed and the Lost

> In Russia, the power of the state can be authoritarian or even totalitarian over a very long period of time. . . . A chorus of souls demanding, "Shoot them like mad dogs" is easily coaxed from the mighty bosom of the God-fearing Russian people.
> —ANDREI PIONTKOVSKY, 2006[42]

The disappointed generation may not have a clear memory of the end of the Soviet Union, but it certainly does of the 1990s—and in many cases it is unlikely to be a positive one. It was the experience of social upheaval and uncertainty then that caused the "disappointment," as the promise of a new post-Soviet beginning soured.

This has led to current polling results showing a majority of Russians in favor of restoring the Soviet Union, up to and including Stalinism.[43] Many of those polled will be individuals old enough to remember what life in the Soviet Union entailed, but that does not affect the preference they state. According to one Russian view, hankerings for the USSR should not be dismissed as "nostalgic withdrawal or as escapist fantasies. . . . They are not. The narrators are neither self-delusional fools . . . nor unrepentant apologists for Communist terror. They know what they've survived."[44] And yet some aspects of this nostalgia—referred to by author Masha Gessen as retro-totalitarianism[45]—rely on an effective resurrection of the myth of Stalin as a benevolent ruler and the Stalinist era as a golden age of Russian accomplishment.[46]

This preference for the Soviet past enjoys substantial support among people, some now in their thirties, who were born too late to have any memory at all of life under communism. This generation has an even more positive image of the Soviet era than those who lived through it, thanks in particular to propagandist Soviet popular culture and films being treated as historical sources describing realistically how things were during the Soviet

Union.[47] In effect, Soviet myths have been transferred effectively to the generation of Russians who did not have firsthand experience against which to measure them. This has led to a dilution and suppression of folk memory of how grim and unpleasant life in the Soviet Union actually was, including the very real challenges of shortages of key foodstuffs, essential goods, and especially housing. Symptoms of this false nostalgia include wide circulation on social media of images intended to demonstrate that there were in fact no food shortages in the USSR. On analysis, these images turn out to be propaganda shots, heavily edited, or even photographs of American supermarkets altered by the addition of Cyrillic signs and labels.[48] In this way they provide a perverse echo of *Amerika*, a magazine about life in the United States that, under an obscure bilateral agreement, was permitted to be printed in the Soviet Union in limited numbers and with restricted circulation. One front cover in 1990 was a simple photograph of a set of U.S. supermarket shelves stacked with produce; no caption was required to demonstrate the contrast with Russia's empty food shops.

Other, more dangerous myths arise from the idealization of the Soviet past. It allows the challenges to Soviet happiness that are portrayed in this culture—the West, "fascism," and Western liberal ideas and decadence—to be more readily accepted as threats to present-day Russia, and consequently to provide grounds for ever more radical steps to defend Russia against them.

Similarly, members of the next, "lost" generation have little direct memory of the "chaos" and "humiliations" of the 1990s that they hear about on television and from parents and older relatives. They have spent most of their lives being fed consistent Russian state narratives about the disaster of *demokratiya*, the treachery of the West in bringing down the Union and then exploiting Russia in its weakened state, and the need for assertiveness and military strength in order to head off further Western encroachments. Consequently, members of this generation experience both the respect and nostalgia for the power and glory of the Soviet Union enjoyed by the preceding generation, and an even stronger rejection of the West and of unconstrained democratization. This is reflected not only in trust in President Putin but also in distrust of other politicians. In fact, research in 2008 found this generation saw "most youths agreeing with their elders that Russia needs to be ruled with a strong hand."[49]

As a result, even many of those who travel to the West and enjoy being there do not hold Western values in high esteem, or even consider them relevant. Combined with education in the approved version of twentieth-century history and the criminalization of any discussion of the Soviet Union's more heinous acts, this creates an alarming worldview in which this generation may be the most likely to support more assertive foreign policy lines abroad and more repressive ones at home. Throughout the Putin era the authorities have had little difficulty mobilizing or inducing large numbers in this age bracket to participate in patriotic or pro-Putin movements and events. By contrast, the election protests of 2011–12 involved only a tiny fraction of the younger generation at the time—just as, contrary to portrayals in Western media, they only involved a tiny fraction of the Russian population as a whole.[50] Moreover, this fraction was unrepresentative; it was drawn primarily from urban dwellers with more opportunities for exposure to alternative views than most young people in Russia, including the critical enablers of higher education, foreign contacts, and overseas travel. For the remainder of Russians of this generation, the impact on their appetite for political participation may be different. Attitudes toward both the viability and the desirability of protest will have been formed by observing the 2011–12 display of defiance against the authorities, and in particular by experiencing the slow tightening of repressive measures that followed it. Members of this generation may not necessarily conclude from these observations that participating in politics, or even calling for social change, is a productive or healthy life choice.

Parallels between Russia today and Germany in the late 1930s are often overstated; but in this case the creation of a like-minded generation with a carefully nurtured sense of grievance suggests an alarming similarity. As described by Jeffrey Mankoff in 2010, "This generation . . . is notable for its support of Russia's great power ambitions, its xenophobia, and its heightened sense of political efficacy, or ability to have an impact on the larger world."[51] Just as dangerously, such a view "encourages young Russians to value elements in the nation's history that set it at odds with the West, as well as with neighbors who resent the legacy of Russian colonial domination that represented the USSR."[52]

The Generation of the Future

> I really don't know very much about that period of history.
> —RUSSIAN ANALYST, *aged twenty-five, referring to the 1990s*

But the youngest generation—Pastukhov's "generation of the future"—is displaying an entirely different attitude to political power in its country.

This generation not only has no memory of the Soviet Union or of the 1990s, it has no memory of anything other than Putinism. And it receives a significant proportion of its political information online, through channels that are far less tightly controlled by the state.[53] Measures that have been put in place to insulate Russians from unapproved opinions do not have an effect if those Russians are watching the *Kaktus* "morning political show" on YouTube rather than the evening news on the television.[54] Social media in particular, while they do not have a bigger audience than state television, do have a different one, less subject to state influence: Russia's information security measures, including soft filters on the internet, are aimed at excluding unapproved media content rather than at controlling unmoderated conversations internally and on a mass basis. In addition, young Russians, like young people anywhere, are demonstrating an instinctive use of social media, including arriving at methods of bypassing security measures, providing both the security services and their parents with new challenges on top of constantly having to catch up with the arrival of new services for communicating and sharing information.[55] In short, adolescents in Russia are far more likely to inhabit a common information space with their peers abroad, based on common tools of communication, than any other Russian social group.

According to Tatiana Stanovaya, the current young generation has little interest in mainstream politics, but at the same time it is far less fearful of possible repression and far readier to act and to defend its interests.[56] This observation is borne out by the extreme youth not only of many participants in the March 2017 protests across Russia[57] but also of many activists in grassroots campaigns on local issues.[58] The consequence appears to be signs of entirely unrestrained willfulness, independence, and expressions of dissatisfaction.[59] In particular, the very youngest Russian citizens are so far removed from any experience of generalized repression and persecution for expressing political views as to be unaware that defying the authorities can lead to severe personal problems—an awareness that was intuitive for previous generations. After the March 2017 protests, numerous videos posted online showed schoolteachers and college lecturers remonstrating with their pupils and students for joining the rallies or for being sympathetic to the Navalny campaign. When appeals to be respectful of authority and not be gulled by foreign-backed subversives like Navalny were rejected,[60] those of the older generation betrayed their genuine concern by resorting to appeals to their young charges not to get involved because they did not understand how much trouble it could cause them.[61] This lack of consciousness and comprehension among the very young that traditional responses of locking up or even murdering citizens for expressing relatively innocent opinions might also be applied to them is indicative of how far Russia has progressed from its repressive past. And, importantly, their lack of fear is unprecedented in Russian history.

This does not mean that substantial political change driven by eighteen-year-olds in Russia is imminent. Long-serving U.S. diplomat Thomas Graham notes that the durability of youth discontent should not be taken for granted, and that "we will have to wait and see how effective the Kremlin's coercive apparatus will be."[62] Civil activist Zhanna Nemtsova is not optimistic, believing that "for many youngsters, this is like a game—it won't last."[63] But thanks to social media, the vastly increased number of individuals who are discontented and able to communicate with one another and mobilize to express their discontent could have a lasting impact in the future once this new generation gains influence and power. Ivan Kurilla notes that, just as "the 1960s generation (the *shestidesyatniki*) were a leading force in the early perestroika years, and the perestroika generation led the election protests in 2011–12," so too the young generation currently developing a taste for protest may be at its most influential a decade or two from now. At that point, "the number of these people will be much greater than in previous rounds of reform. This is not a guarantee of success, but provides a better basis for it."[64] Sociologist Lev Gudkov thinks it may take even longer: "The cynicism and incompetence in the key political and administrative spheres will generate radical protest a generation later—among the children of the current young generation."[65]

This impression of political activism was called into question by polling data released in February 2018, one month before the presidential election. These data suggested that the under-twenty-fives were in fact not the sector of the population most interested in radical change. But this was a misleading artifact of polling, resulting from comparison with large numbers of older, less well-educated, economically disadvantaged Russians. In this latter group, yearning for stability clashes with dissatisfaction at the status quo to produce a paradoxical situation in which some of the greatest advocates of substantial reform would in fact prefer regressive measures and a step away from economic liberalism.[66] What is not in doubt is that an unusually sustained period of relative liberalism in Russia has combined with the near-ubiquitous availability of online tools for communication and organization to produce a young generation that is like no other in Russian history. As a result, after decades of false hopes, there may now be grounds to believe that political change in Russia might finally be accompanied by fundamental societal change.

Patience, Resilience, and Anger

> Russian history has always provided examples of surprising and sudden change. The quality of *stikhiinost'*, or spontaneity, has spawned totally unexpected outbursts of rebellion and revolution.
> —MARVIN KALB, 2015[67]

However, for all its uniqueness in Russian history, the youngest generation will not be in a position to influence Russian state behavior for a long time, even if its current attitudes persist into adulthood. In the meantime, Russia is faced with a different perennial problem: the extent to which the broad mass of its population will tolerate impositions by its leadership.

Throughout this book, examples have been provided of state behavior that would be considered intolerable in much of Europe or North America being accepted in Russia because it conforms with persistent fundamental assumptions about the relationship between the state and the individual. The exception to this rule has repeatedly proved to be the material conditions of ordinary Russians. Once these deteriorate beyond a certain point, usually as a result of the state's pursuit of military grandeur, the consequences in terms of popular unrest have typically escalated rapidly and unpredictably. In fact, excessive spending on the military has traditionally been the major contributor to state collapse in Russia. This happened at least twice during the twentieth century: in 1991 at the end of the Cold War and in 1917 as a result of World War I, and, more debatably, in 1905 following the Russo-Japanese War; but it also routinely served as the catalyst for major social upheaval in previous centuries.

Here as elsewhere, historical parallels should not be overstated. It is true that Russia has a considerable history of exposing its citizens to privation in pursuit of military aims and has never previously considered the welfare of its subjects as significant when compared with the aspiration to greater military power.[68] President Putin and his closest associates have a background exclusively in security, not economics, and career experience of working with effectively unlimited budgets; despite the experience of the 1980s they may not fully realize that the damage caused by subordinating economic reality to military aspirations is not temporary and reversible but potentially fatal over the long term. The most recent versions of Russia's National Security Strategy may now aspire to ensure the material satisfaction of the population and to build economic power as an accompaniment to straightforward military might. But persistent unwillingness or failure to undertake substantial economic reform belies these ambitions. Economic setbacks might have been expected to challenge the current regime or induce it to change policy toward real development. Nevertheless, Russia has continued in the pattern set after the global financial crisis of 2007–08, where

> even though the economic crisis proved harmful to the Russian economy and people's living standards, it has nonetheless failed to make the elite revise its policy. . . . The crisis failed to force the elite to implement deeper structural and political reforms. Moreover, it has actually reinforced existing tendencies, such as state control over the economy and its oil-oriented character, the elite's economic expansion at the expense of private businesses, and the preservation of political power. Thus, the crisis has so far failed to dismantle Putinism, indeed quite the reverse—it has in fact contributed to its becoming "set in stone."[69]

Russians, especially those who remember the 1990s, find it easy to agree with their leaders that their economic woes are the result of hostile foreign intervention rather than Russia's own failure to modernize and adapt its economy. For now, Putin and his state leadership are able to disregard such fundamental problems as structural economic weaknesses, claiming that the roots of the problems lie elsewhere: for instance, the falling standard of living of Russians after mid-2014, partly due to a collapse in the ruble exchange rate, was presented as the result of Western sanctions.[70]

But even within this context, the challenges posed by simultaneous military modernization, economic deterioration, and sanctions, though important, risk being overstated. The reduction in purchasing power of ordinary Russians while funds are diverted to fueling military regeneration is unlikely to have the same social effect as it would in a developed Western nation, and is offset to a surprising extent by the boost in national pride that results. Polls show substantial popular support for military spending, even at the cost of the broader economy and standards of living.[71] As described in a Russian editorial in late October 2015:

> So if the economic collapse in Russia continues, pride in the army still cannot fully make up for people [for] the absence of conditions for a normal life. But for now—in a situation where the authorities live by tactics and not by strategy—the army and military mobilization of the nation really look like a national idea, and a panacea for the crisis, and a means of supporting a high rating.[72]

Even more fundamentally, economic deterioration would have to be on an extraordinary scale to produce anything like the conditions that have previously provoked substantial unrest in Russia. In addition to its unprecedented degree of freedom from repression—even taking into account recent steps back toward authoritarianism—Russian society today enjoys levels of income and material benefits that are far less backward in comparison to European neighbors than has been the case in past centuries. In particular, the modest decline in standards of living that has accompanied macroeconomic changes in the current decade bears no comparison with the genuine privation and hunger that led to mass unrest in previous centuries—or even with the challenges of the early 1990s. The persistent claim that current expenditure on military modernization and rearmament is not sustainable in the short term ignores the relative resilience of the Russian economy, and the fact that by 2016–17 the most expensive phases of these programs had already been completed and the relative cost burden had eased.[73] As a result, according to senior Russian journalist Andrey Kolesnikov, at present there is "little reason to believe that the middle class will react to the ongoing financial and economic crisis with protests or renewed calls for change."[74] In fact, a vogue for self-denial for patriotic purposes—in effect, conspicuous nonconsumption—suggests that the regime still has substantial reserves of goodwill among its subjects.[75]

Perversely, the radical change needed to ensure the future well-being of Russia's citizens could well be the step that presents the most danger to the leadership. A long-overdue process of restructuring and diversification is essential to avert economic stagnation and prevent decline relative even to Russia's friends and neighbors. But this, like so much else, is a familiar situation in Russia's history. The need to modernize is postponed until it is unavoidable, and then, as described in 2006 by Andrei Piontkovsky, a consistent critic of the Russian leadership:

> The moderniser embarks upon a frenzy of mobilisation, and as a rule successfully accomplishes his mission. At the cost of enormous sacrifices, he catches up with the eternally alluring and eternally hated West. . . . For some reason, though, after every triumph of modernisation by every moderniser, Russia finds herself back beside the broken trough. A new ruler appears who has to repeat the same exhortation: "We have fallen behind."[76]

A decade on, a Russian Academy of Sciences assessment of Russia's place in the world duly reported that "Russia . . . faces a tough challenge—it risks permanently falling behind in its development as a modern power."[77] Thomas Graham agrees, echoing other predictions of the demise of the Putin regime, but for a substantially different reason:

> Russia is reaching a point where regime change is increasingly likely because the economy is not able to back up its ambitions to be a great power. The system that worked for 500 years does not when competition is based on flexibility, creativity and innovation. All of these present a need to consider the welfare of the population—which Russia does not traditionally do well. . . . Creativity needs to extend through broad swathes of society, and this is not compatible with a political regime that makes decisions for individuals. In an open world, individuals have choices.[78]

On each previous occasion, the decision to modernize was avoided for so long that when it was finally taken, "enormous sacrifices" on the part of the population were essential and forced through by the regime. This was the case not only in Soviet times, most notably under Stalin. A biography of Peter the Great published in 1898 noted that "it would mean an enormous waste of wealth, labour and even human life, but the strength of Russia and the secret of her destiny has always consisted to a great extent in the readiness and power to ignore the cost in obtaining a desired result."[79] Almost exactly 100 years later, the diagnosis of post-Soviet Russia was the same: "They are prepared to sacrifice everything, once again, that might assist Russia to become a good country for its people in order to restore Russia as a great power."[80]

If the Russian leadership succumbs once again to this temptation, including in order once again to "catch up with the West," the most realistic challenge arising for the regime may well be the limited patience of today's Russian population with more substantial reductions in their living standards resulting from the need to fund national projects. While it is true that Russian populations historically have been far more tolerant of this situation than Western liberal democracies, it is also true that the tipping point at which the population has had enough is unpredictable; and when it arrives, it will be highly damaging. Not only Western analysts but also Russian leaders themselves have been historically extremely bad at predicting when this tipping point is likely to occur. Leadership statements suggest that President Putin is fully aware of the danger of Russia, like the Soviet Union, spending itself into the grave. The question is instead whether this present regime will be any better than its predecessors at assessing the point at which ordinary Russians will begin to protest in earnest.

Russia's economic meltdown in the summer of 1998 was a sudden and unexpected demonstration of how rapidly and badly things could go wrong even under relatively benign circumstances, and with unanticipated consequences for the outside world as well. In conditions of a sustained state effort at economic transformation, the disruption for ordinary Russians would be even more severe. In this case, the challenge for the leadership would be to avoid repetition of another consistent historical pattern, namely "that typical Russian character-pattern, described by Russian and foreign observers alike, at all periods—the pattern shown in very long spells of uncomplaining endurance and acquiescence, breaking out only at long intervals, and in extreme circumstances, into brief orgies of uncontrollable violence and rage."[81]

The current state of affairs whereby Russians are not routinely engaging in mass murder of their fellow citizens, whether as a result of civil disorder or on the instructions of the state, is anomalous in history. It might seem far-fetched to fear that previous behavior might return if Russian society were put under sufficient stress. But liberal commentators do fear that the behaviors exhibited by Russia at war in previous centuries and still today in Syria, including in particular a relative disregard for civilian life, could once again be turned against the country's own population. In 1911, Maurice Baring described how Russians "learn to bear suffering with stoicism, and therefore to inflict it with insensibility when the occasion arises."[82] Today Lev Gudkov refers to "the belief that collective unity can only be expressed and experienced as a form of violence (toward the country's own citizens or someone else)."[83] According to film director Yuriy Bykov, "People just want a bit of bread and a roof over the heads, that's the basic demand. They won't go out to protest unless things are really, really bad. But then, once they do, they won't go out demanding dialogue, they'll go out with pitchforks demanding blood."[84]

Russia's leadership appears to be preparing for this challenge as best it can. In addition to the slow tightening of measures intended to monitor, constrain, suppress, or divert discontent, the National Guard (described in chapter 9) has been established to provide a reliable force for violent repression of protest.[85] It has been provided with capabilities to inflict mass casualties on an enormous scale in the name of public order. If it were ever ordered to use them, this would signal a return to the darkest eras of Russia's history.

CONCLUSION

The Way Forward

Continuity

> In order to understand them, both to comprehend their past and to forecast their future, we must take full account not only of the period since 1917 but also Russia's age-old experience, much of it tragic, through many centuries. Then we must ask ourselves now what has changed and what is the same in the underlying sources or causes of Russian attitudes and policies toward the West.
> —FREDERICK L. SCHUMAN, *1962*[1]

This book has argued that there are consistent themes throughout Russian history and Russian social and geographic reality that induce its leaders to act in consistent ways when faced with challenges. If this is true, it means that Russia is not as unpredictable as it is often described. In 2008, Finnish Russia-watcher Hanna Smith compiled a survey of forecasts of Russian development written over the previous century. She found common threads that had been valid throughout the whole period as well as today, and concluded: "Perhaps it would be safe to assume that they will also be valid for the next one hundred years."[2] If this is so, it should still be possible for outsiders to attempt to see the world through the prism of Russian social attitudes, and use an understanding of the roots of the Russian view of the world not only to interpret and decipher, but also to some extent to predict Russian statements and actions.

In the near term, there is little prospect for a change of direction from Russia. Even in the current context of accelerating change, it is hard to envisage a major shift in policy without the cooperation of the security elite; and there is no evident incentive at present for it to disrupt the system that has restored its previous prestige and prosperity and endorsed its view of what constitutes national security and status for Russia.[3] Poll results suggest a shift in attitudes among the public on the criterion of greatness, from military strength to the population's standard of living,[4] but there is no reason to expect this shift to be reflected in official policy. Russia's default view is that territory, political status, national prestige, and the requirements of hard security are valued more highly than the rights and quality of life of its citizens. This assumption is institutionalized in the country's political, economic, social, and cultural realities and is unlikely to change soon.

In this as in so much else, the country is returning to the historical norm.[5] History is important to Russia, and historical parallels do carry weight and meaning. The "thousand-year narrative" referred to by President Putin may be unrecognizable from abroad, but it needs to be taken into consideration as part of the framework of his decisions and a provider of models to emulate. According to a prediction from 2007 based on historical analysis, Moscow "may be on its way to a restoration of Stalin's dreams, or to an apotheosis as capital of a new Eurasian antagonist for the West."[6] Just over a decade later, elements of both phenomena are already visible.

In Part I it was suggested that the question of whether the narrative of a hostile and dangerous West that seeks to destroy Russia is based on a genuine assessment of the threat or is a fabrication for domestic propaganda purposes is irrelevant: either way it is accepted as fact, and drives Russian actions. Even if a narrative of this kind begins its life solely as a legitimating device, it creates a reality of its own, since consistently framing policy in its rhetoric cannot fail to establish it as the real decision-making framework for the leadership.[7] The effect is amplified by Russia's zero-sum approach to security, grounded in a perception that there is a finite amount of security to go around and so any increase in the security of its neighbors must necessarily be detrimental to Russia's own position.

President Putin himself is not the issue. Enduring Russian concerns, rather than Putin's personal preferences, are the drivers for Russia's current policy priorities, and his successor (if and when one might appear) is highly unlikely to abandon altogether the strain of conservative nationalism that serves Russia well today. Putin is enacting, rather than inventing, Russian state assumptions and ambitions that have been consistent over the long term and remained unchanged even during the period when Russia was treated as a friend and partner by the West. What has changed dramatically in the last decade is Russia's capability to achieve these ambitions. In addition, fundamental Russian assumptions about the nature of relations between states—now put into action by Putin—have two inevitable consequences: first, innocent Western actions are portrayed as threatening to Russia, and second, actions that Russia perceives as normal and natural appear morally unacceptable to the West. The inescapable conclusion is that Russia will continue to present a challenge to the West for the foreseeable future. Consequently, rather than 2014–19 being treated as just a "current crisis," managing the Russia problem needs to involve long-term planning.

The aspects of Moscow's current behavior that so surprise and dismay Western leaders are in fact manifestations of Russia reverting to type. But they also provide pointers for how the West can behave in order to manage relations with Moscow effectively. It bears reemphasizing that Russia is not unique in every way, and some features of its governance are recognizable elsewhere. For instance, the systematic embrace of falsehood and deception as an instrument of policy, previously regarded by the West as a strikingly distinctive feature of Soviet and Russian life, no longer looks quite so exceptional after the arrival in power of President Donald Trump. But in combination, these features create a singularity where all Western assumptions must be put aside. The key to the Russian enigma is not only Russian national interest, which is easily understood. It is also the toxic blend of paranoia, delusion, isolation, and inability to adjust to the notion of cooperation for the common good that dictates how Moscow perceives and pursues this interest. And that is far harder to grasp.

Comprehension

Russia is a fact humanity has had plenty of time to grasp.
—LEV TIKHOMIROV, 1888[8]

The defining characteristic of Western approaches to Russia in the post–Cold War period has been repetition of the same action while expecting different results. This stems from ignoring the fact that what the West may habitually expect, or assume, or hope is not a driving factor in what the Russian leadership decides to do. Accepting this reality requires both modesty on the part of Western leaders and policymakers and the ability to disregard their own ideas of what constitutes a logical and rational course of action, because Russia is not guided by their preconceptions.

Policymakers habitually ask binary questions about Russia, expecting an answer that is either black or white, yes or no. And yet most questions asked about Russia have more than one possible answer. Those seeking to genuinely understand Russia—or to understand the explanations of Russian conduct they are presented with—must, like Russians themselves, be adept at simultaneously holding mutually exclusive views and perceptions. In addition, Russia's gift for flexibility of strategic planning must be factored in, together with the possibility of combinations of multiple policy objectives, not all of which are realistic. Consequently, the temptation to assess the options available to Moscow from the standpoint of what appears rational in Washington or Brussels must be resisted.

As noted at the start of this book, language represents a key obstacle to understanding. This is not only because some fundamental Russian concepts cannot be conveyed in English and therefore cannot be assessed through translated material alone. It is also because there are Western terms that have been adopted in Russian but have acquired entirely different connotations, especially when applied in descriptions of Russia's political system. Finally, there are those terms that do translate, but misleadingly—because identical terms often mean very different things in Russian- and in English-language foreign policy documents.

All of this argues the need for far more widespread, detailed and close study of Russia to guide policy. Both the complexity and the otherness of

Russia mean that superficial analysis of the country and its likely actions is misleading and potentially dangerous. It leads to the presumption that Russians will act in a particular way because that is what appears logical in the West, an assumption that routinely delivers unwelcome surprises.[9]

Hence a corps of knowledgeable individuals who can advise on policy toward Moscow on the basis of a deep understanding of Russia is invaluable to any country that wishes to manage the relationship successfully. But—crucially—"understanding" in itself is not sufficient to generate policy advice that will make the situation better rather than worse. Previous chapters have described how even individuals who are highly intelligent and deeply conscious of the reality of Russia can misguidedly promote claims, assertions, or rationales from Moscow that are seductive to their egos or intellects but pernicious to the security of the West. These arguments can be made with the best of intentions and need not necessarily mean that the presenter is acting under instructions from the Kremlin, but they are no less damaging for that. At its most innocent, for liberal-minded academics and observers in particular, translating an understanding of Russia into sensible policy advice requires overcoming a persistent tendency for optimism to triumph over evidence.

It was unfortunate, but hardly surprising, that expertise on Russia became devalued after the end of the Cold War. In the general perception that the threat from Russia had evaporated, it was entirely sensible to focus on the rapid emergence of new challenges from other regions.[10] But this does not excuse the marginalization of the Russia expertise that remained readily available even when it was deeply unfashionable. In the words of a senior American Russia-watcher, "In all the years I've done this, I don't think anything I've ever said has ever got through."[11] In addition, a challenge inherent in the current surge in demand for commentary on Russia is that, just as in the early days of advice on Afghanistan and Iraq, a substantial amount of it is highly superficial and therefore dangerously misguided. It should not even need to be pointed out that "you're not a 'Russia expert' if you don't know Russian and have never been to Russia."[12]

The same challenge of deficit of expertise pertains in reverse. The availability of informed assessments by intelligent Russians who know and understand the West does not mean that Russia's leaders are not at times also dangerously misguided about the drivers of Western decision making. The

Soviet leadership would on occasion make announcements that, seen from the West, appeared incomprehensible to the point of being deranged. But it was assumed generally that private discussions by that same leadership behind closed doors were rational in Western terms. Not until after the end of the Soviet Union did it become clear that its decision making had been rational only in terms of the self-contained universe of its leadership, operating in a parallel reality to what was taken for granted by the West.

Miscommunication breeds miscalculation, and Russian policy today is again built around misreading and misunderstanding of the West.[13] As Russia retreats further into itself, and the scope for real dialogue on security issues is constrained by domestic politics in the United States and NATO's policy of restricting contact, there are fewer and fewer points of reference for reality checks on both sides. The obstacles to understanding between Russia and the West are not yet as formidable as they were during the Cold War, but the trend is toward the same kind of complete disconnection between the West's and Russia's perceptions of events that in 1983, for example, risked causing accidental nuclear war during NATO's "Able Archer" exercise.[14]

It follows that President Putin and his advisers need help in not misreading the West. This means that messaging to Russia must be clear and direct, rather than couched in diplomatic niceties. The approach that President Putin adopts when expressing himself clearly provides a model for passing messages back to him in a manner that will be immediately understood.

Confrontation

> The regime's perception of reality [was] the proposition that Russia was a besieged fortress, and ultimately the belief that a Russia risen from its knees meant that others, and especially its ex-Soviet neighbours, had to fall on theirs.
>
> —SIR ANDREW WOOD, *2015*[15]

Instances of malignant behavior by Russia, such as ongoing military involvement in Ukraine, the shooting down of Malaysia Airlines Flight MH17, attempts to subvert democratic processes in the United States and Europe, the nerve agent attack in Salisbury, England, and more, should not be treated as isolated incidents. Instead, they are the presenting symptoms of a deeper disorder, namely the deep-seated and long-term incompatibility between two views of the world. Pretense at all-encompassing strategic partnership with Moscow was only possible while Russia was in a position of relative weakness and the perceived threat from the West was hypothetical rather than immediate. Now that Moscow feels itself both under greater threat and more capable of taking action to counter that threat, the long-term outlook is for a return to normal in relations with Russia: namely, continued conflict and confrontation.

Russia's trajectory toward confrontation depends on objective factors. This means that any change of policy by the United States or any other Western country may not in fact influence this trajectory at all. The relationship as a whole is not amenable to change through policy steps because it rests on the fundamental incompatibility between Russian interests and Western values. Russia not only defines its own security as the insecurity of its neighbors but also requires buffer states against cultural and economic threats, in the same way that it has developed anti-access and area denial (A2/AD) capabilities against military threats in order to keep them at a distance. As such, its interests are incompatible with Euro-Atlantic values, which hold that small states should be sovereign and independent. Consequently, the most immediate expression of this incompatibility remains the front-line states in Europe. The danger of precipitate action by Russia will persist for as long as the West supports the independence and unqualified sovereignty of those countries that Russia perceives as its fiefdom.

Living next to Russia and remaining independent will continue to entail difficult political and strategic choices: Moscow insists it is entitled to a sphere of legitimate interests, but a problem arises when these other countries do not wish to be within that sphere. If in addition those who argue that President Putin needs to legitimize himself through foreign adventures are right, then an essential prerequisite for stability within Russia is the creation of still more instability abroad. In effect, as a result of Russia's assumption of entitlement to dominion over its neighbors, Europe as a whole has become the scene of an unresolved conflict, of which at present Ukraine is just the most obvious expression.

Russia also appears to expect that major European partners and the United States share its own willingness to join in Yalta-style agreements to allocate spheres of great-power influence. In Putin's eyes, the Yalta settlement provided decades of stability.[16] In addition, the U.S. retreat from global leadership and the domestic political chaos that have accompanied the Trump presidency provide Russia with a unique opportunity to advance its own interests. The potential fracturing of a wide range of relationships that had previously centered on the United States serves Moscow well, enabling it to further weaken Western alliances, and it is in Moscow's interest to encourage these processes by any means available. And yet, whether or not enlargement was a mistake for NATO, it is a fact. NATO must now live with the consequences of its decision—either stand firm and make the necessary investment to do so credibly, or retreat from both territory and principles and thereby show itself to be the useless anachronism that Russia claims it is. The choice, as noted above, is between values and interest. To suggest that the front-line states should be recognized as within Russia's "sphere of influence" means abandoning core values that unite the Euro-Atlantic community.

Russia under Putin—and, in all probability, his successors—will continue to be proactive, and will exploit opportunities for advantage where they occur. This exploitation may still, under specific circumstances of threat or opportunity for Russia, include the use of military force in Europe.[17] Russia has, for instance, consistently warned of plans for military action against the U.S. ballistic missile defense sites in Poland and Romania.[18] Postnationalist Europe may consider this approach to resolving security challenges outdated, but this is immaterial because Russia is perfectly capable of acting militarily in circumstances where such a response would never have occurred to a European state. This is the most obvious example of a poor relationship with Russia incurring not just an opportunity cost but an existential threat to neighbors and potentially to countries further abroad.

Just as history provides pointers for understanding and predicting Russian behavior, so it also provides precedents for how the United States and Europe can deal with the challenge.[19] A key lesson is the necessity of political will to use hard and soft power to defend boundaries and values—since superior U.S. and NATO capability is useless without the will to use it. This will must be maintained in the face of Russian tactics of attrition, combining a barrage of information operations with diplomacy, insistence, persistence, and the dedication of more resources than the West imagines feasible in a bid to exhaust the United States and cause it to withdraw from the defense of Europe. Political will also requires a demonstrable readiness to resort to force in this defense, and under no circumstances to allow Moscow to become convinced that it can act without consequences. As noted by Samuel Greene of the Russia Institute at King's College London: "The costs of geo-economic and geopolitical competition with Moscow will be unsustainable, as long as Moscow is willing to countenance military confrontation and Europe is not."[20]

Suggestions persist that various developments since 1991 mean we now find ourselves in a "new Cold War." Widely differing rationales are put forward for the comparison.[21] But if we are indeed at the start of such a cold war, we are in the period before the rules that made the original Cold War stable have been laid down and agreed on. This means that ahead of us there still lie the Korean War, the Cuban missile crisis, Vietnam, and a patchwork of small but deeply unpleasant proxy wars in Africa, Asia, and Central America. Meanwhile, Western observers of Russia who are fully aware of the dangers that lie ahead are still trying collectively to write a new version of Kennan's Long Telegram. If there is scope for optimism, it lies only in the hope that Russia's actions since 2014 have removed all doubt in Europe as to the nature of the challenge and the necessity for unity to withstand it. In the early Cold War, John Foster Dulles defined the moment of greatest danger as when "the perceived threat from the East had begun to fade—[when] allies would become quarrelsome, collective security arrangements would begin to seem outdated, neutralism would gain respectability."[22] With luck, thanks to Russia, this moment has already passed.

Containment

We have every reason to assume that the infamous policy of containment, led in the 18th, 19th and 20th Centuries, continues today.
—VLADIMIR PUTIN, *March 2014*[23]

Containment is a highly loaded term. To Western ears it recalls the early years of the Cold War, while to Russia it evokes a much longer period of generalized Western hostility to Russia. But at its simplest, the notion of containing Russia is precisely what is needed for maintaining a relationship while limiting the scope for dangerous escalation of conflicts, or for adverse consequences for Russia's immediate neighbors. In essence, containment in this sense should consist of removing opportunities for Russia to do damage.

At the end of the Cold War, the widespread assumption was that integration of the whole of the former Soviet Union with the West would be beneficial for all concerned, and would help Russia become prosperous and secure. A conscious decision was made to treat Russia as the legitimate successor to the Soviet Union, and as such to grant it a status in the world that was out of all proportion to its new diminished stature and relevance. Today, the idea that today's Russia is not the same actor as the former USSR is undermined by the simple fact that it is sitting in the USSR's seat on the United Nations Security Council. Granting this seat was not automatic but a deliberate choice by international partners. Similarly, Russia's membership in the former G-8 was granted out of politeness rather than because it qualified in any way for membership in a club of democratically inclined major economic powers.

Choices like these were made to encourage integration, and as part of building up a thick web of relationships both at state level and through local and regional economic partnerships. This policy of integration was the opposite of containment, and it continued—including in the form of the Obama "reset" after the war with Georgia—long after the post–Cold War euphoria had dissipated. And yet President Putin and Russia's political system reject many of these relationships and initiatives—especially those based on an assumption of independent private enterprise, the rule of law, and property rights—because they present an implicit threat to that system. In the same way, Russia is bound to attack NGOs, even nonpolitical ones and those without foreign backing, because any attempt to hold the state accountable is in itself an attack on the state.

Russia perceives both internal and external threats to the regime, but over the past decade it has been able to take significant steps to mitigate them. In the case of the entirely misplaced perception that the West harbors hostile intentions toward Russia and would like to see it destabilized, long-term military reorganization has significantly reduced Russia's vulnerabilities in hard-power terms. Meanwhile, domestic measures to prevent external influences on the population have significantly curtailed the reach of the West in terms of soft power. This easing of Moscow's sense of acute vulnerability has reduced apprehension at the prospect of confrontation with the West, and hence has contributed directly to increased assertiveness abroad. Moscow can be expected to continue acting in its current manner for as long as this seems to bring success by continuing to expand Russia's reach and influence and hence enhancing its status and perception of power.

The failures of sundry resets show that fundamental conflicts remain. Even more: Russian ambitions lead unavoidably to a need to damage the standing and interests of the United States and its major allies, and as such must be countered. At times Russia has succeeded admirably in causing its international partners to forget that it is by no means a military or economic superpower. And even though continued predictions of imminent economic collapse remain driven more by optimism than by evidence, there is no doubt that Russia's long-term prospects remain dire. Currently, however, Russian power is a function of Western incoherence, division, and disunity. These, and the resultant lack of clarity on the boundaries of acceptable behavior, are inherently destabilizing; as described in one Russian study, "The lack of strategic goal-setting by Western partners hinders the shaping and implementation of the Kremlin's foreign policy, thereby forcing it to continue feeling its way."[24]

It follows from all of this that in the absence of internal restraint of the expansionist instinct within Russia, external constraints are essential. Conflict is likely if Russia's leaders misjudge these constraints, particularly if they underestimate the West's readiness and ability to resist them. Thus deterrence of Russian adventurism in Europe requires ensuring that Russia does not perceive deficits of political, military, or societal power—or the will to employ them. As described by Thomas Graham, the task is to ensure that Russia's periphery consists of countries with "well-organized competent societies and competent militaries. This will render subversion ineffective, as domestic cohesion is an effective barrier."[25]

In addition, it should not be assumed that Moscow's ambitions are limited to the immediate focus of conflict, whether geographically or politically. Throughout both recent and more distant history, Russia has shown itself content to take two steps forward and one step back in order to advance its position. In seizing Crimea and then attacking eastern Ukraine, it has given an incentive to the international community to recognize Russian entitlement to Crimea, with the implication that this would then bring an end to operations on the Ukrainian mainland. In the same way, in 2008 Russia seized South Ossetia and Abkhazia together with additional Georgian territory, then retreated from the rest of Georgia once it had achieved a cease-fire agreement that recognized and cemented its control of the two northern territories. Here and elsewhere, there is a consistent pattern: Moscow demands the whole of somebody else's cake and then graciously settles for only half.

It is axiomatic—and demonstrated repeatedly over history—that Russia respects strength and despises compromise and accommodation. This strength must necessarily include military power, present and ready for use, to provide a visible counter to Russia's own new capabilities. Some Western countries may have felt that maintaining strong standing armies and investing in hardware and manpower represented an outmoded metric of national security. But Russia's traditional and persistent respect for brute military force as the key determinant of national status and the right to assert national interests means that the United States and Western alliances must respond in kind. Maintaining superior conventional military capability is essential in ensuring that Russia does not perceive opportunities to further its interests—or to remove notional threats to itself—by military means.

Conclusion

Today's challenge is not how to see Russia crushed again, as it was when the Soviet Union collapsed; it's about constraining its worst tendencies as it revives. That requires showing unrelenting firmness on what matters most to the United States . . . and in the meantime remaining alert for issues on which American and Russian interests converge enough to permit at least limited cooperation

—JOHN MCLAUGHLIN, *August 2017*[26]

> If the United States would have some sort of list of items on which it doesn't want to cooperate with us and another list on which it wants to cooperate with us, when we have this list, we would certainly understand better how we ourselves should proceed on this relationship.
> —SERGEY LAVROV, *September 2008*[27]

Assumptions that Russia was a partner to the West and shared its interests prevailed for over two decades after the end of the Cold War in the face of mounting evidence to the contrary. It is crucial that these assumptions now be discarded and the reality of disagreement recognized. But this in itself should not lead inevitably to outright and open hostility. One lesson of the Cold War is that coexistence is possible while accepting that the strategic interests of Moscow and the West are incompatible. Once the irreconcilable differences between the West and the Soviet Union had been recognized, the security policies of both came to be geared to managing rather than resolving the conflict between the two sides. There was no coordinated attempt by either side to reconcile these opposing views of the world, since this did not appear possible or perhaps even necessary.

Today there is another opportunity to recognize that Western values and vital interests are not reconcilable with those of Russia, and to adjust for that reality in long-term management of the relationship. If the West renounces its hope that Russia will, after all, in the end turn out to think just like the West does, then practical cooperation should be possible as long as issues are ring-fenced. There should be no reason in principle why Russia and Western nations cannot work practically in those few areas where their interests coincide, despite their differences in others.

It follows, according to experienced Russia-watcher Kadri Liik, that the main aim of communicating with Russia should be to "agree on the nature of disagreements. If this could be achieved, then the differences would still be there, but they would be less dangerous."[28] Ivan Kurilla too identifies failure to communicate about differing worldviews and failure to accept and recognize disagreement as key factors in the repetitive cycle of confrontation between Russia and the West.[29] The alternative is to continue the cycle of crisis followed by "reset," the crises becoming deeper and more dangerous with each iteration.

Cooperation with Russia on specific bilateral issues is possible. But the boundaries of these issues must be firmly and explicitly laid down in order to avoid another cycle of disappointment in the relationship. For example, the Russian default position is that "nothing serious in the world can happen without us." If this is not acceptable to other states in specific instances, then this must be stated clearly. In particular, if and when proposals for cooperation made by Russia are declined, the reasons for the rebuff need to be communicated—it has to be clear that this is not just happening through intransigence or instinctive disdain for Russia or for Putin himself.

A similar approach should be applied to Russia's engagement or participation in those multilateral organizations, agreements, or endeavors to which it is still a party or in which it is still showing an interest. It was suggested in the introduction to this book that as Russia is not part of the West, there is limited utility in assessing it by Western criteria or judging it by Western standards. Ideally, of course, Russians should have the opportunity to enjoy Western standards in fields such as human rights, democracy, and the rule of law; but the trend is against this happening any time soon. The exception to this principle comes when Russia seeks membership in Western or even global institutions that are founded on an understanding of common values and behavior. To make allowances for Russian exceptionalism in this case devalues the institutions themselves. But here again, the refusal to make allowances should be clearly and consistently communicated.

A constructive relationship at arm's length would also allow the West to make best use of future opportunities that may arise if and when levels of hostility from Moscow diminish. These opportunities are rare and depend entirely on internal Russian circumstances, but they do occur. The brief retreat from confrontation by the USSR during Khrushchev's early tenure as Soviet leader in the mid-1950s saw uncharacteristic conciliatory moves from Moscow, including not only the closure of exposed and strategically redundant overseas bases such as Port Arthur in China and Porkkala in Finland but also the far more significant withdrawal of Soviet occupation troops from Austria. While at present there is no indication of an imminent softening in Russia's security posture that would allow tensions to be reduced, the United States and its allies should be prepared to engage fully with any move toward de-escalation that might be sensed coming from Moscow.

Former U.S. senior diplomat Daniel Fried argues the following: "A sound Russia policy would mean resisting Russian aggression and helping others resist it; identifying areas of potential cooperation, without expecting too much or rewarding Russia for its cooperation in areas of supposed mutual interest; stabilizing the relationship where possible, including by keeping up dialogue, civilian and military; and looking to a better future relationship with a better Russia."[30] All of this is true, but to look for a better Russia is to look far, far into the future. Optimism of this kind is perennial and only human, but it should be contained for the sake of a better chance at a functional relationship with the Russia that exists, rather than the Russia one might hope for. In particular, it must constantly be recalled that change in Russia is not always for good, and not always really change: as with the instances recounted in this book, what can appear to be evolution or reform is usually no more than a temporary aberration.

Thus, in attempting to live with Russia, the aim should be to build a working relationship by recognizing and publicly stating differences, not by pretending they do not exist. The longer-term goal is to assist Russia, where possible, in its transition to a postimperial mentality, while hoping that this does not necessarily involve the kind of war, with Russia on the losing side, that has been an essential part of the process for other former imperial powers. In the meantime, it does need to be consistently pointed out—even though it will not be welcome news—that good relations with Moscow are not the only foreign policy goal for the United States and Europe and they should not be allowed to obscure or distort other and more vital interests.

Understanding and accepting this basic clash of interests and worldviews inevitably means that the West must invest heavily and for the long term in deterring Russia from aggressive and hostile actions. This deterrence must include willingness to impose costs and consequences on Russia in response to military adventurism, cyber and information assaults, or any of the other ways in which Russia endangers the integrity of Western states or the lives and livelihoods of their citizens. The process, inevitably, will be costly and damaging for both sides—but it has to be remembered that a failure to deter Moscow invites consequences that are far more costly and far more damaging. Western policymakers, politicians, and populations will need to be constantly reminded not only that Russia is not like them and does not wish to be like them, but also that other methods of dealing with it have been repeatedly tried and failed, and that being willing to accept confrontation and invest in prevailing in it is the proven way of constraining Russian ambition and hostile intent. It is this understanding, coupled with the strategic patience required to act on it consistently and for as long as necessary, that will provide the basis for safeguarding peace between Russia and the West.

Notes

Introduction

1. Maria Lipman, "Putin's 'Besieged Fortress' and Its Ideological Arms," in *The State of Russia: What Comes Next?*, edited by Maria Lipman and Nikolay Petrov (London: Palgrave Macmillan, 2015), p. 111.

2. Paul Hollander, *Political Pilgrims: Travels of Western Intellectuals to the Soviet Union, China and Cuba, 1928–78* (New York: Oxford University Press, 1981).

3. Astolphe de Custine, *Lettres de Russie: La Russie en 1839*, edited by Pierre Nora (Paris: Gallimard, 1975), p. 240. (Author's translation throughout.)

4. For accounts of Russia in the mid-eighteenth century that describe official and personal behavior that will be familiar to modern visitors, see Jonas Hanway, *An Historical Account of the British Trade with the Caspian with a Journal of Travels from London through Russia into Persia and back through Russia, Germany and Holland* (London, 1753), and M. l'abbé Chappe d'Auteroche, *Voyage en Sibérie fait par ordre du roi en 1761, contenant les moeurs, les usages des Russes et l'état actuel de cette puissance* (Paris, 1768), available at http://gallica.bnf.fr/ark:/12148/btv1b8620782c/f9.image.

5. "Many simple explanations of [Russia's] behavior or misbehavior are available, ranging from total depravity and original sin to totalitarian despotism, World Revolution, capitalist villainy, Pan-Slavic imperialism, the Russian soul, and Wall Street plots. Each of these explanations appears to afford adequate emotional satisfaction to those accepting it." Frederick L. Schuman, *The Cold War, Retrospect and Prospect* (Louisiana State University Press, 1962), p. 7.

Chapter 1

1. Gonzague de Reynold, *Le Monde russe* (Paris: Librairie Plon, 1950), p. 25.
2. Thomas Gomart, *Russian Foreign Policy: Strange Inconsistency* (Shrivenham, U.K.: Conflict Studies Research Centre, March 2006).
3. Andrew Monaghan, *The New Politics of Russia: Interpreting Change* (Manchester University Press, 2016), p. 49.
4. Fiona Hill, "Putin: The One-Man Show the West Doesn't Understand," *Bulletin of the Atomic Scientists* 72, no. 3 (2016), pp. 140–44.
5. Interview with Ivan Kurilla, European University at St. Petersburg, August 2017.
6. Monaghan, *The New Politics of Russia*, p. 39.
7. Natalia Zubarevich, "The Relations between the Center and the Regions," in *The State of Russia: What Comes Next?*, edited by Maria Lipman and Nikolay Petrov (London: Palgrave Macmillan, 2015), p. 61.
8. Natalia Zubarevich, "Four Russias: Rethinking the Post-Soviet Map," OpenDemocracy.net, March 29, 2012 (https://www.opendemocracy.net/od-russia/natalia-zubarevich/four-russias-rethinking-post-soviet-map).
9. "Russian Combat Methods in World War II," Department of the Army pamphlet, quoted in Catherine Merridale, *Ivan's War: The Red Army 1939–1945* (London: Faber and Faber, 2005), p. 27.
10. Laurens van der Post, *Journey into Russia* (Harmondsworth: Penguin, 1965), throughout.
11. Walter Bedell Smith, Introduction to *Journey for Our Time. The Journals of the Marquis de Custine* (London: George Prior, 1980), pp. 12–13.
12. "How Russia Went Wrong, As Told from the Inside," *The Economist*, September 16, 2017 (https://www.economist.com/news/books-and-arts/21728877-andrei-kovalev-says-things-no-outsider-could-about-russias-megalomania-persecution).
13. Henry Kissinger, *World Order* (New York: Penguin Press, 2014), p. 50.
14. Gerald Seymour, *A Damned Serious Business* (London: Hodder & Stoughton, 2018), p. 147.
15. "Ivangorod-Narva: Yevrosoyuz na tom beregu" [Ivangorod-Narva: The EU on the other bank of the river], Varlamov.ru, June 21, 2017 (http://varlamov.ru/2434012.html).
16. In the 1960s, Laurens van der Post noted that in the borderlands, "People use the same language about Russians as a South African fanatic of apartheid will use about his black countrymen." *Journey into Russia*, p. 316. In the current century in Finland, different standards of social and communal responsibility among Russian immigrants mean that "minor conflicts related to cultural misunderstandings over life in apartment buildings can escalate to the point of civil unrest." "Racist Online Agitation Spreads in Finland," *YLE News*, May 5, 2008.

17. Russia can still appear "remarkable and strange" to neighbors despite centuries of interaction. Still taking the example of Finland, see Arto Mustajoki and Ekaterina Protassova, "The Finnish-Russian Relationships: The Interplay of Economics, History, Psychology and Language," *Vestnik Rossiyskogo universiteta druzhby narodov. Seriya: Lingvistika* [Bulletin of the Peoples' Friendship University of Russia, Linguistics Series] 4 (2015), pp. 69–80 (https://cyberleninka.ru/article/n/the-finnish-russian-relationships-the-interplay-of-economics-history-psychology-and-language).

18. Barry Petchesky, "A User's Guide to the Bizarre Toilets of Sochi," *Deadspin*, February 5, 2014 (http://deadspin.com/a-users-guide-to-the-bizarre-toilets-of-sochi-1516518904).

19. "Russian Official: Our Video Surveillance of Sochi's Showers Proves Sabotage," *The Atlantic*, February 6, 2014 (https://www.theatlantic.com/politics/archive/2014/02/russian-official-our-video-surveillance-sochis-showers-proves-sabotage/357801/).

20. Andrey Makarychev, "FIFA 2018 Countdown: Rethinking the Sochi Legacy," PONARS Eurasia, July 6, 2017 (http://www.ponarseurasia.org/article/fifa-2018-countdown-rethinking-sochi-legacy).

21. Iwona Wiśniewska and Jadwiga Rogoża, "The 2018 FIFA World Cup in Russia: Circuses instead of Bread?," OSW, September 17, 2018 (https://www.osw.waw.pl/en/publikacje/osw-commentary/2018-09-17/2018-fifa-world-cup-russia-circuses-instead-bread).

22. Ibid.; author's interviews with soccer fans after their return from Russia, summer 2018.

23. Steve Rosenberg, "Why Russian Workers Are Being Taught How to Smile," *BBC News*, June 9, 2018 (https://www.bbc.co.uk/news/av/world-europe-44415769/why-russian-workers-are-being-taught-how-to-smile); Damien Sharkov, "Russia Is Giving Smiling Lessons for World Cup to Make Locals Look Friendly," *Newsweek*, June 12, 2018 (https://www.newsweek.com/russia-giving-smiling-lessons-world-cup-make-locals-look-friendly-973031).

24. Author's interviews with soccer fans after their return from Russia, summer of 2018.

25. David Satter, *The Less You Know, the Better You Sleep* (Yale University Press, 2016), p. xiii.

26. "There is a certain mythology that Russia is a land of irregularities and paradoxes, to a large extent impenetrable to outsiders. At the level of cliché, the 'Russian soul' and 'Russian chaos' claim some implicit explanatory power." Alena V. Ledeneva, *How Russia Really Works: The Informal Practices That Shaped Post-Soviet Politics and Business* (Cornell University Press, 2006), p. 10.

27. Edward Crankshaw, *Putting Up with the Russians* (London: Macmillan, 1984), p. xi.

28. Text available at http://lib39.ru/kray/literature/writers-2/solzhenitsyn/prussian_nights.php (author's translation).

29. Emil Pain, "The Imperial Syndrome and Its Influence on Russian Nationalism," in *The New Russian Nationalism: Imperialism, Ethnicity and Authoritarianism 2000–15*, edited by Pål Kolstø and Helge Blakkisrud (Edinburgh University Press, 2016), pp. 46–74.

30. Vladimir Baranovsky, "Russia: A Part of Europe or Apart from Europe?," *International Affairs* 76, no. 3 (2000), pp. 443–58.

31. Tibor Szamuely, *The Russian Tradition* (London: Secker & Warburg, 1974), p. 126.

32. Ibid.

33. Lev Gudkov, "Putin's Relapse into Totalitarianism," in *The State of Russia*, edited by Lipman and Petrov, p. 99.

34. Interview with Ivan Kurilla, European University at St. Petersburg, August 2017.

35. Sergey Lavrov, "Russia's Foreign Policy in a Historical Perspective," *Russia in Global Affairs*, March 30, 2016 (http://eng.globalaffairs.ru/number/Russias-Foreign-Policy-in-a-Historical-Perspective-18067).

36. See Iver B. Neumann, *Russia and the Idea of Europe* (London: Routledge, 2017).

37. Alexei G. Arbatov, Karl Kaiser, and Robert Legvold, eds., *Russia and the West: The 21st Century Security Environment* (Armonk, N.Y.: M. E. Sharpe for the EastWest Institute, 1999), p. 7.

38. Vladimir Putin, "Poslanie Federal'nomu Sobraniyu Rossiyskoy Federatsii" [Address to the Federal Assembly of the Russian Federation], April 25, 2005 (http://kremlin.ru/events/president/transcripts/22931).

39. The first clause of a *Nakaz*, a combined manifesto declaration and statement of legal principles for Russia in 1767. An English translation is available at http://www2.stetson.edu/~psteeves/classes/catherineinstruction.html.

40. Dmitry Trenin, "Russia Leaves the West," *Foreign Affairs*, July/August 2006. (https://www.foreignaffairs.com/articles/russia-fsu/2006-07-01/russia-leaves-west).

41. Andrey Kozyrev, *Izvestiya*, January 2, 1992, quoted in Iver B. Neumann, "Russia's Return as True Europe, 1991–2017," *Conflict and Society* 3, no. 1 (2017), pp. 78–91 (https://www.berghahnjournals.com/view/journals/conflict-and-society/3/1/arcs030107.xml).

42. As quoted in Suzanne Crow, *The Making of Foreign Policy in Russia under Yeltsin* (Munich: Radio Free Europe/Radio Liberty, 1993), p. 76.

43. Gudkov, "Putin's Relapse into Totalitarianism," p. 100.

44. André Gide, *Back from the USSR* (London: Secker & Warburg, 1937), p. 15.

45. Mark Bassin, Sergey Glebov, and Marlene Laruelle, eds., *Between Europe and Asia: The Origins, Theories, and Legacies of Russian Eurasianism* (Pittsburgh University Press, 2015).

Chapter 2

1. A senior Russian academician from the Institute for US and Canadian Studies, Moscow, speaking to the Conflict Studies Research Centre, Royal Military Academy Sandhurst, summer of 1994.

2. Mark Galeotti, speaking at King's College London, April 26, 2018.

3. As described in Ingmar Oldberg, *Russia's Great Power Strategy under Putin and Medvedev*, UI Occasional Paper 1 (Stockholm: Swedish Institute of International Affairs, June 2010).

4. Jeffrey Mankoff, *Russian Foreign Policy: The Return of Great Power Politics* (Lanham, Md.: Rowman & Littlefield, 2009).

5. Anatoly Reshetnikov, "Frozen Transition: Russia and Great Power Crisis Management," *New Perspectives* 24, no. 1 (2016), p. 102. See also S. Frederick Starr, ed., *The Legacy of History in Russia and the New States of Eurasia* (Armonk, N.Y.: M. E. Sharpe, 1994), p. 6.

6. Dmitri Trenin, director, Carnegie Moscow Center, speaking at the Council on Foreign Relations "Perspectives on Russia" symposium, New York, April 13, 2017 (https://www.cfr.org/event/perspectives-russia).

7. Aleksandr Pushkin, "O nichtozhestve literatury russkoy" [On the nullity of Russian literature], 1834 (http://rvb.ru/pushkin/01text/07criticism/02misc/1053.htm).

8. For a clear and direct expression of this common belief, see "Zoya Zotova: Rossiya spasla ot fashistskoy chumy narody vsego mira" [Zoya Zotova: Russia saved the peoples of the whole world from the fascist plague], EthnoInfo.ru, n.d. (http://www.ethnoinfo.ru/statji/1859-zoja-zotova-rossija-spasla-ot-fashistskoj-chumy-narody-vsego-mira).

9. Compare Scott Wilson, "Obama Dismisses Russia as 'Regional Power' Acting out of Weakness," *Washington Post*, March 24, 2014 (https://www.washingtonpost.com/world/national-security/obama-dismisses-russia-as-regional-power-acting-out-of-weakness/2014/03/25/1e5a678e-b439-11e3-b899-20667de76985_story.html), and "Putin—The Interview (Part 2): 'We Do Not Claim the Role of a Superpower,'" *Bild*, January 12, 2016 (http://www.bild.de/politik/ausland/wladimir-putin/russian-president-vladimir-putin-the-interview-44096428.bild.html).

10. "On Affirming the Strategic Course of the Russian Federation with the Member States of the Commonwealth of Independent States," *Rossiyskaya gazeta*, September 23, 1995, p. 4; "Fundamentals of Russian Federation Border Policy," *Rossiyskaya gazeta*, November 6, 1996, p. 4; and "Treaty on Cooperation in the Protection of the Borders of the Participants in the Commonwealth of Independent States with States That Are Not Members of the Commonwealth," *Rossiyskaya gazeta*, July 7, 1995, p. 4.

11. Bertil Nygren, *The Rebuilding of Greater Russia. Putin's Foreign Policy to-*

wards the CIS Countries (Abingdon: Routledge, 2008); and Marcin Kaczmarski, *Russia's Revisionist Policy Towards the West* (Warsaw: Center for Eastern Studies, 2009), p. 5.

12. "Putin Calls for 'Eurasian Union' of Ex-Soviet Republics," BBC News Online, October 4, 2011 (http://www.bbc.co.uk/news/world-europe-151725190).

13. Interview with Tatiana Stanovaya, head of the analytical department at Moscow's Center for Political Technologies, July 2017.

14. Henry Kissinger, *World Order* (New York: Penguin, 2014), p. 53.

15. For a description of the "mental remapping" involved in this process, see Mikhail Suslov, "Geographical Metanarratives in Russia and the European East: Contemporary Pan-Slavism," in *Eurasian Geography and Economics* 53, no. 5 (2012), pp. 575–95 (http://dx.doi.org/10.2747/1539-7216.53.5.575).

16. The evidence was circulated on Twitter: Nigel Gould-Davies, "Enemies once airbrushed out," Twitter post, July 9, 2017 (https://twitter.com/nigelgd1/status/883978032028897283).

17. Described by Russian officials as a component of Western information warfare against Russia. See Keir Giles, *Handbook of Russian Information Warfare*, Fellowship Monograph 9, Research Division (Rome: NATO Defense College, November 2016), p. 40.

18. Neil MacFarquhar, "That Devious Plot to 'Zombify' Russia: The Fidget Spinner," *New York Times*, July 18, 2017 (https://mobile.nytimes.com/2017/07/18/world/europe/russia-fidget-spinner-plot.html).

19. Jeffrey Mankoff, "Generational Change and the Future of U.S.-Russian Relations," *Journal of International Affairs* 63, no. 2 (Spring/Summer 2010), pp. 1–15.

20. Interview with Ivan Kurilla, European University at St. Petersburg, August 2017.

21. Dmitriy Suslov, speaking at the Lennart Meri conference in Tallinn, May 13, 2017.

22. Tibor Szamuely, *The Russian Tradition* (London: Secker & Warburg, 1974), p. 69.

23. Vladimir Safronkov, Russian deputy envoy to the United Nations, speaking to Matthew Rycroft, the United Kingdom's permanent representative to the United Nations. Quoted in Andrew Roth, "'Don't You Look Away from Me!': How a Russian Diplomat's Tirade Broke U.N. Tradition," *Washington Post*, April 13, 2017 (https://www.washingtonpost.com/news/worldviews/wp/2017/04/13/dont-you-look-away-from-me-how-a-russian-diplomats-tirade-broke-u-n-tradition/).

24. Vladimir G. Baranovsky and Alexei G. Arbatov, "The Changing Security Perspective in Europe," in *Russia and the West: The 21st Century Security Environment*, edited by Alexei G. Arbatov, Karl Kaiser, and Robert Legvold, (Armonk, N.Y.: M. E. Sharpe for the EastWest Institute, 1999), p. 55.

25. Keir Giles, "Assessing Russia's Reorganized and Rearmed Military" (Washington: Carnegie Endowment for International Peace, May 4, 2016).

26. A. Kennaway, *The Russian "Black Hole"* (Shrivenham, U.K.: Conflict Studies Research Centre, November 1996), p. 1.

27. As stated in a formal briefing to the NATO Defense College by the Military Academy of the Russian General Staff (which could reasonably be expected to take this view) in November 2007. The relative weight of military issues in the National Security Strategy adopted in December 2014 is dramatically greater than in Western European equivalents, and progress in military modernization is listed as a key determinant of national security. See also Isabelle Facon, "Russia's National Security Strategy and Military Doctrine and Their Implications for the EU," EU Directorate-General for External Policies, January 2017 (http://www.europarl.europa.eu/RegData/etudes/IDAN/2017/578016/EXPO_IDA%282017%29578016_EN.pdf).

28. Pavel K. Baev, "Russia Celebrates Its Newly Revived Old-Fashioned Militarism," *Eurasia Daily Monitor* (Jamestown Foundation) 14, no. 61 (May 8, 2017) (https://jamestown.org/program/russia-celebrates-newly-revived-old-fashioned-militarism/). See also "Mobilizing Patriotism in Russia," *Russian Analytical Digest* 2017 (Zurich: Center for Security Studies, 2017) (http://www.css.ethz.ch/content/specialinterest/gess/cis/center-for-securities-studies/en/publications/rad/details.html?id=/n/o/2/0/no_207_mobilizing_patriotism_in_russianr).

29. "Russian Military Training: In Kindergarten," *Moscow Times*, March 29, 2017 (https://themoscowtimes.com/articles/russian-military-training-in-kindergarten-57573).

30. "By 2009, the chief of the general staff acknowledged that Kaliningrad was effectively demilitarised with the only remaining units tasked with territorial defence." "Fortress Kaliningrad Key to Russia's Assertive Shield," *Oxford Analytica*, July 21, 2017.

31. A. Dynkin, V. Baranovsky, I. Kobrinskaya, and others, "Russia and the World 2017: IMEMO Forecast," *New Perspectives* 25, no. 1 (2017), p. 89.

32. For a classic example, see Zoie O'Brien, "Are You Watching NATO? Putin Rolls Out THIS Terrifying Russian Armada across World," *Daily Express*, July 31, 2017 (http://www.express.co.uk/news/world/834816/North-Korea-news-trump-Russia-latest-Navy-USA-Vladimir-Putin).

33. Fiona Hill, "Putin: The One-Man Show the West Doesn't Understand," *Bulletin of the Atomic Scientists* 72, no. 3 (2016), pp. 140–44.

34. "Venäjän media ilkkuu Helsingin tunneleille: 'Tunnelit eivät pelasta: venäläiset bunkkeripommit yltävät suomalaisiin maan alle asti'" [Russian media embrace Helsinki tunnels: "Tunnels cannot save you: Russian bunker bombs will reach Finns underground"], *Ilta-Sanomat*, Ulkomaat, July 18, 2017 (https://www.is.fi/ulkomaat/art-2000005295084.html); and "'Russia's Bunker Busters Will Reach Finns Underground': How to Ridicule and Threaten at Once," *EU vs*

Disinfo, July 28, 2017 (https://euvsdisinfo.eu/russias-bunker-busters-will-reach-finns-underground-how-to-ridicule-and-threaten-at-once/).

35. Dynkin and others, "Russia and the World 2017: IMEMO Forecast," p. 88.

36. Dima Adamsky, *The Culture of Military Innovation* (Stanford University Press, 2010), p. 40.

37. "The Russian Mindset," Chatham House, February 17, 2009, p. 2.

38. Kimberly Marten, "President Trump, Keep in Mind That Russia and the West Think about Negotiations Very, Very Differently," *Washington Post*, July 25, 2017 (https://www.washingtonpost.com/news/monkey-cage/wp/2017/07/25/president-trump-keep-in-mind-that-russia-and-the-west-think-about-negotiations-very-very-differently/).

39. "Proyavleniye myagkotelosti chrevato" [Showing weakness is fraught with consequences], Znak.com, April 13, 2017 (https://www.znak.com/2017-04-13/v_kremle_sochli_normalnymi_rezkie_slova_zama_postpreda_rf_pri_oon_predstavitelyu_britanii).

40. Aaron Mehta, "Interview: Swedish Minister of Defence Peter Hultqvist," *Defense News*, May 31, 2017 (https://www.defensenews.com/pentagon/2017/05/31/interview-swedish-minister-of-defence-peter-hultqvist/).

41. "Russia Issues Fresh Threats against Unaligned Nordic States," *Defense News*, May 5, 2016 (http://www.defensenews.com/story/defense/international/2016/05/05/russia-issues-fresh-threats-against-unaligned-nordic-states/83959852/). Damien Sharkov, "Putin Vows Military Response to 'Eliminate NATO Threat' If Sweden Joins US-Led Alliance," *Newsweek*, June 2, 2017 (http://www.newsweek.com/vladimir-putin-vows-eliminate-nato-threat-sweden-joins-619486).

42. "Stöd för Nato-medlemskap nu större än motståndet" [Support for NATO membership now greater than opposition], Dagens Nyhetter, June 5, 2016 (http://www.dn.se/debatt/stod-for-nato-medlemskap-nu-storre-an-motstandet/).

43. Arbatov, Kaiser, and Legvold, eds., *Russia and the West*, p. 13.

44. Sergey Lavrov, statement at the opening session of the OSCE Annual Security Review Conference, Vienna, June 23, 2009 (http://www.mid.ru/en/vistupleniya_ministra/-/asset_publisher/MCZ7HQuMdqBY/content/id/288306).

45. Peter Calvocoressi, *Survey of International Affairs 1949–1950* (London: Royal Institute of International Affairs, 1953), p. 13.

46. Lilia Shevtsova, "How the West Misjudged Russia: Part 2. The Pragmatists," *American Interest*, January 20, 2016 (https://www.the-american-interest.com/2016/01/20/how-the-west-misjudged-russia-part-2-the-pragmatists/).

47. For histories of this process, see Martin A. Smith, "A Bumpy Road to an Unknown Destination: NATO-Russia Relations, 1991–2002," *European Security* 2, no. 4 (2002), pp. 59–77; Angela Stent, *The Limits of Partnership: U.S.-Russian Relations in the Twenty-First Century* (Princeton University Press, 2014); and Keir Giles, "The State of the NATO-Russia Reset" (Shrivenham, U.K.: Conflict Studies Research Centre, September 2011).

48. Telegram, George Kennan to George Marshall, February 22, 1946 (https://www.trumanlibrary.org/whistlestop/study_collections/coldwar/documents/pdf/6-6.pdf).

49. Kissinger, *World Order*, p. 52.

50. Mikhail Suslov, "Po ty storony imperii: Prostransvenniye konfiguratsii identichnostei v rossiiskikh literaturnykh utopiyakh rubezha XIX–XX gg." [On the other side of the Empire: Spatial configurations of identities in Russian literary Utopias at the turn of the twentieth century], *Ab Imperio: Theory and History of Nationalism and Empire in the Post-Soviet Space* 4 (2011), pp. 325–56.

51. When drawing up simple contracts in Moscow in the early 1990s, the author was gently teased for constructing them along Western lines. If a document was based on a presumption of good faith and not bulging with punitive clauses, "that's a gentleman's agreement, not a contract." Developments in Russian business culture since that period have been rapid, but not transformational. See Nigel Holden, Cary L. Cooper, and Jennifer Carr, *Dealing with the New Russia: Management Cultures in Collision* (New York: John Wiley & Sons, 1998). Although now twenty years old, this manual's grounding in Russian history and social studies makes it still instructive and relevant today.

52. Geoffrey Hosking, "Putin Is Part of a Continuum That Stretches Back to the Tsars," *The Guardian*, April 4, 2017 (https://www.theguardian.com/commentisfree/2017/apr/04/putin-continuum-tsars-russia).

53. Discussed in detail in Marten, "President Trump, Keep in Mind."

54. Pavel Baev, "Russia Reinvents Itself as a Rogue State in the Ungovernable Multi-Polar World," in *The State of Russia: What Comes Next?*, edited by Maria Lipman and Nikolay Petrov (London: Palgrave Macmillan, 2015), p. 77.

55. David Sanger, "Putin Revels in His Role as Disrupter of U.S. Plans," *International New York Times*, October 1–2, 2016, p. 1.

56. Don Jensen, conversation with the author, April 2017.

57. Alex Stamos, "An Update on Information Operations on Facebook," September 6, 2017 (https://newsroom.fb.com/news/2017/09/information-operations-update/).

58. Ben Collins, Kevin Poulson, and Spencer Ackerman, "Russia Used Facebook Events to Organize Anti-Immigrant Rallies on U.S. Soil," *Daily Beast*, September 11, 2017 (http://www.thedailybeast.com/exclusive-russia-used-facebook-events-to-organize-anti-immigrant-rallies-on-us-soil).

59. Edward Crankshaw, "Russia's Imperial Design," *Atlantic Monthly*, November 1957, pp. 39–45.

60. See "Agreement Between the Government of The United States of America and the Government of The Union of Soviet Socialist Republics on the Prevention of Incidents On and Over the High Seas" (U.S. State Department, May 25, 1972) (https://www.state.gov/t/isn/4791.htm).

61. Andrey Ostroukh, "Russia, EU Need to Improve Relations, Says Putin,"

Wall Street Journal, June 17, 2016 (http://www.wsj.com/articles/russia-eu-need-to-improve-relations-says-putin-1466166833).

62. Andrey Kortunov, "How Not to Talk with Russia" (European Council on Foreign Relations, April 1, 2016).

63. Serhii Plokhy, *Lost Kingdom: The Quest for Empire and the Making of the Russian Nation* (New York: Hachette, 2017), p. xii.

64. Edward L. Keenan, "On Certain Mythical Beliefs and Russian Behaviors," in *The Legacy of History in Russia and the New States of Eurasia,* edited by S. Frederick Starr (Armonk, N.Y.: M. E. Sharpe, 1994), p. 24.

65. Lev Gudkov, "Putin's Relapse into Totalitarianism," in *The State of Russia,* edited by Lipman and Petrov, p. 89.

66. Letter from Lev Tolstoy to *The Times,* June 27, 1904 (https://babel.hathitrust.org/cgi/pt?id=hvd.hndprs;view=1up;seq=9).

67. John Reshetar, *Problems of Analyzing and Predicting Soviet Behavior* (New York: Doubleday, 1955), p. 20.

68. As described by Russian military leaders quoted in Giles, *Handbook of Russian Information Warfare.*

69. James Nixey, Head, Russia and Eurasia Programme, Chatham House, speaking at the Council on Foreign Relations "Perspectives on Russia" symposium, New York, April 13, 2017 (https://www.cfr.org/event/russian-foreign-policy).

70. Interview with Tatiana Stanovaya, head of the analytical department at Moscow's Centre for Political Technologies, July 2017.

71. Alina Polyakova, Director of Research, Europe and Eurasia, Atlantic Council, speaking at the Council on Foreign Relations "Perspectives on Russia" symposium, New York, April 13, 2017 (https://www.cfr.org/event/russian-foreign-policy/).

72. Fiona Hill and Pamela Jewett, *Back in the USSR: Russia's Intervention in the Internal Affairs of the Former Soviet Republics and the Implication for United States Policy toward Russia,* Occasional Paper, Strengthening Democratic Institutions Project (Cambridge, Mass.: Belfer Center for Science and International Affairs, Harvard Kennedy School, January 1994); Marek Menkiszak, "The Putin Doctrine: The Formation of a Conceptual Framework for Russian Dominance in the Post-Soviet Area," OSW Commentary 131, March 28, 2014 (https://www.osw.waw.pl/sites/default/files/commentary_131.pdf).

73. Speaking at the Lennart Meri conference in Tallinn, May 13, 2017.

74. President of Russia, "Address by President of the Russian Federation," Moscow, March 18, 2014 (http://en.kremlin.ru/events/president/news/20603).

75. "Russia's Investigative Committee Opens Cases over Rehabilitation of Nazism in Ukraine," TASS, January 14, 2018 (http://tass.com/politics/985019/).

76. Robert Hunter, "Geopolitics and the Problem of Russian Power," *Prism* 6, no. 2 (2016), p. 12.

77. This process is examined in more detail in Keir Giles, *The Turning Point*

for Russian Foreign Policy (Carlisle, Pa.: Strategic Studies Institute, U.S. Army War College, May 2017), p. 44.

78. Flemming Splidsboel Hansen, "Past and Future Meet: Aleksandr Gorchakov and Russian Foreign Policy," *Europe-Asia Studies* 54, no. 3 (May 2002), pp. 377–96.

79. "It is surprising how easily the transition from an all-Russia to an all-Slav to an all-Orthodox and finally to a crusade against the whole West has been made." Stuart Ramsay Tompkins, *The Russian Mind* (University of Oklahoma Press, 1953), p. 187.

80. Gonzague de Reynold, *Le Monde russe* (Paris: Librairie Plon, 1950), p. 372.

81. See John P. Ledonne, *The Grand Strategy of the Russian Empire, 1650–1831* (Oxford University Press, 2003).

82. John Lough, *The Place of Russia's "Near Abroad"* (Sandhurst: Soviet Studies Research Centre, January 28, 1993), p. 12.

83. See, for instance, what journalist Ben Smith calls an "astonishing video justifying Russian empire-building along the lines of the British 'white man's burden.'" Ben Smith, "What If Trump TV Was Good?," *BuzzFeed*, July 18, 2017. For a colorful expression of this mindset, see also "I'm a Russian Occupier," video, YouTube, February 27, 2015 (https://www.youtube.com/watch?v=o01nS_M3PQY). (The video is in Russian. A version with English-language subtitles was deleted from YouTube for violating policies on hate speech.)

84. Interview with Ivan Kurilla, European University at St. Petersburg, August 2017.

85. Iver B. Neumann, "Russia's Standing as a Great Power, 1492–1815," in *Russia's European Choices*, edited by Ted Hopf (New York: Palgrave, 2008), pp. 11–34; Iver B. Neumann, "Russia As a Great Power, 1815–2007," *Journal of International Relations and Development* 11, no. 2 (2008), pp. 128–51.

86. Fedor Lukyanov, "Putin's Foreign Policy: The Quest to Restore Russia's Rightful Place," *Foreign Affairs*, May/June 2016, pp. 30–37.

87. Mark Galeotti, "The Plaintive Voice of Russia's Embattled Foreign Policy Establishment," *New Perspectives* 24, no. 1 (2016), p. 121.

88. Sir Tony Brenton, British ambassador to Russia 2004–08, letter to *Financial Times*, May 24, 2017 (https://www.ft.com/content/20479d3a-3fb6-11e7-82b6-896b95f30f58).

89. Frederick L. Schuman, *The Cold War: Retrospect and Prospect* (Louisiana State University Press, 1962), p. 22.

90. Andrew Wood, "Russia's Damaging Obsession with Cold War Myths," Chatham House, May 12, 2016 (https://www.chathamhouse.org/expert/comment/russias-damaging-obsession-cold-war-myths).

91. John Mearsheimer, "Why the Ukraine Crisis Is the West's Fault," *Foreign Affairs* 93, no. 5 (2014), pp. 77–89. Among the many ripostes to Mearsheimer,

see Alexander Motyl, "The Ukraine Crisis According to John J. Mearsheimer: Impeccable Logic, Wrong Facts," European Leadership Network, October 21, 2014 (https://www.europeanleadershipnetwork.org/commentary/the-ukraine-crisis-according-to-john-j-mearsheimer-impeccable-logic-wrong-facts/).

92. Zbigniew Brzezinksi, "Russia Needs to Be Offered a 'Finland Option' for Ukraine," *Financial Times*, February 22, 2014 (https://www.ft.com/content/e855408c-9bf6-11e3-afe3-00144feab7de); Henry Kissinger, "How the Ukrainian Crisis Ends," *Washington Post*, March 6, 2014 (http://www.henryakissinger.com/articles/wp030614.html).

93. Michael E. O'Hanlon, *Beyond NATO: A New Security Architecture for Eastern Europe* (Brookings, August 2017), p. 3.

94. Samuel Greene, "Conditionality beyond Sanctions: Identifying and Pursuing Interests in the EU-Russia Relationship," Policy Memo 460, PONARS, February 2017 (http://www.ponarseurasia.org/memo/conditionality-beyond-sanctions-identifying-and-pursuing-interests-eu-russia-relationship).

95. Nolan D. McCaskill and David Cohen, "Trump Vows 'to Move Forward' with Putin," *Politico*, July 9, 2017 (http://www.politico.eu/article/trump-vows-to-move-forward-with-putin/).

96. Discussed in detail in Ion Ratiu, *Moscow Challenges the World* (London: Sherwood Press, 1986), p. 4; and Edward Crankshaw, "The Price Brezhnev Should Be Asked to Pay," *The Observer*, 1977, reprinted in *Putting Up with the Russians* (London: Macmillan, 1984).

97. "Do We Achieve World Order through Chaos or Insight?," interview with Henry Kissinger, Spiegel Online International, November 13, 2014 (http://www.spiegel.de/international/world/interview-with-henry-kissinger-on-state-of-global-politics-a-1002073.html).

98. Mark Kramer, "NATO, the Baltic States, and Russia: A Framework for Sustainable Enlargement," *International Affairs* 78, no. 4 (October 2002), pp. 731–56.

99. As described in Robert Gellately, *Stalin's Curse* (Oxford University Press, 2013).

100. As described in Jim Kovpak, "The Desperation of Stephen Cohen," StopFake.org, 12 July 12, 2017 (http://www.stopfake.org/en/the-desperation-of-stephen-cohen/). See also Stephen J. Blank, *Towards A New Russia Policy* (Carlisle, Pa.: Strategic Studies Institute, U.S Army War College, February 2008).

101. Astolphe de Custine, *Lettres de Russie: La Russie en 1839*, edited by Pierre Nora (Paris: Gallimard, 1975), p. 109.

102. The mixed cynicism, naivety, self-deception, and moral vacuity of British communist visitors to the USSR is depicted scathingly in Laurens van der Post, *Journey into Russia* (Harmondsworth: Penguin, 1965), p. 147.

103. David Satter, *The Less You Know, the Better You Sleep* (Yale University Press, 2016), p. xii.

104. For a colourful introduction to the Valdai scene, see Dmitry Gorenburg, "Valdai 2017: Reactions from a Newbie," *Russian Military Reform* (blog), October 30, 2017 (https://russiamil.wordpress.com/2017/10/30/valdai-2017-reactions-from-a-newbie/).

Chapter 3

1. "James Clapper Says Watergate 'Pales' in Comparison with Trump Russia Scandal," *The Guardian*, June 7, 2017 (https://www.theguardian.com/us-news/2017/jun/07/james-clapper-says-watergate-pales-in-comparison-with-trump-and-russia-scandal).

2. In conversation with the author, September 2016.

3. Peter Baker, "Pressure Rising as Obama Works to Rein In Russia," *New York Times*, March 2, 2014 (http://www.nytimes.com/2014/03/03/world/europe/pressure-rising-as-obama-works-to-rein-in-russia.html).

4. Gleb Pavlovskiy, "Putin v dni Velikoy russko-ukrainskoy revolutsii. Yego press-konferentsiya ob Ukraine" [Putin in the days of the Great Russian-Ukrainian Revolution: His press conference on Ukraine], *Gefter*, March 14, 2014 (http://gefter.ru/archive/11640).

5. Edward Crankshaw, *Putting Up with the Russians* (London: Macmillan, 1984), p. 152.

6. S. G. Chekinov and S. A. Bogdanov, "Initial Periods of Wars and Their Impact on a Country's Preparations for a Future War," *Military Thought* (English edition) 4 (2012).

7. John Foreman, "The Determinants of Recent Russian Behaviour: What Do These Mean for NATO Decision Makers?" (Rome: NATO Defense College, October 2016), p. 1.

8. Andrew Monaghan, "'An Enemy at the Gates' or 'From Victory to Victory'? Russian Foreign Policy," *International Affairs* 84, no. 4 (2008), pp. 717–33.

9. "Russia's NATO Envoy Accuses Obama's Team of Scuppering ABM Talks," BBC Monitoring, translation of Rossiya 24 news channel broadcast, July 6, 2011.

10. Major-General Anatoliy Nikonov, professor of operational arts at the Russian General Staff Academy, speaking at the NATO Defense College, Rome, November 14, 2007.

11. Ronald Reagan, *The Reagan Diaries: Volume 1. January 1981–October 1985*, edited by Douglas Brinkley (New York: HarperCollins, 2009).

12. "Kontrrazvedka: Shpionov segodnya lovyat tak . . ." [Counterintelligence: This is how you catch spies today . . .], interview with Nikolai Patrushev, *Argumenty i Fakty*, October 9, 2007 (http://www.aif.ru/society/330).

13. Neighbors of Russia were concerned over the possibility of dangerous instability well into Putin's tenure. See the report based on the "Stable Russia"

project commissioned by the Finnish Ministry of Defense in 2007 for an expression of this concern: *Russia of Challenges* (Helsinki: Finnish Ministry of Defense, 2007).

14. George Kennan, quoted in John Gaddis, *Strategies of Containment* (Oxford University Press, 1982), p. 20.

15. Stephen J. Blank, *Towards a New Russia Policy* (Carlisle, Pa.: Strategic Studies Institute, U.S. Army War College, February 2008), p. v.

16. Crankshaw, *Putting Up with the Russians*, p. xii.

17. Alexei G. Arbatov, Karl Kaiser, and Robert Legvold, eds., *Russia and the West: The 21st Century Security Environment* (Armonk, N.Y.: M. E. Sharpe for the EastWest Institute, 1999), p. 5.

18. Pobedoved, "Security: If a War Comes . . . ," *Za pskovskiy narod*, March 9, 2006 (https://dlib.eastview.com/browse/doc/9167510).

19. "Rossiyane nazvali glavnykh vragov strany" [Russians name the main enemies of the country], RBK, January 10, 2018 (https://www.rbc.ru/politics/10/01/2018/5a549d4b9a79476120fe5065).

20. President of Russia, "Meeting with Students at the Mining University," Moscow, January 26, 2015 (http://en.kremlin.ru/events/president/news/47519).

21. Aydyn Mekhtiyev, "Nezazhivayushchiye rany Sredney Azii: Kak SShA sozdayut dugu nestabil'nosti v podbryushch'ye Rossii" [Wounds that do not heal in Central Asia: How the U.S. creates an arc of instability in Russia's underbelly], *Pravda*, July 17, 2017 (https://www.pravda.ru/world/17-07-2017/1342238-middle_asia-0/).

22. Described in detail in Keir Giles, "Russia's National Security Strategy to 2020" (Rome: NATO Defense College, June 2009) (http://www.conflictstudies.org.uk/files/rusnatsecstrategyto2020.pdf).

23. As detailed in Gleb Pavlovskiy, "Sistema RF: Istochniki rossiyskogo strategicheskogo povedeniya. Metod George F. Kennan" [The Russian Federation system: Sources of Russian strategic behavior. The George F. Kennan method] (Moscow: Izdatel'stvo Evropa, 2015).

24. Katri Pynnöniemi and András Rácz, "Threat Perception Affects Operational Doctrines," FIIA Comment 2 (Helsinki: Finnish Institute of International Affairs, January 2016).

25. Polina Nikolskaya and Andrew Osborn, "Putin Dials Up Anti-U.S. Rhetoric, Keeps Mum on Re-election," Reuters, October 19, 2017 (https://www.reuters.com/article/us-russia-putin-usa-energy/putin-dials-up-anti-u-s-rhetoric-keeps-mum-on-re-election-idUSKBN1CO2CX).

26. The theme of the West as a destabilizing influence that must be resisted is explored at length in two essential studies of Russian civilization and culture originally published in the 1970s: Tibor Szamuely, *The Russian Tradition* (London: Secker & Warburg, 1974), and Richard Pipes, *Russia under the Old Regime* (New York: Scribner, 1974).

27. Henry W. Nevinson, *The Dawn in Russia* (London: Harper & Bros., 1906), p. 166.

28. Astolphe de Custine, *Lettres de Russie: La Russie en 1839*, edited by Pierre Nora (Paris: Gallimard, 1975), p. 108.

29. Keir Giles and Mark A. Smith, *Russia and the Arctic: The "Last Dash North"* (Shrivenham, U.K.: Conflict Studies Research Centre, September 2007), p. 14 (https://www.academia.edu/929852/Russia_and_the_Arctic_the_Last_Dash_North_ p. 14).

30. Nikolskaya and Osborn, "Putin Dials Up Anti-U.S. Rhetoric."

31. The cyclical or even seasonal nature of these relations is explored in detail in Keir Giles, "The State of the NATO-Russia Reset" (Shrivenham, U.K.: Conflict Studies Research Centre, September 2011) (http://www.conflictstudies.org.uk/files/csrc_nato-russia-reset_preview.pdf).

32. See, for example, interview with Sergey Karaganov in *Rossiyskaya gazeta*, April 24, 2014 (https://rg.ru/2014/04/23/karaganov-site.html) (in Russian).

33. Polina Devitt, "Lavrov Accuses West of Seeking 'Regime Change' in Russia," Reuters, November 22, 2014 (http://www.reuters.com/article/us-ukraine-crisis-idUSKCN0J609G20141122).

34. Yegor Gaidar, "The Soviet Collapse" (American Enterprise Institute, April 19, 2007) (http://www.aei.org/issue/foreign-and-defense-policy/regional/europe/the-soviet-collapse/).

35. This concern over instability is stated, for example, in Government of Russia, Ministry of Foreign Affairs, "Presentation and Responses to Questions by Russian Foreign Minister Sergei Lavrov on Topical Issues of Foreign Policy of the Russian Federation," Moscow, October 20, 2014 (http://www.mid.ru/ru/press_service/minister_speeches/-/asset_publisher/7OvQR5KJWVmR/content/id/716270).

36. Interview with Sergey Lavrov on *Russia Today*, February 3, 2011 (http://www.mid.ru/web/guest/foreign_policy/news/-/asset_publisher/cKNonkJE02Bw/content/id/220154).

37. Fedor Lukyanov, "What to Expect from the Meeting of Russian and US Presidents in Northern Ireland," Russian International Affairs Council, June 3, 2013 (http://russiancouncil.ru/analytics-and-comments/comments/chego-zhdat-ot-vstrechi-prezidentov-rossii-i-ssha-v-severnoy).

38. Tatia Lemondzhava, "In Russia, the Doors Are Closing: How—and Why—Russians Are Losing Their Freedom to Travel Abroad," *Foreign Policy*, April 29, 2016 (http://foreignpolicy.com/2016/04/29/in-russia-the-doors-are-closing-tourism-putin-human-rights/).

39. "CIA and Ex-Nazis Were behind 1956 Hungarian Revolution, Russian State TV Claims," *Hungary Today*, October 25, 2016 (http://hungarytoday.hu/news/cia-ex-nazis-behind-1956-hungarian-revolution-russian-state-tv-claims-78806).

40. President of Russia, "Meeting with Participants of the 'Seliger-2012' Forum," transcript, Moscow, July 31, 2012 (http://kremlin.ru/transcripts/16106).

41. "A Conversation with Vladimir Putin. Continued," live broadcast, all major Russian TV and radio channels, December 15, 2011 (http://archive.government.ru/eng/docs/17409/).

42. Alexander Duleba, "The 'New Normal in Russian Foreign Policy Thinking," *New Perspectives* 24, no. 1 (2016), p. 125.

43. *Germany and Revolution in Russia 1915–1918: Documents from the Archives of the German Foreign Ministry*, edited by S. A. B. Zeman (Oxford University Press, 1958), throughout. See also Douglas Boyd, *Red October: The Revolution That Changed the World* (Stroud: The History Press, 2017).

44. Michael Kramer, "Rescuing Boris: The Secret Story of How Four U.S. Advisers Used Polls, Focus Groups, Negative Ads and All the Other Techniques of American Campaigning to Help Boris Yeltsin Win," *Time*, July 15, 1996 (https://ccisf.org/wp-content/uploads/2016/12/201612201405.pdf).

45. Vladimir Putin, "Putin: Eta operatsiya – bessovestnyy krestovyy pokhod" [Putin: This operation is an unscrupulous crusade], *Argumenty i Fakty*, March 21, 2011 (http://www.aif.ru/society/24194).

46. A. B. Podtserob, "Arab Spring or Islamist Autumn?" (Moscow: Institut Blizhnego Vostoka, August 6, 2012) (http://www.iimes.ru/?p=15284).

47. "Volya naroda vmesto 'arabskoy zimy': Klyuchevye tsitaty Putina" [The will of the people instead of an "Arab Winter": Key quotes from Putin], RBK, March 18, 2014 (https://www.rbc.ru/politics/18/03/2014/570419999a794761c0ce80af).

48. President of Russia, "Address by President of the Russian Federation," news release, Moscow, March 18, 2014 (http://en.kremlin.ru/events/president/news/20603).

49. Vladimir Putin, "Russia and a Changing World," *Moskovskiye novosti*, February 27, 2012 (http://www.mn.ru/politics/78738).

50. Presentations by delegation from Russia's General Staff Academy at NATO Defense College, Rome, November 2013.

51. "The Arab Spring was the harvest of seeds sown by Bush Junior, with the concept of the Greater Middle East and democratization of that entire region." See interview with Sergey Lavrov, *Rossiyskaya gazeta*, October 24, 2012 (http://www.rg.ru/2012/10/23/lavrov-poln.html).

52. Medvedev was speaking at a meeting of the National Anti-Terrorist Committee. "Dmitriy Medvedev provel vo Vladikavkaze zasedaniye Natsionalnogo antiterroristicheskogo komiteta" [Dmitry Medvedev holds a meeting of the National Anti-Terrorist Committee in Vladikavkaz], transcript, Moscow, February 22, 2011 (http://www.kremlin.ru/transcripts/10408).

53. "Security Council Approves 'No-Fly Zone' over Libya, Authorizing 'All Necessary Measures' to Protect Civilians, by Vote of 10 in Favor with 5 Ab-

stentions," news release, United Nations, March 17, 2011 (https://www.un.org/press/en/2011/sc10200.doc.htm).

54. As explained by Fedor Lukyanov, "Let It Be How It Used to Be," *Kommersant*, July 15, 2013 (http://www.kommersant.ru/doc/2219495).

55. Anna Arutyunyan, "Putin Condemns Libya 'Crusade,'" *Moscow News*, March 21, 2011.

56. Government of Russia, Ministry of Foreign Affairs, "Answers by Russian Foreign Minister Sergey Lavrov to Listeners' Questions on Live Broadcasts on Voice of Russia, Radio Russia, and Ekho Moskvy," news release, Moscow, October 21, 2011 (http://www.mid.ru/web/guest/foreign_policy/news/-/asset_publisher/cKNonkJE02Bw/content/id/188914).

57. See, for example, Mohammed El-Katiri, "State-Building Challenges in a Post-Revolution Libya" (Carlisle, Pa.: Strategic Studies Institute, U.S. Army War College, October 2012) (but written at the beginning of 2012, when it still appeared that the situation in Libya was manageable with appropriate intervention).

58. Dmitri Trenin, "Why Russia Supports Assad," *New York Times*, February 9, 2012 (https://www.nytimes.com/2012/02/10/opinion/why-russia-supports-assad.html); Ruslan Pukhov, "Why Russia Is Backing Syria," *New York Times*, July 6, 2012 (http://www.nytimes.com/2012/07/07/opinion/why-russia-supports-syria.html).

59. "Russian MID Does Not Rule Out Insurgent Victory in Syria," RT.com, December 13, 2012 (http://russian.rt.com/inotv/2012-12-13/MID-Rossii-ne-isklyuchaet-pobedi).

60. Glenn Kessler, "President Obama and the 'Red Line' on Syria's Chemical Weapons," *Washington Post*, September 6, 2013 (http://www.washingtonpost.com/blogs/fact-checker/wp/2013/09/06/president-obama-and-the-red-line-on-syrias-chemical-weapons/). See also "A Strike Will Be Carried Out against Syria," Russian International Affairs Council, August 28, 2013 (http://russiancouncil.ru/analytics-and-comments/analytics/udar-po-sirii-budet-nanesen/).

61. As outlined in Keir Giles, "What Russia Learns from the Syria Ceasefire: Military Action Works," Chatham House Expert Comment (London: Royal Institute of International Affairs, March 3, 2016) (https://www.chathamhouse.org/expert/comment/what-russia-learns-syria-ceasefire-military-action-works).

62. President of Russia, news conference, Moscow, December 20, 2012 (http://en.kremlin.ru/events/president/news/17173).

63. Dov Lynch, "'The Enemy Is at the Gate': Russia after Beslan," *International Affairs* 81, no. 1 (January 2005), pp. 141–44.

64. "The very concept of national sovereignty is becoming eroded. . . . Countries that pursue their own policy or simply stand in the way of someone's interests are being destabilized." "Meeting of the Security Council," Russian presidential website, July 22, 2014 (http://kremlin.ru/news/46305).

65. Yevgeniy Satanovsky, "Five Years of War for Oil and Democracy," *Mezhdunarodnaya zhizn* 5 (2008), pp. 3–10.

66. Interview with Deputy Minister Karasin, *Rossiyskaya gazeta*, August 16, 2005.

67. Defined as the "conviction that Russians should define their own democracy and protect themselves from values exported from outside" by Margot Light in "Russia and Europe and the Process of EU Enlargement," in *The Multilateral Dimension in Russian Foreign Policy*, edited by Elana Wilson Rowe and Stina Torjesen (London: Routledge, 2009), pp. 83–96.

68. Speech by Vladimir Putin to expanded meeting of the State Council on Russia's development strategy through to 2020, February 8, 2008 (http://kremlin.ru/events/president/transcripts/24825).

69. Interfax, December 29, 2007.

70. Vitaliy Ivanov, "'Myagche i shirshe'? Nu net!" ["More gently, with a broader view of things?" Well, no!], *Izvestiya*, March 24, 2008.

71. Government of Russia, Ministry of Foreign Affairs, "Foreign Policy and Diplomatic Activities of the Russian Federation in 2007," Moscow, March 18, 2008 (http://www.mid.ru/foreign_policy/news/-/asset_publisher/cKNonkJE02Bw/content/id/345430).

72. "Putin's Prepared Remarks at 43rd Munich Conference on Security Policy," delivered February 10, 2007, *Washington Post*, February 12, 2007 (http://www.washingtonpost.com/wp-dyn/content/article/2007/02/12/AR2007021200555_pf.html).

73. Rob Watson, "Putin's Speech: Back to Cold War?," BBC News, February 10, 2007 (http://news.bbc.co.uk/1/hi/world/europe/6350847.stm).

74. "Putin's Prepared Remarks at 43rd Munich Conference on Security Policy."

75. *Segodnya*, October 20, 1995: summary at http://www.friends-partners.org/friends/news/omri/1995/10/951023I.html.

76. Andrey Kalikh, "Nevoyennye ugrozy v Voyennoy doctrine" [Nonmilitary threats in the Military Doctrine], *Nezavisimoye voyennoye obozreniye*, March 16, 2007 (http://nvo.ng.ru/concepts/2007-03-16/4_doctrina.html).

77. On the growth in Russian capability and consequent increase in assertiveness, see Keir Giles, *Russia's "New" Tools for Confronting the West: Continuity and Innovation in Moscow's Exercise of Power*, Chatham House Research Paper (London: Royal Institute of International Affairs, March 2016).

78. "Security Council: Russia Will Update Its Military Doctrine by Late 2014," RIA Novosti, September 2, 2014 (http://ria.ru/interview/20140902/1022334103.html).

79. Andrzej Wilk, "The Russian Army—the Priority for Putin's Third Term," OSW, July 24, 2013 (http://www.osw.waw.pl/en/publikacje/analyses/2013-07-24/russian-army-priority-putins-third-term).

80. I. N. Vorobyov and V. A. Kiselev, "Gibridnye operatsii kak novyy vid

voyennogo protivoborstva" [Hybrid operations as a new form of armed conflict], *Voyennaya mysl'* 5 (2015), pp. 41–49.

81. For more detail on this, see Keir Giles, "'Information Troops—A Russian Cyber Command?" (Tallinn: NATO Cooperative Cyber Defence Centre of Excellence, June 2011). See also Andrey Soldatov and Irina Borogan, *The Red Web: The Struggle between Russia's Digital Dictators and the New Online Revolutionaries* (New York: PublicAffairs, 2015).

82. Speaking at a meeting of the Shanghai Cooperation Organization (SCO) Regional Anti-Terrorist Structure, March 27, 2012.

83. *Information Security Doctrine of the Russian Federation*, Security Council of the Russian Federation (http://www.scrf.gov.ru/security/information/document5/).

84. De Custine, *Lettres de Russie*, p. 74.

85. President Putin in free discussion at Valdai Club meeting in Sochi, October 22, 2015. Available in a different English translation via "Meeting of the Valdai International Discussion Club," Russian presidential website (http://en.kremlin.ru/events/president/news/50548).

86. Pavel Baev, "Russia Reinvents Itself As a Rogue State in the Ungovernable Multi-Polar World," in *The State of Russia: What Comes Next?*, edited by Maria Lipman and Nikolay Petrov (London: Palgrave Macmillan, 2015), pp. 69–86.

87. Forcefully described in Lev Gudkov, "Putin's Relapse into Totalitarianism," in *The State of Russia*, edited by Lipman and Petrov, pp. 86–110.

88. Telegram, George Kennan to George Marshall, February 22, 1946 (https://www.trumanlibrary.org/whistlestop/study_collections/coldwar/documents/pdf/6-6.pdf).

89. Anna Newby, "Vladimir Putin, Explained," *Order from Chaos* (blog), Brookings, May 10, 2016 (https://www.brookings.edu/blog/order-from-chaos/2016/05/10/vladimir-putin-explained/).

90. Interview with Sergey Karaganov, June 2017.

91. George Kennan, quoted in John Gaddis, *Strategies of Containment* (Oxford University Press, 1982), p. 20.

92. Interview with Thomas Graham, Tallinn, May 13, 2017.

93. "NATO's Defence and Deterrence," infographics on "Ballistic Missile Defence" and "NATO's Forward Presence," NATO website, June 2017.

94. Nancy Morgan, presentation at the RUSI Missile Defence Conference, London, March 18, 2014.

95. Andrew Monaghan, "Russian State Mobilization: Moving the Country onto a War Footing," Chatham House Research Paper (London: Royal Institute of International Affairs, May 2016) (https://www.chathamhouse.org/sites/files/chathamhouse/publications/research/2016-05-20-russian-state-mobilization-monaghan-2.pdf).

Notes to Pages 59–62

Chapter 4

1. President of Russia, "Address by President of the Russian Federation," Moscow, March 18, 2014 (http://en.kremlin.ru/events/president/news/20603).

2. Andrey Kortunov, "Russia and the West: What Does 'Equality' Mean?," in *Coping with Complexity in the Euro-Atlantic Community and Beyond*, edited by Andris Sprūds and Diāna Potjomkina (Riga: Latvian Institute of International Affairs, 2016), p. 85.

3. Interview with Vladimir Ivanov, EastWest Institute, Moscow, July 2017.

4. A collapse that was probably, given time, inevitable. See Yegor Gaidar, *Collapse of an Empire: Lessons for Modern Russia* (Brookings, 2007).

5. "Russian and Chinese Assertiveness Poses New Foreign Policy Challenges: A Conversation with Robert M. Gates," Council on Foreign Relations, May 21, 2014 (www.cfr.org/defense-and-security/russian-chinese-assertiveness-poses-new-foreign-policy-challenges/p35645).

6. Lev Gudkov, "Putin's Relapse into Totalitarianism," in *The State of Russia: What Comes Next?*, edited by Maria Lipman and Nikolay Petrov (London: Palgrave Macmillan, 2015), p. 98.

7. Roger Cohen, "Russia's Weimar Syndrome," *New York Times*, May 1, 2014 (https://www.nytimes.com/2014/05/02/opinion/cohen-russias-weimar-syndrome.html).

8. Vladimir G. Baranovsky and Alexei G. Arbatov, "The Changing Security Perspective in Europe," in *Russia and the West: The 21st Century Security Environment*, edited by Alexei G. Arbatov, Karl Kaiser, and Robert Legvold (Armonk, N.Y.: M. E. Sharpe for the EastWest Institute, 1999), p. 45.

9. Figures on U.S. aid in particular are available in Curt Tarnoff, "U.S. Assistance to the Former Soviet Union 1991–2001: A History of Administration and Congressional Action," Congressional Research Service, January 15, 2002 (research.policyarchive.org/914.pdf). For an example of the backlash from Russia a decade later, see Michael Schwirtz, "Russia Seeks to Cleanse Its Palate of U.S. Chicken," *New York Times*, January 19, 2010 (http://www.nytimes.com/2010/01/20/world/europe/20russia.html).

10. Irina Kobrinskaya, "'Deter and Engage': A New NATO Strategy for Taming Russia," *New Perspectives* 23, no. 2 (2015), p. 134.

11. Kortunov, "Russia and the West," p. 86.

12. As put by Philip Gordon, "Americans assumed the Russians would give it up and just go back home and deal with Russia." Council on Foreign Relations Russia symposium, "How Did We Get Here?," New York, April 13, 2017 (https://www.cfr.org/event/how-did-we-get-here).

13. "We remember that Emperor Aleksandr I took an active part in drafting the decisions of the Congress of Vienna in 1815, which secured the development of the continent without serious armed conflicts for the following forty

years." Sergey Lavrov, "Russia's Foreign Policy in a Historical Perspective," *Russia in Global Affairs*, March 30, 2016 (http://eng.globalaffairs.ru/number/Russias-Foreign-Policy-in-a-Historical-Perspective-18067). See also Andrei Kolesnikov, "Re-defining Yalta: Putin at the UN," Carnegie Moscow Center, October 5, 2015 (http://carnegie.ru/commentary/61486).

14. For a comprehensive listing of sources and arguments, see "NATO-Russia Relations: About the Controversy over the 'NATO Expansion' during Reunification Negotiations," NATO Multimedia Library (http://www.natolibguides.info/nato-russia/controversy).

15. Compare Steven Pifer, "Did NATO Promise Not to Enlarge? Gorbachev Says 'No,'" *Up Front* (blog), Brookings Institution, November 6, 2014 (https://www.brookings.edu/blog/up-front/2014/11/06/did-nato-promise-not-to-enlarge-gorbachev-says-no/) with "Gorbachev Blasts NATO Eastward Expansion," Gorbachev Foundation, April 2, 2009 (http://www.gorby.ru/en/presscenter/publication/show_26613/).

16. Lawrence Freedman, "The New Great Power Politics," in *Russia and the West*, edited by Baranovsky and Arbatov, p. 36.

17. George Kennan, "A Fateful Error," *New York Times*, February 5, 1997.

18. Kimberly Marten, "Reconsidering NATO Expansion: A Counterfactual Analysis of Russia and the West in the 1990s," *European Journal of International Security*, November 1, 2017 (https://doi.org/10.1017/eis.2017.16). See also Dmitry Suslov, "The Russian Perception of the Post–Cold War Era and Relations with the West," lecture (New York: Harriman Institute, Columbia University, November 9, 2016) (https://www.sant.ox.ac.uk/sites/default/files/university-consortium/files/suslov_harriman_lecture_on_post-cold_war_era.pdf).

19. Boris Yeltsin, "Yeltsin's Resignation Speech," BBC, December 31, 1999 (http://news.bbc.co.uk/1/hi/world/monitoring/584845.stm).

20. Olga Irisova, "Where Did the Russian 'Democrats' Disappear To?," IntersectionProject.eu, August 19, 2016 (http://intersectionproject.eu/article/society/where-did-russian-democrats-disappear).

21. Il'ja Rákoš, "Svetlana Alexievich Is No Useful Idiot," interview, IljaRakos.com, August 13, 2016 (http://www.iljarakos.com/svetlana-alexievich-is-no-useful-idiot).

22. Interview available at https://www.youtube.com/watch?v=40gj_tE-FOo.

23. Andrei Piontkovsky, *Another Look into Putin's Soul* (Washington: Hudson Institute, 2006), p. 98.

24. A. (Sasha) Kennaway, *Continuity & Conflict in Russian Government* (Shrivenham, U.K.: Conflict Studies Research Centre, September 1999), p. 13.

25. Andrey Yefremov, "Aleksandr Gurov: V 90-e tol'ko umyshlennykh ubiystv bylo po 32 tysyachi v god" [Aleksandr Gurov: In the 1990s there were 32,000 deliberate murders a year], File-RF, June 17, 2017 (http://file-rf.ru/analitics/169).

26. Vladimir Zubkov, "Flight Safety Over CIS Airlines Remains Unsatisfactory," ConCISe, February 28, 1997, p. 610.

27. Baranovsky and Arbatov, "The Changing Security Perspective in Europe," p. 45.

28. As stated by President Putin in his address to the Federal Assembly on December 4, 2014: "The policy of containment was not invented yesterday. It has been carried out against our country for many years, always, for decades, if not centuries. In short, whenever someone thinks that Russia has become too strong or independent, these tools are quickly put into use." Address available at http://en.kremlin.ru/events/president/news/47173.

29. Philip Gordon, speaking at Council on Foreign Relations Russia symposium, "How Did We Get Here?," New York, April 13, 2017 (https://www.cfr.org/event/how-did-we-get-here).

30. Freedman, "The New Great Power Politics," in *Russia and the West*, edited by Baranovsky and Arbatov, p. 27.

31. Stephen Kotkin, "Russia's Perpetual Geopolitics: Putin Returns to the Historical Pattern," *Foreign Affairs* 95, no. 3 (May/June 2016), pp. 2–9.

32. John Lough, *The Place of Russia's "Near Abroad"* (Shrivenham, U.K.: Soviet Studies Research Centre, January 28, 1993), p. 2. See also "Russia and the West: Still Most Awkward Partners," *The Economist*, May 9, 1998.

33. Baranovsky and Arbatov, eds., *Russia and the West*, p. 16.

34. Vladimir Lukin, letter to Aleksandr Solzhenitsyn, *Literaturnaya gazeta* 14 (April 1, 1992), p. 9.

35. Andrew Monaghan, "'An Enemy at the Gates' or 'From Victory to Victory'? Russian Foreign Policy," *International Affairs* 84, no. 4 (2008), pp. 717–33.

Chapter 5

1. A. (Sasha) Kennaway, *Continuity & Conflict in Russian Government* (Shrivenham, U.K.: Conflict Studies Research Centre, September 1999), p. 2.

2. Tibor Szamuely, *The Russian Tradition* (London: Secker & Warburg, 1974), p. 88.

3. Michael T. Florinsky, *Russia: A History and an Interpretation* (New York: Macmillan, 1955), pp. 1–9.

4. Alain Besançon, *Présent soviétique et passé russe* (Paris: Pluriel, 1980), p. 85.

5. A. (Sasha) Kennaway, *The Russian "Black Hole"* (Shrivenham, U.K.: Conflict Studies Research Centre, November 1996), p. 1.

6. Andrei Tsygankov, *The Strong State in Russia: Development and Crisis* (Oxford University Press, 2014), p. 5.

7. Henry Kissinger, *World Order* (New York: Penguin, 2014), p. 56.

8. Exchange with the author, October 2017.

9. "Aleksandr Akhiyezer: Kogda v Rossii poyavitsya gosudarstvo?" [Aleksandr Akhiezer: When will a state appear in Russia?], *Tolkovatel*, August 17, 2016 (http://bit.ly/ahiezer).

10. Maxim Trudolyubov, "Three Rules of Kremlin Power," *New York Times*, March 23, 2016 (http://mobile.nytimes.com/2016/03/24/opinion/international/three-rules-of-kremlin-power.html).

11. "Vladimir Putin Wants to Forget the Revolution," *The Economist*, October 26, 2017 (https://www.economist.com/news/briefing/21730644-ignoring-its-lessons-dangerous-russia-vladimir-putin-wants-forget-revolution).

12. Gregory Asmolov, "The Kremlin's Cameras and Virtual Potemkin Villages: ICT and the Construction of Statehood," in *Bits and Atoms: Information and Communication Technology in Areas of Limited Statehood*, edited by Steven Livingston and G. Walter-Drop (Oxford University Press, 2014), pp. 30–46.

13. Maxim Trudolyubov, "With Trump's Hands Tied, Putin Is Free to Act," *Russia File* (blog), Kennan Institute of the Woodrow Wilson International Center for Scholars, August 2, 2017 (http://www.kennan-russiafile.org/2017/08/02/with-trumps-hands-tied-putin-is-free-to-act/).

14. Simon Shuster, "Vladimir Putin Doesn't Understand the Limits of Donald Trump's Power," *Time*, August 1, 2017 (http://time.com/4881972/vladimir-putin-donald-trump-executive-power/).

15. Fiona Hill, "Putin: The One-man Show the West Doesn't Understand," *Bulletin of the Atomic Scientists* 72, no. 3 (2016), pp. 140–44.

16. Shuster, "Vladimir Putin Doesn't Understand the Limits of Donald Trump's Power."

17. David Lewis, "The 'Moscow Consensus': Constructing Autocracy in Post-Soviet Eurasia," OpenDemocracy.net, May 25, 2016 (https://www.opendemocracy.net/od-russia/david-lewis/moscow-consensus-constructing-autocracy-in-post-soviet-eurasia).

18. Examples of this approach include Clifford Gaddy and Fiona Hill, *Mr. Putin: Operative in the Kremlin* (Brookings, 2013); Walter Laqueur, *Putinism: Russia and Its Future with the West* (New York: Thomas Dunne Books, 2015); Daniel Treisman, *The Return: Russia's Journey from Gorbachev to Medvedev* (New York: Free Press, 2011); and Angus Roxburgh, *The Strongman: Vladimir Putin and the Struggle for Russia* (London: I. B. Tauris, 2012).

19. As also summarized by Gleb Pavlovsky, "Russian Politics under Putin: The System Will Outlast the Master," *Foreign Affairs*, May/June 2016 (https://www.foreignaffairs.com/articles/russia-fsu/2016-04-18/russian-politics-under-putin).

20. See "Reversal of Fortune," in Keir Giles, "Military Service in Russia: No New Model Army," Russian Series 07/18 (Shrivenham, U.K.: Conflict Studies Research Centre, May 2007).

21. For a recent overview of the unfriendly means Russia adopts to influence its neighbors, see "Russia's Toolkit," in Keir Giles, Philip Hanson, Roderic Lyne, and others, *The Russian Challenge*, Chatham House Report (London: Royal Institute of International Affairs, June 2015) (http://www.chathamhouse.org/publication/russian-challenge-authoritarian-nationalism).

22. Robert Larsson, *Russian Leverage on the CIS and the Baltic States* (Stockholm: FOI [Swedish Defence Research Agency], June 2007) (https://www.foi.se/en/our-services/fois-reports--publications/summary.html?reportNo=FOI-R--2280--SE).

23. Michael Rywkin, "Russian Foreign Policy at the Outset of Putin's Third Term," *American Foreign Policy Interests* 34, no. 5 (September 2012).

24. Geoffrey Hosking, "Putin Is Part of a Continuum That Stretches Back to the Tsars," *The Guardian*, April 4, 2017 (https://www.theguardian.com/commentisfree/2017/apr/04/putin-continuum-tsars-russia).

25. As in, for example, Karen Dawisha, *Putin's Kleptocracy: Who Owns Russia?* (New York: Simon & Schuster, 2014); and Mikhail Zygar, *Vsya kremlevskaya rat'* (Moscow: Alpina Publisher, 2016), translated by Thomas Hodson as *All the Kremlin's Men: Inside the Court of Vladimir Putin* (New York: PublicAffairs, 2016).

26. Arkadiy Ostrovsky, speaking at the Lennart Meri conference, Tallinn, May 13, 2017.

27. Edward Crankshaw, *Russia without Stalin* (London: Michael Joseph, 1956), p. 138.

28. Andrew Monaghan, *The New Politics of Russia: Interpreting Change* (Manchester University Press, 2016), p. 123.

29. Victor Madeira, *Britannia and the Bear* (London: Boydell and Brewer, 2014), p. 2 and throughout.

30. Edward Crankshaw, *Putting Up with the Russians* (London: Macmillan, 1984), p. xiii.

31. Senior Russian military officer commenting on the release of the Panama Papers, April 2016.

32. See also Vyacheslav Glazychev, "The 'Putin Consensus' Explained," in *What Does Russia Think?*, edited by Ivan Krastev, Mark Leonard, and Andrew Wilson (European Council on Foreign Relations, September 2009), pp. 9–14.

33. Dmitriy Oreshkin, quoted in Ezekiel Pfeifer, "Will Putin's Regime Survive the Current Crisis?," Institute of Modern Russia, undated (https://imrussia.org/en/the-rundown/event-briefings/2253-will-putins-regime-survive-the-current-crisis).

34. Wright Miller, *Who Are the Russians?* (London: Faber and Faber, 1973), p. 42.

35. Boris Makarenko, "Post-Crimean Political Order," in *The State of Russia: What Comes Next?*, edited by Maria Lipman and Nikolay Petrov (London: Palgrave Macmillan, 2015), p. 11.

36. Aleksey Levinson, head of Levada Center, speaking at the Lennart Meri conference, Tallinn, May 13, 2017.

37. Stepan Goncharov, "Russia's 'Special' Conservatism," IntersectionProject.eu, June 22, 2015 (http://intersectionproject.eu/article/society/russias-special-conservatism).

38. The czar was "the tender-hearted autocrat whose benevolence was only thwarted by evil counsellors and his ignorance of the truth." Henry W. Nevinson, *The Dawn in Russia* (London: Harper & Bros., 1906), p. 10.

39. James Foote, *Russian and Soviet Imperialism* (London: Foreign Affairs Publishing, 1972), p. 111.

40. As with BBC correspondent Steve Rosenberg's "very Russian conversation" reported on Twitter on September 25, 2018 (https://twitter.com/BBCSteveR/status/1044494708112805888).

41. Aglaya Snetkov, "From Crisis to Crisis: Russia's Security Policy under Putin," *Russian Analytical Digest* 173 (October 12, 2015).

42. Vladimir Milov, "Fresh Protests Are Sign of Change of Dynamics in Russian Politics," *Diplomaatia*, May 2017, p. 9.

43. Veera Laine, Katri Pynnöniemi, and Toivo Martikainen, "Zugzwang in Slow Motion? The Implications of Russia's System-Level Crisis," FIIA Analysis 6 (Helsinki: Finnish Institute of International Affairs, December 2015).

44. Michael Mandelbaum, speaking at the Council on Foreign Relations Russia symposium, "How Did We Get Here?," New York, April 13, 2017 (https://www.cfr.org/event/how-did-we-get-here). See also Pavel K. Baev, "Virtual Militarism Grows into Real Peril for Russia," *Eurasia Daily Monitor* (Jamestown Foundation) 13, no. 90 (May 9, 2016) (https://jamestown.org/program/virtual-militarism-grows-into-real-peril-for-russia/).

45. Interview with Dr. Pavel Luzin, Perm University, July 2017.

46. Daniel Fried, "Russia's Back-to-the-80s Foreign Policy," *The Atlantic*, August 2, 2017 (https://www.theatlantic.com/international/archive/2017/08/cold-war-russia-putin-reagan-trump/535728/).

47. Lev Gudkov, "Putin's Relapse into Totalitarianism," in *The State of Russia*, edited by Lipman and Petrov, p. 96.

48. Angus Roxburgh, "I Thought Nothing in Russia Could Shock Me. Then I Went to a Television Broadcast," *The Guardian*, June 30, 2017 (https://www.theguardian.com/commentisfree/2017/jun/30/russia-putin-protests-police-arrests-tv-show).

49. Telegram, George Kennan to George Marshall, February 22, 1946 (https://www.trumanlibrary.org/whistlestop/study_collections/coldwar/documents/pdf/6-6.pdf).

50. Adam Olearius, "The Voyages and Travells of the Ambassadors Sent by Frederick Duke of Holstein to the Great Duke of Muscovy and the King of Persia" (London, 1669) (https://books.google.co.uk/books?id=UPS_NYFKTzwC).

51. Astolphe de Custine, *Lettres de Russie: La Russie en 1839*, edited by Pierre Nora (Paris: Gallimard, 1975), p. 74.

52. "The Front-Line Diary of a Soviet Officer," CIA, December 4, 1950 (https://www.cia.gov/library/readingroom/docs/CIA-RDP80-00926A0028000 20001-0.pdf). See also Aleksandr Solzhenitsyn's *Prussian Nights* for a memoir of

rape, casual murder, and senseless and self-defeating destruction driven by envy during the advance into Germany.

53. A video of the reaction of Russian troops arriving in Georgian barracks is available at https://www.youtube.com/watch?v=7ped0ddLrNU. A video of the condition of the same buildings after they had departed is available at https://www.youtube.com/watch?v=lGaP-gyxgac.

54. "Nalichiye zagranpasporta i poezdki za rubezh" [Possession of a foreign passport and travel abroad], Levada Center, April 26, 2016 (http://www.levada.ru/2016/04/26/nalichie-zagranpasporta-i-poezdki-za-rubezh/).

55. Tatia Lemondzhava, "In Russia, the Doors Are Closing," *Foreign Policy*, April 29, 2016 (http://foreignpolicy.com/2016/04/29/in-russia-the-doors-are-closing-tourism-putin-human-rights/).

56. "V MVD soglasovali spisok 13 stran dlya otpuska sotrudnikov" [Interior Ministry approves a list of 13 permitted countries for employee vacations], RBC.ru, January 12, 2018 (https://www.rbc.ru/society/12/01/2018/5a5887399a7947237e44edb5).

57. Former NATO official James Greene, speaking at Chatham House, March 31, 2011.

58. Mikhail Suslov, "'Russian World': Russia's Policy towards Its Diaspora," *Russie.Nei.Visions* 103, Ifri (Institut français des relations internationals), July 2017 (https://www.ifri.org/sites/default/files/atoms/files/suslov_russian_world_2017.pdf).

59. Carl Schreck, "Russian Expats Wrestle with Dual-Citizenship Dilemma," Radio Free Europe/Radio Liberty, June 23, 2014 (https://www.rferl.org/a/russia-expatriates-dual-citizenship-law/25432010.html).

60. See "Russian Minorities," in Giles, Hanson, Lyne, and others, *The Russian Challenge*, p. 41.

61. Suslov, "'Russian World.'"

62. Stuart Ramsay Tompkins, *The Russian Mind* (University of Oklahoma Press, 1953), p. 124.

63. For impressions of one such thaw, see Harrison E. Salisbury, *A New Russia?* (New York: Harper & Row, 1962), p. 128.

64. "TV listings from independent newspaper in Russia's Yakutia warn readers of lies and distortions on state channels," Twitter (@SEEnnis), May 28, 2016 (pic.twitter.com/37CzQCIz7y).

65. "Razgovor v lagere: chto prosili u Putina na krymskoy 'Tavride'" [Conversation in the camp: What Putin was asked for at Crimea's "Tavrida"], RBC.ru, August 20, 2017 (http://www.rbc.ru/politics/20/08/2017/5999e1be9a79472cc831860c).

66. See the Meduza website at https://meduza.io/.

67. Nevinson, *The Dawn in Russia*, p. 64.

68. "Russia: Assault on Freedom of Expression," HumanRightsWatch.org,

July 18, 2017 (https://www.hrw.org/news/2017/07/18/russia-assault-freedom-expression).

69. Mikhail Suslov, "The Medium for Demonic Energies: 'Digital Anxiety' in the Russian Orthodox Church," *Digital Icons: Studies in Russian, Eurasian and Central European New Media* 14 (2015), pp. 1–25.

70. "Russian Web Censor Cracks Down Ahead of Next Anti-Corruption Protests," GlobalVoices.org, March 31, 2017 (https://globalvoices.org/2017/03/31/russian-web-censor-cracks-down-ahead-of-next-anti-corruption-protests/).

71. Anna Balashova and Mariya Kolomychenko, "Abonentov Skype zamknut vnutri seti" [Skype subscribers will be locked in the network], *Kommersant*, May 20, 2016 (https://www.kommersant.ru/doc/2990902).

72. "The KGB Tidies Up," editorial, *Daily Telegraph*, June 24, 1972, p. 14.

73. Russia's defensive information security measures are discussed in detail in Keir Giles, *Russia's "New" Tools for Confronting the West: Continuity and Innovation in Moscow's Exercise of Power*, Chatham House Research Paper (London: Royal Institute of International Affairs March 2016) (https://www.chathamhouse.org/publication/russias-new-tools-confronting-west).

Chapter 6

1. Astolphe de Custine, *Lettres de Russie: La Russie en 1839*, edited by Pierre Nora (Paris: Gallimard, 1975), p. 137.

2. David Satter, journalist and author, speaking at a Russia discussion event in Cambridgeshire, February 2013.

3. The survival of this principle into post-Soviet times is described in Sergey Patrushev and Lyudmila Filippova, "Dualism of Mass Consciousness and Typology of Mass Politics," *Politicheskaya nauka* 1 (2017), pp. 13–37, and commentary in Paul Goble, "Post-Soviet Man Resembles Pre-Soviet Predecessor More Than Soviet One, Sociologists Say," *Window on Eurasia*, May 16, 2017 (http://windowoneurasia2.blogspot.co.uk/2017/05/post-soviet-man-resembles-pre-soviet.html).

4. "Russians never became citizens in the true sense of the word and always positioned themselves in opposition to the state, because the government is always trying to take something away from them." Christian Neef, "Understanding Moscow: The Mysteries of the Russian Mindset," *Der Spiegel*, August 22, 2017 (http://www.spiegel.de/international/world/understanding-moscow-the-mysteries-of-the-russian-mindset-a-1162072.html).

5. Interview with Tatiana Stanovaya, head of the analytical department at Moscow's Center for Political Technologies, July 2017.

6. Dima Adamsky, *The Culture of Military Innovation* (Stanford University Press, 2010), p. 39.

7. Stuart Ramsay Tompkins, *The Russian Mind* (University of Oklahoma Press, 1953), p. 97.

8. Tibor Szamuely, *The Russian Tradition* (London: Secker & Warburg, 1974), p. 171.

9. Aleksandr Herzen, *From the Other Shore* (http://altheim.com/lit/herzen-ftos.html).

10. Described in detail in Geoffrey Hosking, "Forms of Social Solidarity in Russia and the Soviet Union," in *Trust and Democratic Transition in Post-Communist Europe*, edited by I. Markova (Oxford University Press, 2004), pp. 47–62.

11. Walter Bedell Smith, introduction to de Custine, *Lettres de Russie*, pp. 12–13.

12. Stepan Goncharov, "Russia's 'Special' Conservatism," IntersectionProject.eu, June 22, 2015 (http://intersectionproject.eu/article/society/russias-special-conservatism).

13. Levada Center, "Vzaimodeystviye grazhdan i gosudarstvo" [Cooperation between citizens and the state], April 6, 2015 (https://www.levada.ru/2015/04/06/vzaimodejstvie-grazhdan-i-gosudarstva/).

14. Giles Fletcher, "Of the Russe Common Wealth" (London, 1591) (https://archive.org/details/russiaatcloseofs20bond).

15. Andrei Piontkovsky, "Another Look into Putin's Soul" (Washington: Hudson Institute, 2006).

16. Sergey Aleksashenko, "The Russian Economy at the Start of the Post-Putin Era," in *The State of Russia: What Comes Next?*, edited by Maria Lipman and Nikolay Petrov (London: Palgrave Macmillan, 2015), p. 35.

17. Alexander Etkind, *Internal Colonization: Russia's Imperial Experience* (Cambridge: Polity, 2011).

18. For an example of an investigation detecting contracted-out soldiers who were entirely satisfied with their "exploitation," see FBIS, "Moscow Military Prosecutor Investigates Charges of Exploitation of Enlisted Men," *Moskovskiy Komsomolets*, March 9, 2006. Conversely, for a well-publicized incident of contracting-out with a lethal outcome, see FBIS, "Russia: Military Procurator Interviewed on Crimes Committed by Officers," *Krasnaya zvezda*, February 10, 2006. The mid-2000s finally saw the beginning of efforts to curtail the practice; see "'Arenda' soldat zapreshchena" [Soldier "rental" banned], *Krasnaya zvezda*, October 11, 2005.

19. Nikki Haley, speaking at an emergency UN Security Council meeting on April 5, 2017. Video available at https://www.youtube.com/watch?v=tSweWsZlHDs.

20. Adamsky, *The Culture of Military Innovation*, p. 44.

21. After a slow start, this process has now been under way for over a decade. See Keir Giles, "Military Service in Russia: No New Model Army," Russian Series 07/18 (Shrivenham, U.K.: Conflict Studies Research Centre, May 2007).

22. See detailed discussion of this and other factors in "Russia's Military Robots," CSIS, October 5, 2017 (https://www.youtube.com/watch?v=s2aqMQ0Sa4w).

23. Patrick Tucker, "The Pentagon Is Nervous about Russian and Chinese Killer Robots," *Defense One*, December 14, 2015 (http://www.defenseone.com/threats/2015/12/pentagon-nervous-about-russian-and-chinese-killer-robots/124465/).

24. "Kalashnikov Gunmaker Develops Combat Module Based on Artificial Intelligence," TASS, July 5, 2017 (http://tass.com/defense/954894).

25. Fletcher, "Of the Russe Common Wealth."

26. De Custine, *Lettres de Russie*, p. 164.

27. N. A. Dobrolyubov, "Russkaya satira Ekaterinskago vremeni" [Russian satire in Catherine's time], in *Sochineniya N. A. Dobrolyubova* [Works of N. A. Dobrolyubov] (St. Petersburg, 1876).

28. "Officials in Russia are better protected in terms of their abilities to speak and to act than an ordinary citizen, just because they are representatives of the State. But probably this is found in the West too." Interview with Vladimir Ivanov, EastWest Institute, Moscow, July 2017.

29. Samuel Greene, "Conditionality beyond Sanctions: Identifying and Pursuing Interests in the EU-Russia Relationship," Policy Memo 460, PONARS, February 2017 (http://www.ponarseurasia.org/memo/conditionality-beyond-sanctions-identifying-and-pursuing-interests-eu-russia-relationship).

30. Interview with Vladimir Ivanov, EastWest Institute, Moscow, July 2017.

31. Sirkka Laihiala-Kankainen, "Continuity and Change in Education: The Russian Experience," paper presented at the European Conference on Educational Research, Lahti, Finland, September 22–25, 1999 (http://www.leeds.ac.uk/educol/documents/00001291.htm).

32. As described at the time by Chief Military Prosecutor Sergey Fridinskiy, the man most directly concerned with dealing with the consequences: "The army is not some isolated part of society that exists all by itself. Young people are drafted into the army from society, and they carry on behaving the way they are used to." See BBC Monitoring, "Criminal Punishment Alone Will Not End Hazing in Army—Prosecutor," ITAR-TASS, April 6, 2007.

33. "I see as compensation for the misfortune of being born under this regime only dreams of arrogance and the hope of domination: it is to this passion for domination that I return each time I try to analyze the moral life of the inhabitants of Russia." De Custine, *Lettres de Russie*, p. 111.

34. A. (Sasha) Kennaway, "The Russian 'Black Hole'" (Shrivenham, U.K.: Conflict Studies Research Centre, November 1996), p. 2.

35. Interview with Vladimir Ivanov, EastWest Institute, Moscow, July 2017.

36. Maurice Baring, *The Russian People* (1911) (https://archive.org/details/russianpeople017102mbp).

37. Alena V. Ledeneva, *How Russia Really Works: The Informal Practices That Shaped Post-Soviet Politics and Business* (Cornell University Press, 2006), p. 13.

38. David Satter, *The Less You Know, the Better You Sleep* (Yale University Press, 2016), p. 84.

39. A foreigner's blundering encounters with these boundaries during the Cold War are described in Laurens van der Post, *Journey into Russia* (Harmondsworth: Penguin, 1965).

40. Kirill Rogov, "Switch On, Switch Off: How Law Sustains the Russian System," OpenDemocracy.net, December 17, 2010 (https://www.opendemocracy.net/od-russia/kirill-rogov/switch-on-switch-off-how-law-sustains-russian-system).

41. Maxim Trudolyubov, "Moscow Seeks to Pull the Plug on Cultural Liberalization," *Russia File* (blog), Kennan Institute of the Woodrow Wilson International Center for Scholars, August 25, 2017 (http://www.kennan-russiafile.org/2017/08/25/moscow-seeks-to-pull-the-plug-on-cultural-liberalization/).

42. Compare the similar accounts of "Tatiana" in Alena Ledeneva's *How Russia Works* and Yana Yakovleva in Peter Pomerantsev's *Nothing Is True and Everything Is Possible: The Surreal Heart of the New Russia* (New York: PublicAffairs, 2014).

43. "Ministr yustitsii Aleksandr Konovalov: Uvazehnie k zakonu v povsednevnoi zhizni v Rossii ne bylo nikogda" [Minister of Justice Aleksandr Konovalov: Russia has never known respect for the law in everyday life], NTV, July 2, 2008 (http://polit.ru/article/2008/06/02/interview/).

44. Aleksandra Ageyeva, "Tak i popadayesh' v istoriyu" [That's how you make history], Twitter, June 14, 2017 (https://twitter.com/ageevasana/status/874936331276779520).

45. Henry W. Nevinson, *The Dawn in Russia* (London: Harper & Bros., 1906), p. 233.

46. Fletcher, "Of the Russe Common Wealth."

47. N. R. Shushanyan and A. V. Ledeneva, "Telefonnoye pravo v Rossii" [Telephone law in Russia] (Higher School of Economics, 2008) (https://www.hse.ru/pubs/share/direct/document/72384970).

48. Ivan Zhdanov, "Resheniye po Lyaskinu slovo v slovo sovpadayet s resheniyem po Volkovu, mozhem za sud'yu chitat'" [The Lyaskin verdict is word for word the same as the Volkov verdict, you can read it for the judge], Twitter, August 3, 2017 (https://twitter.com/ioannzh/status/893168592509964288).

49. Jacob Miller, "Union of Soviet Socialist Republics," in *World Survey 1962* (London: George Newnes, 1962), p. 259.

50. A. Kennaway, *Continuity & Conflict in Russian Government* (Shrivenham, U.K.: Conflict Studies Research Centre, September 1999), p. 4.

51. Lev Gudkov, "Putin's Relapse into Totalitarianism," in *The State of Russia*, edited by Lipman and Petrov, p. 100.

52. As with the legislative changes following the armed conflict in Georgia ensuring that identical military action abroad would in the future be legal. See also Sergey Aleksashenko, "The Russian Economy at the Start of the Post-Putin Era," in *The State of Russia*, edited by Lipman and Petrov, p. 34.

53. Jason C. Vaughn, *A Socio-Political Model of Lies in Russia* (Lanham, Md.: University Press of America, 2016), p. 95.

Notes to Pages 98–105   205

54. Tatyana Pavlovskaya, "Na Kubani razgorelsya skandal vokrug svad'by docheri krayevogo sud'i" [Scandal erupts in Kuban over wedding of daughter of regional judge], *Rossiyskaya gazeta*, July 17, 2017 (https://rg.ru/2017/07/17/reg-ufo/kubani-skandal-vokrug-svadby-docheri-sudi.html).
55. Ledeneva, *How Russia Really Works*, p. 13.
56. Ibid., p. 191.
57. J. Michael Waller, "Russia's Biggest 'Mafia' Is the KGB," *Wall Street Journal Europe*, June 22, 1994.
58. Alena Ledeneva and Stanislav Shekshnia, "Doing Business in Russia: Informal Practices and Anti-Corruption Strategies," *Russie.Nei.Visions* 58, March 2011 (https://www.ifri.org/en/publications/enotes/russieneivisions/doing-business-russia-informal-practices-and-anti-corruption).
59. Pomerantsev, *Nothing Is True and Everything Is Possible*, p. 205.
60. Lauri Mälksoo, *Russian Approaches to International Law* (Oxford University Press, 2015), p. 185.

Chapter 7

1. Protoierey Ioann Garmash, interviewed in "Pride, Patriotism and How Putin Helped Redefine What It Means to Be a 'True Russian,'" PBS, July 10, 2017 (http://www.pbs.org/newshour/bb/pride-patriotism-putin-helped-redefine-means-true-russian/).
2. "Om Sverige går med i Nato kommer vi att vidta nödvändiga åtgärder" [If Sweden joins NATO, we will take necessary steps], Sergey Lavrov, interview with *Dagens Nyheter*, April 28, 2016 (http://fokus.dn.se/lavrov/).
3. Aleksandr Osipovich, "Church Offers Atomic Blessing," *Moscow Times*, September 5, 2007.
4. Helpfully summarized by Marlene Laruelle in "Space As a Destiny. Legitimizing the Russian Empire through Geography and Cosmos," in *Empire De/Centered: New Spatial Histories of Russia and the Soviet Union*, edited by Sanna Turoma and Maxim Waldstein (Farnham: Ashgate, 2013), pp. 85–101.
5. See Charles Clover, *Black Wind, White Snow: The Rise of Russia's New Nationalism* (Yale University Press, 2016).
6. Maxim Trudolyubov, "Hard Work vs. Magic," *Russia File* (blog), Kennan Institute of the Woodrow Wilson International Center for Scholars, April 19, 2016 (https://www.wilsoncenter.org/article/hard-work-vs-magic).
7. Frederick L. Schuman, *The Cold War: Retrospect and Prospect* (Louisiana State University Press, 1962), p. 60.
8. James Foote, *Russian and Soviet Imperialism* (London: Foreign Affairs Publishing, 1972), p. 111.
9. Discussed in Anna Arutyunyan, *The Putin Mystique* (Northampton, Mass.: Olive Branch Press, 2015), p. 41 and throughout.
10. In the early 1990s, arguably Russia's most popular public personality

was Anatoly Kashpirovsky, a psychiatrist and trained hypnotist who conducted televised healing sessions.

11. The broadcasts ran from 1993 to early 1995. "Russian Radio Ends Cult Broadcasts," UPI, March 23, 1995.

12. Maria Domanska, "Russia Marks the 70th Anniversary of the Victory over Nazism: What Significance Does It Have in an Epoch of Global Confrontation?," OSW, May 20, 2015..

13. A video of the protest is available on YouTube. See timurnechaev77, "Pussy Riot Gig at Christ the Savior Cethedral (Original Video)," YouTube, July 2, 2012 (www.youtube.com/watch?v=grEBLskpDWQ).

14. Maksim Kolomiets, "Pokemon-provokator: Vse, chto nuzhno znat' ob areste blogera Sokolovskogo" [Pokémon the provocateur: Everything you need to know about the arrest of the blogger Sokolovskiy], Ridus, September 4, 2016 (https://www.ridus.ru/news/230846.html).

15. Government of Russia, Ministry of Foreign Affairs, "Report on the Human Rights Situation in the European Union," unofficial translation (https://archive.org/stream/RussianReportOnHumanRightsInTheEu_2014/Russian-ReportOnHumanRightsInTheEu_2014_djvu.txt).

16. "Strategiya natsionalnoy bezopasnosti Rossiyskoy Federatsii" [National Security Strategy of the Russian Federation], December 31, 2015 (http://kremlin.ru/acts/bank/40391), Article 78.

17. "Zakat Evropy" [The decline of Europe], *Izvestia*, October 11, 2007 (http://izvestia.ru/news/329597).

18. Dr. Strangelove, "Russian President Putin Defends Christian Culture, Western Values, Condemns Political Correctness," YouTube video, February 28, 2014, from the Valdai Discussion Group, September 19, 2013. Translation available at http://en.kremlin.ru/events/president/news/19243.

19. Petr Konečný, "Nahý jsem masturboval pro gaye, chlapsky přiznal Jakub Janda," Expres.cz, September 17, 2015 (http://www.expres.cz/jakub-janda-porno-video-0vp-/zpravy.aspx?c=A150917_113804_dx-zpravy_bk).

20. George Packer, "The Quiet German," *New Yorker*, December 1, 2014 (www.newyorker.com/magazine/2014/12/01/quiet-german).

21. Sergei Prozorov, "Russia and the Missing World," *New Perspectives* 24, no. 1 (2016), p. 111.

22. Government of Russia, Ministry of Foreign Affairs, "Report on the Human Rights Situation in the European Union," unofficial translation (https://archive.org/stream/RussianReportOnHumanRightsInTheEu_2014/Russian-ReportOnHumanRightsInTheEu_2014_djvu.txt).

23. "Resolution of 6 February 2014 on the EU-Russia Summit," European Parliament (http://www.europarl.europa.eu/sides/getDoc.do?pubRef=-//EP//NONSGML+TA+P7-TA-2014-0101+0+DOC+PDF+V0//EN).

24. Tatiana Riabova and Oleg Riabov, "'Gayromaidan': Gendered Aspects

of the Hegemonic Russian Media Discourse on the Ukrainian Crisis," *Journal of Soviet and Post-Soviet Politics and Society* 1, no. 1 (2015), pp. 83–108.

25. Sergey Patrushev and Lyudmila Filippova, "Dualism of Mass Consciousness and Typology of Mass Politics," *Politicheskaya nauka* 1 (2017), pp. 13–37; and commentary in Paul Goble, "Post-Soviet Man Resembles Pre-Soviet Predecessor More Than Soviet One, Sociologists Say," *Window on Eurasia* (blog), May 16, 2017 (http://windowoneurasia2.blogspot.co.uk/2017/05/post-soviet-man-resembles-pre-soviet.html).

26. "Public Opinion in Russia: Russians' Attitudes on Foreign Affairs and Social Issues," Chicago, Associated Press–NORC Center for Public Affairs Research, undated (survey conducted in late 2014) (http://www.apnorc.org/projects/Pages/HTML%20Reports/public-opinion-in-russia-russians-attitudes-on-foreign-affairs-and-social-issues0401-6253.aspx).

27. Vladimir Putin, speaking on Rossiya 24 TV, 1205 GMT, January 17, 2014.

28. Valerie Sperling, *Sex, Politics, and Putin* (Oxford University Press, 2015), p. 5.

29. Maria Engström, "The New Antiquity versus the New Middle Ages," IntersectionProject.eu, June 27, 2017 (http://intersectionproject.eu//article/politics/new-antiquity-versus-new-middle-ages).

30. Stepan Goncharov, "Russia's 'Special' Conservatism," IntersectionProject.eu, June 22, 2015 (http://intersectionproject.eu/article/society/russias-special-conservatism).

31. See James Kirchik, "How the GOP Became the Party of Putin," *Politico*, July 18, 2017 (http://www.politico.com/magazine/story/2017/07/18/how-the-gop-became-the-party-of-putin-215387); Larry Diamond, "Russia and the Threat to Liberal Democracy," *The Atlantic*, December 9, 2016 (https://www.theatlantic.com/international/archive/2016/12/russia-liberal-democracy/510011/); and Geoffrey Hosking, "Putin Is Part of a Continuum That Stretches Back to the Tsars," *The Guardian*, April 4, 2017 (https://www.theguardian.com/commentisfree/2017/apr/04/putin-continuum-tsars-russia). See also Andreas Umland, "Post-Soviet Neo-Eurasianism, the Putin System, and the Contemporary European Extreme Right," *Perspectives on Politics* 15, no. 2 (June 2017), pp. 465–76.

32. Roman Skaskiw, "A Look at Russian Civilization: Power, Truth, Trust, and War," *Small Wars Journal*, March 30, 2016 (http://smallwarsjournal.com/jrnl/art/a-look-at-russian-civilization-power-truth-trust-and-war).

33. Keir Giles, "The Unimportance of Truth," in *Russia's "New" Tools for Confronting the West: Continuity and Innovation in Moscow's Exercise of Power*, Chatham House (London: Royal Institute of International Affairs, March 2016), pp. 37ff.

34. Russia is hardly unique in this respect. Western overreliance on the significance of plausibility can be a significant handicap in confrontational en-

counters with other cultures as well. For a vivid description of the difficulties of cross-examination when the subject has no concept of being trapped in a lie, see Tony Lagouranis and Allen Mikaelian, "Fear Up Harsh: An Army Interrogator's Dark Journey through Iraq" (London: NAL/Penguin, 2007).

35. Viktor Znakov, "Comprehension of Lies: A Russian View," in *States of Mind: American and Post-Soviet Perspectives on Contemporary Issues in Psychology*, edited by Diane F. Halpern (Oxford University Press, 1997), p. 90.

36. Adapted from Alena V. Ledeneva, *How Russia Really Works: The Informal Practices That Shaped Post-Soviet Politics and Business* (Cornell University Press, 2006), p. 198.

37. Z. E. Aleksandrova, *Slovar sinonimov russkogo yazyka* [Dictionary of synonyms of the Russian language], 5th ed. (Moscow: Russkiy yazyk, 1986).

38. Interview with Martti Kari, Assistant Chief of Finnish Defense Staff, April 2017.

39. For an exploration of the difference between "*lozh*" and "*vranye*" in particular, see "Lozh' i vran'ye v yazykovoy kartine mira russkogo cheloveka: Lektsiya Alekseya Shmeleva" ["*Lozh*" and "*vranye*" in the Russian's linguistic image of the world: Lecture by Alexia Shmeleva], video, *Monokler* (https://monokler.ru/lozh-i-vranyo-v-soznanii-rossiyan/).

40. Laurens van der Post, *Journey into Russia* (Harmondsworth: Penguin, 1965), p. 285.

41. To take one example, the declaration in 2011 that multichild families would be given land. See Nadezhda Andreeva, "Zemlya na vyrost" [Land to grow], *Novaya gazeta*, July 3, 2015 (https://www.novayagazeta.ru/articles/2015/07/03/64768-zemlya-na-vyrost).

42. "Putin prosledit za stroitel'stvom domov dlya pogorel'tsev po videokameram" [Putin will use video cameras to watch housing being built for those burned out], *Moskovskiy Komsomolets*, August 3, 2010 (http://www.mk.ru/politics/news/2010/08/03/520786-putin-prosledit-za-stroitelstvom-domov-dlya-pogoreltsev-po-videokameram.html).

43. Jason C. Vaughn, *A Socio-Political Model of Lies in Russia* (Lanham, Md.: University Press of America, 2016), p. ix.

44. Kimberly Marten, "President Trump, Keep in Mind That Russia and the West Think about Negotiations Very, Very Differently," *Washington Post*, July 25, 2017 (https://www.washingtonpost.com/news/monkey-cage/wp/2017/07/25/president-trump-keep-in-mind-that-russia-and-the-west-think-about-negotiations-very-very-differently/).

45. Astolphe de Custine, *Lettres de Russie: La Russie en 1839*, edited by Pierre Nora (Paris: Gallimard, 1975), p. 66.

46. Russia's distinctive basis of morality is further explained by sympathetic academics like Nicolai Petro, "Russia's Moral Framework and Why It Matters," *National Interest*, September 24, 2015 (http://nationalinterest.org/feature/russia%E2%80%99s-moral-framework-why-it-matters-13923).

47. Émile Montégut, "Perspectives sur le temps présent," *Revue des Deux-Mondes*, July 1854, p. 205.

48. Ion Ratiu, *Moscow Challenges the World* (London: Sherwood Press, 1986), p. 206.

49. "Stephen Harper at G20 Tells Vladimir Putin to 'Get Out of Ukraine,'" CBC, November 15, 2014 (http://www.cbc.ca/news/world/stephen-harper-at-g20-tells-vladimir-putin-to-get-out-of-ukraine-1.2836382).

50. Aleksandra Ageyeva, "Tak i popadayesh' v istoriyu" [That's how you make history], Twitter, June 14, 2017 (https://twitter.com/ageevasana/status/874936331276779520).

51. Vladimir Pastukhov, "Sindrom otklyuchennogo soznaniya" [Unplugged consciousness syndrome], BBC Russian Service, December 8, 2014 (http://www.bbc.com/russian/blogs/2014/12/141208_blog_pastoukhov_syndrome_unplugged_consciousness).

52. Vaughn, *A Socio-Political Model of Lies in Russia*, p. 18.

53. De Custine, *Lettres de Russie*, p. 35.

54. This phenomenon is explored in depth from two different angles in Orlando Figes, *The Whisperers: Private Life in Stalin's Russia* (London: Allen Lane, 2007); and Catherine Merridale, *Ivan's War: The Red Army 1939–45* (London: Faber and Faber, 2005).

55. A. V. Manoylo, "Creating an Alternative Reality: Western Narratives on the Russian Intervention in the Syrian Conflict," *Bulletin of Moscow State Regional University, History and Political Sciences Series* 5 (2015). See also Vladislav Inozemtsev, "Pyat' mifov ob Amerike, tirazhiruemykh v Rossii" [Five myths about America that are promoted in Russia], Slon.ru, March 22, 2016 (https://slon.ru/posts/65486).

56. Tom Balmforth, "Russian Archive Chief Out after Debunking Soviet WW II Legend," Radio Free Europe/Radio Liberty, March 17, 2016 (http://www.rferl.mobi/a/mironenko-state-archive-chief-removed-from-post-panfilov-legend/27619460.html).

57. Aleksei Levinson and Lyubov Borisyak, "'Znak uvazheniya': Kak rossiyane otnosyatsya k korruptsii" ["A sign of respect": How Russians view corruption], RBC.ru, March 24, 2016 (http://www.rbc.ru/opinions/society/24/03/2016/56f271cd9a7947f9c25d740b).

58. Andrey Kolesnikov, "Misremembering Russia's War," Carnegie Moscow Center, originally published as "Armiya, flot, Asad" [Army, Navy, Asad], *Novoye vremya*, June 28, 2017 (http://newtimes.ru/stati/xroniki/kopiya-armiya,-flot,-asad-kopiya.html).

59. Andrey Chernykh, "V SPIDe ne nashli nichego russkogo" [Nothing Russian found in AIDS], *Kommersant*, May 31, 2016 (http://kommersant.ru/doc/3000818).

60. Stuart Ramsay Tompkins, *The Russian Mind* (University of Oklahoma Press, 1953), p. 120.

61. Peter Pomerantsev, *Nothing Is True and Everything Is Possible* (New York: PublicAffairs, 2014), p. 199.

62. André Gide, *Back from the USSR* (London, 1937), p. 15.

63. Inozemtsev, "Five Myths about America That Are Promoted in Russia." See also Denis Volkov, "Supporting a War That Isn't: Russian Public Opinion and the Ukraine Conflict," Carnegie.ru, September 9, 2015 (http://carnegieendowment.org/publications/?fa=61236).

64. Interviewed by Ben Smith, "What If Trump TV Was Good?," *BuzzFeed*, July 18, 2017 (https://www.buzzfeed.com/bensmith/what-if-trump-tv-was-good).

65. Merridale, *Ivan's War*, p. 6.

66. Mariya Y. Omelicheva and Lidiya Zubytska, "An Unending Quest for Russia's Place in the World: The Discursive Co-evolution of the Study and Practice of International Relations in Russia," *New Perspectives*, 24, no. 1 (2016), p. 21.

67. Maria Lipman, "Putin's 'Besieged Fortress' and Its Ideological Arms," in *The State of Russia: What Comes Next?*, edited by Maria Lipman and Nikolay Petrov (London: Palgrave Macmillan, 2015), p. 123.

68. Giles Fletcher, "Of the Russe Common Wealth" (1591) (https://archive.org/details/russiaatcloseofs20bond).

69. Lev Tikhomirov, *Russia, Political and Social* (London: Swan Sonnenschein, Lowrey & Co., 1888) (https://archive.org/details/russiapoliticals01tikhuoft).

70. E. B. Lanin (pseudonym of Emile Joseph Dillon, *Daily Telegraph* correspondent in St. Petersburg), *Russian Characteristics* (London: Chapman and Hall, 1892).

71. The phrase is from de Custine, *Lettres de Russie*, p. 221.

72. Elena Fell, "Macro-reasoning and Cognitive Gaps: Understanding Post-Soviet Russians' Communication Styles," *ESSACHESS: Journal for Communication Studies* 7, no. 1 (13) (2014), pp. 91–110.

73. Ibid.

74. Dima Adamsky, *The Culture of Military Innovation* (Stanford University Press, 2010), p. 39.

75. Fell, "Macro-reasoning and Cognitive Gaps."

76. Failures of cross-cultural communication work both ways. Fell's guide for Russian academics on how to communicate effectively with their British counterparts, based largely around how best to convince them that they are worthy interlocutors for the British "middle class," makes enlightening reading for the British academics described in it. See Elena Fell, "Znacheniye kommunikativnoy kompetentsii dlya uspeshnogo vzaimodeystviya russkoy intelligentsii i britanskogo srednego klassa v obrazovatel'nom prostranstve" [Russian intelligentsia and the British middle class: The importance of communicative competence for successful communication in educational space], *Vestnik nauki Sibiri* 2, no. 17 (2015), pp. 213–22 (http://bit.ly/2uTVjzc).

77. In fact, "sedulously maintaining the myths . . . makes it impossible for Russia to look truth in the face and wake up and start behaving like a grown-up power instead of a great clumsy idiot child with nasty domestic habits for whom we are for ever having to make allowances." Edward Crankshaw, *Putting Up with the Russians* (London: Macmillan, 1984), p. 145.

Chapter 8

1. James Foote, *Russian and Soviet Imperialism* (London: Foreign Affairs Publishing, 1972), p. 257.

2. See Andrew Monaghan, *The New Politics of Russia: Interpreting Change* (Manchester University Press, 2016), p. 63.

3. A point explored in detail in Keir Giles, *The Turning Point for Russian Foreign Policy* (Carlisle, Pa.: U.S. Army War College, May 2017).

4. The description is from Alex Pravda, *Leading Russia: Putin in Perspective* (Oxford University Press, 2005), Introduction, p. 1

5. Henry Kissinger, *World Order* (New York: Penguin, 2014), p. 50.

6. This included matters of fine detail. Conscious or unconscious continuity in organs of repression extended to the light blue color of the uniform of the czarist Special Corps of Gendarmes resurfacing in the epaulettes, collar flashes, and cap bands of the uniformed KGB.

7. See, for example, John Reshetar, *Problems of Analyzing and Predicting Soviet Behavior* (New York: Doubleday, 1955), p. 2; and Frederick L. Schuman, *The Cold War: Retrospect and Prospect* (Louisiana State University Press, 1962), p. 7.

8. Edward Crankshaw, *Putting Up with the Russians* (London: Macmillan, 1984), p. 151.

9. Ion Ratiu, *Moscow Challenges the World* (London: Sherwood Press, 1986), p. 375.

10. Laurens van der Post, *Journey into Russia* (Harmondsworth: Penguin, 1965), p. 332.

11. "Presidential Address to the Federal Assembly," December 12, 2012, Russian presidential website (http://kremlin.ru/news/17118).

12. Maria Lipman, "Putin's 'Besieged Fortress' and Its Ideological Arms," in *The State of Russia: What Comes Next?*, edited by Maria Lipman and Nikolay Petrov (London: Palgrave Macmillan, 2015), p. 117.

13. Edward Crankshaw, "The Price Brezhnev Should Be Asked to Pay," *The Observer*, 1977, reprinted in *Putting Up with the Russians*.

14. Edward L. Keenan, "On Certain Mythical Beliefs and Russian Behaviors," in *The Legacy of History in Russia and the New States of Eurasia*, edited by S. Frederick Starr (Armonk, N.Y.: M. E. Sharpe, 1994), p. 19.

15. Astolphe de Custine, *Lettres de Russie: La Russie en 1839*, edited by Pierre Nora (Paris: Gallimard, 1975), pp. 236–37.

16. Lipman, "Putin's 'Besieged Fortress' and Its Ideological Arms," p. 126.

17. "Russian Historians Preparing Textbooks on 'Novorossiya,'" Euromaidan Press, August 30, 2014 (http://euromaidanpress.com/2014/08/30/russian-historians-preparing-textbooks-on-novorossiya/).

18. Madeline Roache, "'Russian History Competition Turns Schoolchildren into Extremists,' Russian Historians Are Told," Euromaidan Press, May 4, 2015 (http://euromaidanpress.com/2017/05/04/russian-history-competition-turns-schoolchildren-into-extremists-russian-historians-are-told/).

19. Article 79, National Security Strategy of the Russian Federation, December 31, 2015 (http://www.ieee.es/Galerias/fichero/OtrasPublicaciones/Internacional/2016/Russian-National-Security-Strategy-31Dec2015.pdf).

20. Article 13 (c), Military Doctrine of the Russian Federation, December 25, 2014 (https://rusemb.org.uk/press/2029).

21. Ivan Kurilla, "The 'Return of Stalin': Understanding the Surge of Historical Politics in Russia," PONARS Policy Memo, May 19, 2016; Andriy Kohut, "Control over the Past: Russia's Archival Policy and Second World War Myths," Euromaidan Press, June 30, 2015 (http://euromaidanpress.com/2015/06/30/control-over-the-past-russias-archival-policy-and-second-world-war-myths/).

22. Tom Balmforth, "Russian Archive Chief Out after Debunking Soviet WW II Legend," Radio Free Europe/Radio Liberty, March 17, 2016 (http://www.rferl.mobi/a/mironenko-state-archive-chief-removed-from-post-panfilov-legend/27619460.html); Anton Krasovskiy, "Byvshiy direktor Gosarkhiva Sergey Mironenko: 'Deputatu Nosovu ya by porekomendoval tshchatel'no obsloedovat'sya'" [Former director of the State Archive Sergey Mironenko: "I think MP Nosov should get professional (medical) help"], Snob.ru, March 18, 2016; Harry Bone, "Putin Backs WW2 Myth in New Russian Film," BBC Monitoring, October 11, 2016 (http://www.bbc.co.uk/news/world-europe-37595972).

23. Lamia Estatie, "Russia and Ukraine's 'Twiplomatic' Spat," BBC News, May 31, 2017 (http://www.bbc.co.uk/news/blogs-trending-40105483).

24. Wright Miller, *Who Are the Russians?* (London: Faber and Faber, 1973), p. 38.

25. Stuart Ramsay Tompkins, *The Russian Mind* (University of Oklahoma Press, 1953), p. 188.

26. Interview with Vladimir Ivanov, EastWest Institute, Moscow, July 2017.

27. See Neil MacFarquhar and Sophia Kishkovsky, "Russian History Receives a Makeover That Starts with Ivan the Terrible," *New York Times*, March 31, 2015, p. A4.

28. Sofi Oksanen, "Your Silence Will Not Protect You," UpNorth.eu, February 28, 2017 (https://upnorth.eu/your-silence-will-not-protect-you/); Gudrun Persson, "The Patriotic Great Power: History and National Security in Russia," in *Coping with Complexity in the Euro-Atlantic Community and Beyond*, edited by

Andris Sprūds and Diāna Potjomkina (Riga: Latvian Institute of International Affairs, 2016), p. 117.

29. Vera Chelishcheva, "Verkhovnyy sud ostavil v sile prigovor blogeru za repost 'VKontakte'" [Supreme Court upholds sentence of blogger for repost on VKontakte], *Novaya gazeta*, September 1, 2016 (https://www.novayagazeta.ru/news/2016/09/01/124619-verhovnyy-sud-ostavil-v-sile-prigovor-blogeru-za-repost-vkontakte).

30. Natalya Portyakova, "Rossiya otvetit Pol'she asimmetrichno" [Russia will respond to Poland asymmetrically], *Izvestiya*, July 31, 2017 (http://iz.ru/624836/portiakova-nataliia/moskva-otvetit-polshe-assimetriei).

31. "Shkol'nik uvidel kosvennuyu vinu Pol'shi v podpisanii pakta Molotova-Ribbentropa" [Shkolnik sees the indirect fault of Poland in the signing of the Molotov-Ribbentrop pact], Lenta.ru, August 8, 2017 (https://lenta.ru/news/2017/08/08/true/); Halya Coynash, "Russia Says Poland, Not USSR, Was Hitler's Ally and Responsible for Holocaust," *Prava lyudiny v Ukrainy*, September 25, 2015 (http://khpg.org/en/index.php?id=1443091855).

32. Serhii Plokhy, *Ukraine and Russia: Representations of the Past* (University of Toronto Press, 2014).

33. For instance, "Pozor Dyunkerka: Kak Yevropa s gotovnost'yu preklonilas' pered Gitlerom" [The shame of Dunkirk: How Europe readily bowed down to Hitler], Zvezda TV (Russian Ministry of Defense TV channel) (https://m.tvzvezda.ru/news/qhistory/content/201707310904-1vri.htm/amp/).

34. Andrew Wood, "Russia's Damaging Obsession with Cold War Myths," Chatham House, May 12, 2016 (https://www.chathamhouse.org/expert/comment/russias-damaging-obsession-cold-war-myths).

35. As with, for example, South Africa's Truth and Reconciliation Commission.

36. Keenan, "On Certain Mythical Beliefs and Russian Behaviors," p. 34.

37. Il'ja Rákoš, "Svetlana Alexievich Is No Useful Idiot," IljaRakos.com, August 13, 2016 (http://www.iljarakos.com/svetlana-alexievich-is-no-useful-idiot/).

38. "Gulag Grave Hunter Unearths Uncomfortable Truths in Russia," *The Guardian*, August 3, 2017 (https://amp.theguardian.com/world/2017/aug/03/gulag-grave-hunter-yury-dmitriyev-unearths-uncomfortable-truths-russia).

39. As with the classic example of Katyn/Khatyn. See Keir Giles, "The Next Phase of Russian Information Warfare" (Riga: NATO Strategic Communications Centre of Excellence, November 2015), pp. 7–8.

40. A phrase used by Oleg Rumyantsev, then chairman of Russia's Parliamentary Constitutional Committee, in William C. Bodie, "The Threat to America from the Former USSR," *Orbis* 37, no. 4 (Fall 1993), pp. 510–11.

Chapter 9

1. Reprinted in *Komsomolskaya Pravda*, September 9, 2017.

2. Nikolay Petrov and Anders Aslund, "Social Benefits Crisis: Domestic Policy Change for Putin," Carnegie Endowment for International Peace, February 2, 2005 (http://carnegieendowment.org/2005/02/02/social-benefits-crisis-domestic-policy-change-for-putin-event-752); "Novyye protesty dal'noboyshchikov: chto izmenilos' god spustya?" [New protests by long-distance drivers: What has changed a year later?], Varlamov.ru, April 9, 2017 (http://varlamov.ru/2322726.html).

3. Vladimir Ryzhkov, "United Russia Wins Elections but Not Respect," *Moscow Times*, September 22, 2014 (https://themoscowtimes.com/articles/united-russia-wins-elections-but-not-respect-39646).

4. At the time of the 2011–12 protests, "there were certain valves, sociopolitical valves in place to allow limited avenues for independent, weird self-expression in political thought. [Now] there's been a kind of hardening of the Kremlin line . . . there's just less patience, less flexibility, less interest in playing that game. And the Putin system is more directly, at times, repressive. There's less pretending these days." Russia correspondent Joshua Yaffa, interviewed by Isaac Chotiner, "The Dots Are Never Going to Connect," Slate, July 17, 2017 (http://www.slate.com/articles/news_and_politics/interrogation/2017/07/the_russia_scandal_dots_are_never_going_to_connect.html).

5. Paul Goble, "Putin's Russian Guard Is True 'Heir to the NKVD,' Its Deputy Commander Says," *Window on Eurasia* (blog), June 4, 2017 (http://windowoneurasia2.blogspot.no/2017/06/putins-russian-guard-is-true-heir-to.html). See also Paul Goble, "Putin Gives National Guard Powers Even NKVD Didn't Have: The Question Now Is Why? Gorevoy Says," *Window on Eurasia* (blog), June 5, 2017 (http://windowoneurasia2.blogspot.co.uk/2017/06/putin-gives-national-guard-powers-even.html).

6. Pavel Luzin, "The Ominous Rise of Russian National Guard," IntersectionProject.eu, July 21, 2017 (http://intersectionproject.eu/article/security/ominous-rise-russian-national-guard); and Sergey Sukhankin, "Russian National Guard: A New Oprichnina, 'Cyber Police' or Something Else?," *Eurasia Daily Monitor* (Jamestown Foundation), March 21, 2017 (https://jamestown.org/program/russian-national-guard-new-oprichnina-cyber-police-something-else-2/).

7. "Boytsam Rosgvardii zakupayut reaktivnyye pekhotnyye ognemety 'Shmel'" [Shmel infantry rocket flamethrowers will be bought for National Guard troops], Centre for Analysis of World Arms Trade, Moscow, April 26, 2017 (http://armstrade.org/includes/periodics/news/2017/0426/073540715/detail.shtml); "Granatomet blizhnego boya GM-94" [GM-94 close combat grenade launcher] *Voyenno-promyshlennyy kuryer*, February 3, 2017 (https://vpk-news.ru/news/35053).

8. Aleksandr Solzhenitsyn, "The Exhausted West," *Harvard Magazine*, July–

August 1978, pp. 20–26. See also Aleksandr Solzhenitsyn, "How We Must Rebuild Russia," *Komsomolskaya Pravda*, September 18, 1990.

9. As put by Ivan Kurilla, "Russia can become democratic eventually, but not as easily as democratic people in Russia would like it to be. We appeal to the West with this description of what is happening but this is not the whole truth." Interview with the author, August 2017.

10. Laurens van der Post, *Journey into Russia* (Harmondsworth: Penguin, 1965), p. 62.

11. Sergey Patrushev and Lyudmila Filippova, "Dualism of Mass Consciousness and Typology of Mass Politics," *Politicheskaya nauka* 1 (2017), pp. 13–37; and commentary in Paul Goble, "Post-Soviet Man Resembles Pre-Soviet Predecessor More Than Soviet One, Sociologists Say," *Window on Eurasia* (blog), May 16, 2017 (http://windowoneurasia2.blogspot.co.uk/2017/05/post-soviet-man-resembles-pre-soviet.html).

12. "Predstoyashchiye vybory i obraz nyneshney Gosdumy" [The upcoming elections and the image of the current State Duma] (Moscow: Levada Center, July 18, 2016) (http://www.levada.ru/2016/07/18/predstoyashhie-dumskie-vybory-i-obraz-nyneshnej-gosdumy/).

13. "Rossiyane snyali s sebya otvetstvennost' za stranu" [Russians renounce responsibility for the country], *Kommersant*, July 13, 2016 (https://www.kommersant.ru/doc/3037200).

14. "At a Russian Polling Station, Phantom Voters Cast Ballots for the 'Tsar,'" Reuters, September 12, 2017 (https://uk.reuters.com/article/uk-russia-election-fraud-exclusive/exclusive-at-a-russian-polling-station-phantom-voters-cast-ballots-for-the-tsar-idUKKCN1BN15N).

15. "Study: Russia's Most Active Protesters Are Its Least Active Voters," *Moscow Times*, March 31, 2017 (https://themoscowtimes.com/news/study-russias-most-active-protesters-its-least-active-voters-57596).

16. Andrei P. Tsygankov, "Nobody Loves Russia: How Western Media Have Perpetuated the Myth of Putin's 'Neo-Soviet Autocracy,'" *European Politics and Policy* (LSE blog), August 17, 2015 (http://bit.ly/1LgfZng).

17. Veera Laine, "The Spring That Never Came," FIIA Comment 6 (Helsinki: Finnish Institute of International Affairs, February 25, 2016) (http://www.fiia.fi/en/publication/569/the_spring_that_never_came/). See also "Russian Authorities Take Aim at Supporters of Opposition Politician Alexei Navalny," OVD-INFO via Open Democracy Russia, July 14, 2017 (https://www.opendemocracy.net/od-russia/ovd-info/russian-authorities-take-aim-at-supporters-of-opposition-politician-alexei-navalny).

18. "V Peterburge avtor posta 'VKontakte' poluchil dva goda strogogo rezhima za unizheniye chinovnikov" [VKontakte post author gets two years of strict regime in Petersburg for insulting civil servants], Fontanka.ru, November 27, 2017 (http://www.fontanka.ru/2017/11/27/034/).

19. Madeline Roache, "Punitive Psychiatry Reemerges in Post-Soviet States," Eurasianet.org, July 5, 2017 (http://www.eurasianet.org/node/84246); Anne Applebaum, "A Chip Off the Old Gulag, in Russia Today, with Torture," *Washington Post*, May 11, 2017 (http://wapo.st/2q6vlWC); "Is Russia Borrowing from Stalin's Playbook to Bury the Past?," *Coda*, January 12, 2018 (https://codastory.com/disinformation-crisis/news/is-russia-borrowing-from-stalins-playbook-to-bury-the-past).

20. Alisa Kustikova, "Noveyshaya istoriya rossiyskogo donosa ot pervogo litsa" [Latest first-person history of the Russian denunciation], *Novaya gazeta*, May 10, 2017 (https://www.novayagazeta.ru/articles/2017/05/10/72393-noveyshaya-istoriya-rossiyskogo-donosa-ot-pervogo-litsa).

21. Ilja Rákoš, "Svetlana Alexievich Is No Useful Idiot" (interview), IljaRakos.com, August 13, 2016 (http://www.iljarakos.com/svetlana-alexievich-is-no-useful-idiot).

22. Angus Roxburgh, "I Thought Nothing in Russia Could Shock Me. Then I Went to a Television Broadcast," *The Guardian*, June 30, 2017 (https://www.theguardian.com/commentisfree/2017/jun/30/russia-putin-protests-police-arrests-tv-show). One indication that these campaigns are effective came in a 2015 survey when Russians were asked to name politicians whom they distrusted. Mikhail Khodorkovsky, despite not technically being a politician, had sought or acquired sufficient political influence to feature prominently in the responses. Levada Center, "Mayskiye reytingi odobreniya i doveriya" [May ratings of approval and trust], Levada.ru, May 27, 2015 (https://www.levada.ru/2015/05/27/majskie-rejtingi-odobreniya-i-doveriya-2/).

23. President of Russia, "Address by President of the Russian Federation," Moscow, March 18, 2014 (http://en.kremlin.ru/events/president/news/20603).

24. "The Price of Campaigning for the Opposition in Russia," Human Rights Watch, November 15, 2017 (https://www.hrw.org/news/2017/11/15/price-campaigning-opposition-russia).

25. Lika Kedrinskaya, "Armiya nauchit lyubit' kogo nado" [The Army will teach you to love whom you need to], *Novaya gazeta—Region*, October 31, 2017 (http://novayareg.ru/news/armiya-nauchit-lyubit-kogo-nado).

26. "Vladimir Putin, in First Remarks on Russian Protests, Warns of Potential Chaos," *New York Times*, March 30, 2017 (https://www.nytimes.com/2017/03/30/world/europe/putin-russia-protests.html); "Putin Compares Anti-Corruption Protests to 'Arab Spring' and 'Euromaidan'," *Moscow Times*, March 30, 2017 (https://themoscowtimes.com/news/putin-compares-anti-corruption-protests-to-arab-spring-and-euromaidan-57586).

27. Interview with Tatiana Stanovaya, head of the analytical department at Moscow's Center for Political Technologies, July 2017.

28. David Satter, *The Less You Know, the Better You Sleep* (Yale University Press, 2016).

29. Elaborated in James Foote, *Russian and Soviet Imperialism* (London: Foreign Affairs Publishing, 1972), pp. 257ff.

30. Benjamin Parker, "The Other Russia: Poisonings, 'Accidents,' and Assassinations," *Weekly Standard*, July 24, 2017 (http://www.weeklystandard.com/the-other-russia-poisonings-accidents-and-assassinations/article/2008974).

31. Vladimir Kara-Murza, speaking on *PBS NewsHour*, "The Deadly Risk of Standing Up to Putin," July 13, 2017 (http://www.pbs.org/newshour/bb/deadly-risk-standing-putin/). See also interview with Vladimir Kara-Murza, *USA Today*, May 2, 2017 (https://www.usatoday.com/story/news/world/2017/05/02/dozens-russian-deaths-cast-suspicion-vladimir-putin/100480734/).

32. Heidi Blake and others, "Poison in the System," *BuzzFeed*, June 12, 2017 (https://www.buzzfeed.com/heidiblake/poison-in-the-system) (and subsequent reports). See also "Outspoken Putin Critic Survives Assassination Attempt," *Financial Times*, June 2, 2017 (https://www.ft.com/content/349300d4-47dd-11e7-8519-9f94ee97d996).

33. Dexter Filkins, "Are Russian Operatives Attacking Putin Critics in the U.S.?," *New Yorker*, June 19, 2017 (https://www.newyorker.com/news-desk/are-russian-operatives-attacking-putin-critics-in-the-us); and Jason Leopold, "High-Profile Russian Death in Washington Was No Accident—It Was Murder, Officials Say," *BuzzFeed*, July 28, 2017.

34. Jeff Stein, "How Russia Is Using LinkedIn As a Tool of War against Its U.S. Enemies," *Newsweek*, August 3, 2017 (http://www.newsweek.com/russia-putin-bots-linkedin-facebook-trump-clinton-kremlin-critics-poison-war-645696).

35. Andrei Piontkovsky, *Another Look into Putin's Soul* (Washington: Hudson Institute, 2006), p. 26.

36. Mark Galeotti, "Reasons to Be Cheerful, 1, 2, 3: What Lies Ahead for Russian Politics," *Moscow Times*, July 5, 2017 (https://themoscowtimes.com/articles/reasons-to-be-cheerful-1-2-3-what-lies-ahead-for-russian-politics-58298).

37. *Potential Challenges to Public Order and Social Stability in the Russian Federation: A CSRC Review* (Oxford: Conflict Studies Research Centre, August 2011) (http://www.conflictstudies.org.uk/files/20110810_csrc_russia_social.pdf).

38. Marc Bennetts, "In Moscow, Putin's Opponents Chalk Up a Symbolic Victory," *Politico*, September 15, 2017 (https://www.politico.eu/article/moscow-vladimir-putin-election-opponents-chalk-up-symbolic-victory/).

39. "Krasnaya Knopka — Pravozashchita dlya vsekh" [Red Button—Human rights for all] (http://bit.ly/krasknopka).

40. "In Russia, Opposition Grows as Fear of the State Fades," *PBS NewsHour*, July 15, 2017 (http://www.pbs.org/newshour/bb/putin-faces-growing-opposition-lead-4th-term/).

41. Aleksei Levinson, "O molodezhi staroy i novoy" [On the old and

new youth], *Vedomosti*, May 22, 2017 (https://www.vedomosti.ru/opinion/columns/2017/05/23/690975-molodezhi).

42. "KGB_Resident," post 340 on a thread on the British Army Rumour Service (ARRSE) forum, "The Baltics—Should Britain Be Rushing to Their Defence?," March 29, 2017 (https://www.arrse.co.uk/community/threads/the-baltics-should-britain-be-rushing-to-their-defence.211956/page-340#post-7810149).

43. Aleksandr Baunov, "Demolition Drama in Moscow," *Foreign Affairs*, May 19, 2017 (https://www.foreignaffairs.com/articles/russian-federation/2017-05-19/demolition-drama-moscow).

44. "Plan to Relocate 1.6 Million Muscovites Turns Middle-Class Russians into Protesters," *Washington Post*, June 10, 2017 (https://www.washingtonpost.com/world/europe/plan-to-relocate-16-million-muscovites-turns-middle-class-russians-into-protesters/2017/06/10/724021c6-49e2-11e7-b69d-c158df3149e9_story.html). Viktor Khamrayev, Aleksandr Voronov, and Valeriya Mishina, "Renovatsiya bez revolyutsii" [Renovation without revolution], *Kommersant*, May 20, 2017.

45. Natalia Antonova, "New Wave Russian Activism in Wake of a Massive Resettlement Scheme," MobilisationLab.org, July 7, 2017 (https://mobilisation-lab.org/new-wave-russian-activism-resettlement/).

Chapter 10

1. Interview with Ivan Kurilla, European University at St. Petersburg, August 2017.

2. See Andrew Monaghan, "'Putin in Crisis' and Russian Public Opinion," Chatham House Comment (London: Royal Institute of International Affairs, February 21, 2013) (https://www.chathamhouse.org/media/comment/view/189545).

3. "Putin's Downfall: The Coming Crisis of the Russian Regime," promotion for talk by Nikolay Petrov, European Council on Foreign Relations, June 2, 2016. The publication was "Putin's Downfall: The Coming Crisis of the Russian Regime," European Council on Foreign Relations, April 19, 2016 (http://www.ecfr.eu/publications/summary/putins_downfall_the_coming_crisis_of_the_russian_regime7006?mc_cid=db575c9c25&mc_eid=52bb31fcfe).

4. Arkady Moshes, "The Sun Is Setting on Putin's System," FIIA Comment 1 (Helsinki: Finnish Institute of International Affairs, January 12, 2012) (https://www.fiia.fi/en/publication/the-sun-is-setting-on-putins-system).

5. As in, for instance, Lilia Shevtsova, "Has the Russian System's Agony Begun?," *American Interest*, March 17, 2015.

6. Maria Lipman and Nikolay Petrov, eds., *The State of Russia: What Comes Next?* (London: Palgrave Macmillan, 2015), p. 3.

7. Pavel K. Baev, "Virtual Militarism Grows into Real Peril for Russia," *Eurasia Daily Monitor* (Jamestown Foundation), May 9, 2016 (https://jamestown.org/program/virtual-militarism-grows-into-real-peril-for-russia/).

8. Michael Kofman, "The Seven Deadly Sins of Russia Analysis," *War on the Rocks*, December 23, 2015 (http://warontherocks.com/2015/12/the-seven-deadly-sins-of-russia-analysis/).

9. Keir Giles, *The State of the NATO-Russia Reset* (Shrivenham, U.K.: Conflict Studies Research Centre, September 2011) (http://www.conflictstudies.org.uk/files/csrc_nato-russia-reset_preview.pdf).

10. As described in Stephen J. Blank, *Towards a New Russia Policy* (Carlisle, Pa.: United States Army War College, February 2008).

11. Michael McFaul, "Getting Russia Right," *Foreign Policy*, Winter 1999–2000, pp. 58–73.

12. For instance, Zbigniew Brzezinski, "Russia, Like Ukraine, Will Become a Real Democracy," *Financial Times*, December 11, 2013.

13. David Satter, *The Less You Know, the Better You Sleep* (Yale University Press, 2016), p. 18.

14. Andrew Monaghan, *The New Politics of Russia: Interpreting Change* (Manchester University Press, 2016), p. 93.

15. *The European Union and Russia: Before and Beyond the Crisis in Ukraine*, European Union Committee, House of Lords, 6th Report of Session 2014–2015 (London: HMSO, February 2015), p. 23.

16. Ulrich Kühn, "More Realism, Please! A Reply to Ditrych, Kulesa and Kobrinskaya," *New Perspectives* 23, no. 2 (2015).

17. As, for instance, Daniel Fried, "Russia's Back-to-the-80s Foreign Policy," *Defense One*, August 3, 2017 (http://www.defenseone.com/threats/2017/08/russias-back-80s-foreign-policy/139978).

18. See also David Filipov, "The Angst of the Liberal Democrats Who Once Thought Russia's Future Was in Their Hands," *Washington Post*, August 17, 2017 (https://www.washingtonpost.com/world/europe/the-liberal-democrats-who-once-thought-russias-future-was-in-their-hands/2017/08/17/77335b28-8298-11e7-9e7a-20fa8d7a0db6_story.html).

19. Interview with Ivan Kurilla, European University at St. Petersburg, August 2017.

20. James Foote, *Russian and Soviet Imperialism* (London: Foreign Affairs Publishing, 1972), p. 58.

21. For a study of these cycles in the relationship specifically with the United States, see Angela Stent, *The Limits of Partnership: U.S.-Russia Relations in the Twenty-First Century* (Princeton University Press, 2014).

22. "One had the right to ask oneself will they now at last lift up their heads?" André Gide, *Back from the USSR* (London, 1937), p. 15. "But, I wondered, could not this all be changing now?" Laurens van der Post, *Journey into Russia* (Harmondsworth: Penguin, 1965), p. 62.

23. The extent to which these developments were understood or even noticed abroad at the time provides interesting insight into the successes and failures of

Russia analysis during the Cold War. For one highly perceptive assessment, see Edouard Krakowski, *Histoire de Russie: L'Eurasie et L'Occident* (Paris: Editions des Deux-Rives, 1954).

24. Kathleen E. Smith, *Moscow 1956: The Silenced Spring* (Harvard University Press, 2017), p. 6.

25. As described regarding earlier eras in *The Realignment of Europe*, edited by Arnold Toynbee (Oxford University Press, 1955).

26. Edward Crankshaw, *Russia and the Russians* (London: Macmillan, 1947), p. 3.

27. Ion Ratiu, *Moscow Challenges the World* (London: Sherwood Press, 1986), p. 4.

28. Henry W. Nevinson, *The Dawn in Russia* (London: Harper & Bros., 1906), p. 243.

29. Wright Miller, *Who Are the Russians?* (London: Faber and Faber, 1973), p. 109.

30. For a useful collection of original documents on this period, see Sven F. Kraemer, *Inside the Cold War from Marx to Reagan* (Washington: American Foreign Policy Council; Lanham, Md.: University Press of America, 2015), p. 20.

31. Ratiu, *Moscow Challenges the World*, p. 16.

32. Gleb Pavlovskiy, *Sistema RF. Istochniki rossiyskogo strategicheskogo povedeniya. Metod George F. Kennan* [The Russian Federation system: Sources of Russian strategic behavior. The George F. Kennan method] (Moscow: Izdatel'stvo Evropa, Moscow, 2015), p. 24.

33. Interview with Ivan Kurilla, European University at St. Petersburg, August 2017.

34. Interview with Dr. Pavel Luzin, Perm University, July 2017.

35. Van der Post, *Journey into Russia*, p. 62.

36. Frederick L. Schuman, *The Cold War: Retrospect and Prospect: Three Lectures* (Louisiana State University Press, 1962), p. 27.

37. Email discussion with Tatiana Stanovaya, head of the analytical department at Moscow's Center for Political Technologies, July 2017.

38. Speaking at the Lennart Meri conference, Tallinn, May 13, 2017.

39. "With 84 Million Users, Russia's Internet Penetration Rate Has Nearly Doubled in Five Years," *East-West Digital News*, February 8, 2016 (http://www.ewdn.com/2016/02/08/with-84-million-users-russias-internet-penetration-rate-has-nearly-doubled-in-five-years/).

40. Eva Hartog and Lev Gudkov, "The Evolution of Homo Sovieticus to Putin's Man," *Moscow Times*, October 13, 2017 (https://themoscowtimes.com/articles/the-evolution-of-homo-sovieticus-to-putins-man-59189).

41. Vladimir Pastukhov, "Teoriya o pokoleniyakh Rossii: Ot 'frontovikov' – k 'pokoleniyu bez budushchego' i dal'she" [Theory on the generations of Russia: From the "front-line soldiers" to the "generation without a future"

and beyond], *Novaya gazeta*, July 18, 2015 (https://www.novayagazeta.ru/articles/2015/07/18/64943-teoriya-o-pokoleniyah-rossii-ot-171-frontovikov-187-8212-k-171-pokoleniyu-bez-buduschego-187-i-dalshe).

42. Andrei Piontkovsky, *Another Look into Putin's Soul* (Washington: Hudson Institute, 2006), p. 99.

43. "Chetvert' rossiyan nazvali stalinskiye repressii neobkhodimost'yu" [One-quarter of Russians called Stalin's repressions essential], Interfax, March 25, 2016 (http://www.interfax.ru/russia/500248).

44. Serguei Oushakine, "Neighbours in Memory," *Times Literary Supplement*, November 18, 2016.

45. Aaron Hicklin, "The Inexorable Rise of Masha Gessen," *Out*, October 31, 2017 (https://www.out.com/out-exclusives/2017/10/31/Masha-Gessen-Russia-Putin).

46. Aleksandr Tverskoy, "Vot i priyekhali," Twitter post, December 21, 2017 (account now deleted).

47. "Vospriyatie molodezhyu novyh nezavisimyh gosudarstv istorii sovetskogo i postsovetskogo periodov" [Youth perception of the history of the Soviet and post-Soviet periods in the new independent states], *Yevraziyskiy monitor* [Eurasia Monitor], April–May 2009 (http://www.zircon.ru/upload/File/russian/publication/1/090909.pdf).

48. "Fake Photo of a Soviet Supermarket Is Actually an American Supermarket," Polygraph.info, January 13, 2018 (https://www.polygraph.info/a/fake-photo-of-soviet-supermarket/28969733.html).

49. Denis Dafflon, "Molodezh Rossii. Portret pokoleniya na perelome" [The Youth of Russia: A portrait of a generation at a turning point], *Vestnik obshchestvennogo mneniya* [Bulletin of Public Opinion] 5, no. 97 (2008), pp. 19–35 (https://elibrary.ru/item.asp?id=12416841).

50. See Monaghan, *The New Politics of Russia: Interpreting Change*, p. 114.

51. Jeffrey Mankoff, "Generational Change and the Future of U.S.-Russian Relations," *Journal of International Affairs* 63, no. 2 (Spring/Summer 2010), pp. 1–15.

52. Ibid.

53. "Russia's YouTube Generation," IntersectionProject.eu, April 7, 2017. http://intersectionproject.eu/article/society/russias-youtube-generation.

54. *Kaktus Morning Political Show*, YouTube channel (https://www.youtube.com/playlist?list=PLMnzjxOFrGPmQRphHcN0u0lJpWJsIqAyv).

55. Responses by the authorities include projects invented to monitor protest potential among students and teachers. See Carolina Vendil Pallin, "Russia's Presidential Domestic Policy Directorate: HQ for Defeat-Proofing Russian Politics," *Demokratizatsiya: The Journal of Post-Soviet Democratization* 25, no. 3 (Summer 2017), pp. 255–78.

56. Email discussion with Tatiana Stanovaya, head of the analytical department at Moscow's Center for Political Technologies, July 2017.

57. "Kto i zachem tyanet Bryanskikh shkol'nikov na miting Naval'nogo?" [Who is drawing Bryansk schoolchildren to the Navalny rally and why?], RVS, March 24, 2017 (http://rvs.su/statia/kto-i-zachem-tyanet-bryanskih-shkolnikov-na-miting-navalnogo); "Schoolchildren at the Navalny Rally" (http://newspolitics.ru/shkolniki-na-mitinge-navalnogo.html).

58. David Kharebov, "How a Small Russian Election Inspired a Big Political Movement," *Moscow Times*, September 8, 2017 (https://themoscowtimes.com/articles/small-election-big-political-movement-58879).

59. Tomila Lankina, "Russians Are Protesting! Part 8. Young Russians Are Joining In, against Expectations," *Washington Post*, March 31, 2017 (https://www.washingtonpost.com/news/monkey-cage/wp/2017/03/31/russians-are-protesting-part-8-young-russians-arent-a-brainwashed-lost-generation-after-all/).

60. See "explanation to youth" that Navalny was trained in the United States to carry out a coup in Russia, issued by National Liberation Movement (NOD), Novokuznetsk, August 2017 (https://twitter.com/twitted_knitter/status/895209441011924992).

61. The following links provide a selection of these videos from across Russia: Lidiya Simakova, "'Vy liberaly-fashisty, kholopy anglosaksov': Politinformatsiya po-tomski" ("You are liberal-fascists and lackeys of the Anglo-Saxons": Political information Tomsk style), Ekho Moskvy, March 30, 2017 (http://echo.msk.ru/blog/echomsk/1953986-echo/); Kevin Rothrock, "This Is How a Russian School Principal Talked to Her Students about Patriotism," *Global Voices*, March 21, 2017 (https://globalvoices.org/2017/03/21/this-is-how-a-russian-school-principal-talked-to-her-students-about-patriotism/amp/); Kirill Vasilyev, "Studentov VlGU sognali v zal i promyli mozgi lektsiyey o 'Gitlere-Naval'nom'" (Vladimir State University students herded into hall for brainwashing with a lecture on "Navalny-Hitler"), *ProVladimir,* April 18, 2017 (https://provladimir.ru/news/life/studentov-vlgu-sognali-v-zal-i-promyli-mozgi-lekciej-o-gitlere-navalnom). See also "Russian University Screens Film Telling Students That Navalny Is Hitler 2.0," *Moscow Times,* April 19 2017, (https://themoscowtimes.com/news/russian-university-shows-students-film-comparing-opposition-leader-to-hitler-57765).

62. Author interview, Tallinn, May 13, 2017.

63. Speaking at Lennart Meri conference, Tallinn, May 13, 2017.

64. Interview with Ivan Kurilla, European University at St. Petersburg, August 2017.

65. Lev Gudkov, "Putin's Relapse into Totalitarianism," in *The State of Russia: What Comes Next?*, edited by Lipman and Petrov, p. 104.

66. Andrei Kolesnikov and Denis Volkov, "The Perils of Change: Russians' Mixed Attitudes toward Reform," Carnegie Moscow Center, February 6, 2018 (http://carnegie.ru/2018/02/06/perils-of-change-russians-mixed-attitudes-toward-reform-pub-75436).

67. Marvin Kalb, *Imperial Gamble: Putin, Ukraine, and the New Cold War* (Brookings, 2015), p. 225.

68. Described at length in A. (Sasha) Kennaway, "The Russian 'Black Hole'" (Shrivenham, U.K.: Conflict Studies Research Centre, December 1996).

69. Jadwiga Rogoża, "'The Power Gained, We Will Never Surrender'— Russian Ruling Elite versus the Succession and Economic Crisis," Punkt Widzenia, OSW, October 2009.

70. Leonid Bershidsky, "Putin Devotes Oil Windfall to Guns, Not Butter," Bloomberg, June 6, 2016 (http://www.bloomberg.com/view/articles/2016-06-06/putin-devotes-oil-windfall-to-guns-not-butter).

71. Andrzej Wilk, "The Russian Army—the Priority for Putin's Third Term," OSW, July 24, 2013 (http://www.osw.waw.pl/en/publikacje/analyses/2013-07-24/russian-army-priority-putins-third-term).

72. "Zato my delayem rakety" [But we make rockets], Gazeta.ru, October 26, 2015 (http://www.gazeta.ru/comments/2015/10/26_e_7846541.shtml), translated for *Russian Defence Policy* (blog) (https://russiandefpolicy.wordpress.com/author/russiandefpolicy/).

73. Julian Cooper, "Military Spending in Russia in 2017 and Planned Spending to 2020: A Research Note," SIPRI, February 3, 2018.

74. Andrey Kolesnikov, "The Russian Middle Class Is a Besieged Fortress," Carnegie Center Moscow, April 6, 2015 (carnegie.ru/publications?fa=59655).

75. Olga Gurova, Ekaterina Kalinina, Jessie Labow and Vlad Strukov, "Patriotic (Non) Consumption: Food, Fashion and Media," *Studies in Russian, Eurasian and Central European New Media* 16 (2016).

76. Piontkovsky, "Another Look into Putin's Soul," p. 29.

77. A. Dynkin, V. Baranovsky, I. Kobrinskaya, and others, "Russia and the World: 2016 IMEMO Forecast," IMEMO-Primakov National Research Institute of World Economy and International Relations, Russian Academy of Sciences, *New Perspectives* 23, no. 2 (2015), p. 100.

78. Interview with Thomas Graham, Tallinn, May 13, 2017.

79. Kazimierz Waliszewski, *Peter the Great* (London: William Heinemann, 1898).

80. Kennaway, "The Russian 'Black Hole,'" p. 5.

81. Miller, *Who Are the Russians?*, p. 59.

82. Maurice Baring, *The Russian People* (1911) (https://archive.org/details/russianpeople017102mbp).

83. Gudkov, "Putin's Relapse into Totalitarianism," p. 97.

84. Interviewed in Shaun Walker, "Unequal Russia: Is Anger Stirring in the Global Capital of Inequality?," *The Guardian*, April 25, 2017 (https://www.theguardian.com/inequality/2017/apr/25/unequal-russia-is-anger-stirring-in-the-global-capital-of-inequality).

85. Galina Ostanovets, "Putin boitsya opyta 1991-go, kogda KGB skazal – net, my strelyat' ne budem" [Putin is afraid of the experience of 1991 when the KGB

said no, we will not shoot], *Delovaya stolitsa*, July 6, 2017 (http://www.dsnews.ua/world/-putin-pokinet-kreml-tolko-vpered-nogami-04072017220000).

Conclusion

1. Frederick L. Schuman, *The Cold War: Retrospect and Prospect* (Louisiana State University Press, 1962), p. 13.

2. Hanna Smith, "Summing Up," in *Russia of Challenges* (Helsinki: Finnish Ministry of Defense, 2008), p. 130 (https://www.defmin.fi/files/1298/Russia_of_Challenges_nettiversio.pdf).

3. Denis Volkov, "Nastroyeniya rossiyskikh elit posle Kryma" [The mood of the Russian elites after Crimea], Carnegie.ru, November 10, 2015 (http://carnegie.ru/2015/11/10/ru-61925/ildv).

4. Yaroslav Fedoseev, "Rossiyane schitayut priznakom velikoy derzhavy dostatok yeye zhiteley" [Russians think the material well-being of its citizens is a sign of a great power], *Kommersant*, June 10, 2016 (https://www.kommersant.ru/doc/3011831).

5. See also Marvin Kalb, *Imperial Gamble: Putin, Ukraine, and the New Cold War* (Brookings, 2015), p. xix.

6. Bill Bowring, "Moscow: Third Rome, Model Communist City, Eurasian Antagonist—and Power As No-Power?," in *Law and the City*, edited by Andreas Philippopoulos-Mihalopoulos (London: Routledge Cavendish, 2007), pp. 39–54.

7. As described in the first decade after the Cold War in *Russia and the West: The 21st Century Security Environment*, edited by Alexei G. Arbatov, Karl Kayser, and Robert Legvold (Armonk, N.Y.: M. E. Sharpe for the EastWest Institute, 1999), p. 8.

8. Lev Tikhomirov, *Russia, Political and Social* (London: Swan Sonnenschein, Lowrey & Co, 1888), p. 7 (https://archive.org/details/russiapoliticals-01tikhuoft).

9. Bruce Allyn, "To Deal with the Russians, America Must Think Like the Russians," *National Interest*, June 22, 2017 (http://nationalinterest.org/feature/deal-the-russians-america-must-think-the-russians-21280).

10. Matthew Crosston, America's Lost Generation: Russian 'Expertise' within Generation X," *Modern Diplomacy*, April 26, 2015 (https://moderndiplomacy.eu/2015/04/26/america-s-lost-generation-russian-expertise-within-generation-x/).

11. Speaking under the Chatham House rule, May 2017.

12. Natalia Antonova, "You're Not a 'Russia Expert' If You Don't Know Russian and Have Never Been to Russia," *Medium*, May 5, 2017 (https://medium.com/the-anti-nihilist-institute/youre-not-a-russia-expert-if-you-don-t-know-russian-and-have-never-been-to-russia-b01e3bb4976b).

13. A helpful summary can be found in Kirk Bennett, "Russia's Virtual Real-

ity," *American Interest*, November 1, 2017 (https://www.the-american-interest.com/2017/11/01/russias-virtual-reality/).

14. Explored in detail in Taylor Downing, *1983: Reagan, Andropov, and a World on the Brink* (New York: Da Capo Press, 2018).

15. Keir Giles, Philip Hanson, Roderic Lyne, and others, *The Russian Challenge*, Chatham House Report (London: Royal Institute of International Affairs, June 2015), p. 51 (https://www.chathamhouse.org/sites/default/files/field/field_document/20150605RussianChallengeGilesHansonLyneNixeySherrWoodUpdate.pdf).

16. Vladimir Putin, "Address to the UN General Assembly," Moscow, September 28, 2015 (http://en.kremlin.ru/events/president/news/50385).

17. Samuel Charap, "Russia's Use of Military Force as a Foreign Policy Tool: Is There a Logic?," Policy Memo 443, PONARS, October 2016 (http://www.ponarseurasia.org/memo/russias-use-military-force-foreign-policy-tool-there-logic).

18. "Putin Warns Romania and Poland That Hosting US Missile Shield System Puts Them in Russia's Cross-Hairs," *The Independent*, May 28, 2016. See also Susanna Capelouto, "Russian President Vladimir Putin warns he'll retaliate against NATO missiles," CNN, May 28, 2016 (http://www.cnn.com/2016/05/28/europe/putin-threatens-romania/index.html).

19. Cold War studies such as John Lewis Gaddis's *Strategies of Containment* (Oxford University Press, 1982) remain highly relevant today.

20. Samuel Greene, "Conditionality beyond Sanctions: Identifying and Pursuing Interests in the EU-Russia Relationship," Policy Memo 460, PONARS, February 2017 (http://www.ponarseurasia.org/memo/conditionality-beyond-sanctions-identifying-and-pursuing-interests-eu-russia-relationship).

21. Compare, for instance, Mark MacKinnon, *The New Cold War: Revolutions, Rigged Elections, and Pipeline Politics in the Former Soviet Union* (New York: Basic Books, 2007), and Edward Lucas, *The New Cold War: How the Kremlin Menaces Both Russia and the West* (London: Bloomsbury, 2008).

22. Quoted in Gaddis, *Strategies of Containment*, p. 145.

23. Putin continued: "They are constantly trying to sweep us into a corner because we have an independent position, because we maintain it and because we call things like they are and do not engage in hypocrisy." "Address by President of the Russian Federation," Moscow, March 18, 2014 (http://en.kremlin.ru/events/president/news/20603).

24. A. Dynkin, V. Baranovsky, I. Kobrinskaya, and others, "Russia and the World: 2017 IMEMO Forecast," *New Perspectives* 25, no. 1 (2017), p. 85.

25. Interview with Thomas Graham, Tallinn, May 13, 2017.

26. John McLaughlin (deputy director and acting director of the CIA from 2000 to 2004), "The Smart Way to Deal with Putin's Russia," *New York Times*, August 9, 2017.

27. Sergey Lavrov, interview by David Remnick, Council on Foreign Relations, Washington, September 24, 2008 (https://www.cfr.org/event/sergey-lavrov).

28. Kadri Liik, "How to Talk with Russia," European Council on Foreign Relations, December 18, 2015 (https://www.ecfr.eu/article/commentary_how_to_talk_to_russia5055).

29. Interview with Ivan Kurilla, European University at St. Petersburg, August 2017.

30. Daniel Fried, "Russia's Back-to-the-80s Foreign Policy," *Defense One*, August 3, 2017 (http://www.defenseone.com/threats/2017/08/russias-back-80s-foreign-policy/139978).

Index

Abkhazia, Russian intervention in, 32, 170
Adamsky, Dima, 20, 116
Akhiezer, Aleksandr, 72
Alexander I, 45
Alexander II, 45
Alexander III, 45
Alexievich, Svetlana, 64, 123
Alienation, 8, 98, 107, 129
Anti-access and area denial (A2/AD) capabilities, 165
Antiblasphemy campaigns, 105–06
Appeasement, 31, 34
Arab Spring, 46–49
Arbatov, Alexei, 39
Asahara, Shoko, 105
Assertiveness, 14, 20, 22, 148
Aum Shinrikyo, 105

Baev, Pavel, 23
Ballistic missile defense (BMD), 56; U.S. sites in Poland and Romania, 166
Baltic states, 30, 51, 56, 63, 66–67. *See also specific countries*

Baluyevsky, Yuriy, 52
Banking crises, 65
Baring, Maurice, 95, 157
Baunov, Aleksandr, 136–37
Berlusconi, Silvio, 73
Borders and border security, 26, 30, 36–37, 62–63, 67, 83, 122
Brenton, Tony, 30
BRICS, 16
Brzezinski, Zbigniew, 31
Bykov, Yuriy, 157

Casualty aversion, 91
Catherine the Great, 11
Cedar Revolution (Lebanon 2005), 43
Censorship, 33, 84–85, 142
Change, prospects for. *See* Prospects for change
Chaos: after Cold War, 68, 94, 148; and destabilization campaigns, 23–24; fear of, 42, 52, 132; and governance structures, 74; management of, 20, 121; and protests, 132; purposeful creation of, 24; regime change as cause of, 52

227

Chechnya, military campaign in, 91
Chirac, Jacques, 73
CIS (Commonwealth of Independent States), 15, 67
Civil society, 53
Clapper, James, 35
Cold War, 59–68, 118, 153. *See also* Soviet era
Collateral damage, 91–92
Collective Security Treaty Organization (CSTO), 15–16
Color revolutions, 43–45
COMECON (Council for Mutual Economic Assistance), 16
Commonwealth of Independent States (CIS), 15, 67
Communalism, 88
Communism: and "disappointed generation," 147–48; and great power self-perception, 14; and individual rights, 88, 93, 143; and moral framework, 104–05
Compromises, 22, 25, 42, 48, 61, 170
Containment, 167–70
Continuity with historical norms, 159–61
Contract law, 23
Cooperation in international relations: continuity with historical norms, 160–61; cycles of, 22–23; prospects for improvement in, 171–73; and threat perceptions, 40, 43, 47, 55; in World War II, 122
Corporate tax rates, 95
Corruption, 7, 78, 84, 90, 98–99, 122, 134
Council for Mutual Economic Assistance (COMECON), 16
Crankshaw, Edward, 24, 36, 38, 76–77, 118, 119, 143
Crimea, intervention in, 29, 32, 48, 56, 170

Crimean War (1853–56), 9, 117
CSTO (Collective Security Treaty Organization), 15–16
Cults, 105
Culture, 5, 8, 9, 79, 103, 114, 120, 148
Cyberattacks, 56, 75
Czars, 26, 72, 78–79, 105, 118, 120, 142. *See also specific individuals*

Decembrist revolt (1825), 82
Deception, 110–11, 113, 161
Decorative democracy, 129–30
De Custine, Astolphe, 33, 41, 82, 87, 111, 113–14, 120
Deference, 12, 15, 16
Democratization, 50, 64–66, 93, 108, 129–30, 142
De Reynold, Gonzague, 3
Destabilization campaigns, 23–24
"Disappointed generation," 147–48
Disinformation campaigns, 109
Domestic policy, 50–51, 65
Double standards, perceptions of, 42
Doublethink, 113–16
Dual citizenship, 83
Dugin, Aleksandr, 104
Dulles, John Foster, 167

Eastern Partnership program (EU), 41
EEU (Eurasian Economic Union), 16
Elections: internet and social media's influence on, 135; and legitimacy, 79; protests of, 44, 127, 135, 149; public perceptions of, 129–30; Western vs. Russian conceptions of, 4
Elites, 6, 133–34, 153
Estonia: cultural differences with Russia, 6; cyberattacks against, 75; history of, 122

Etkind, Alexander, 90
Eurasian Economic Union (EEU), 16
Eurasianism, 104
Europe and European Union: ballistic missile defense in, 166; and Cold War, 61–62, 67; cooperation with Russia's neighbors, 55; Eastern Partnership program, 41; individual rights in, 87, 93; and Russia, 6, 8–12, 25; and Russian expansionism, 26
Expansionist policies, 25–34

Fell, Elena, 115–16
Finland: status of, 31; Russian threats against, 21
Fletcher, Giles, 92, 115
Foote, James, 117, 142
"Four Common Spaces" initiative, 25
Fried, Daniel, 172–73

Gaidar, Yegor, 42
Galeotti, Mark, 13, 29–30, 135
Garmash, Ioann, 103
Gender norms, 108
"Generation of the future," 150–52
Georgia: color revolution in, 43; Russian intervention in, 29, 32, 63, 75–76, 82, 170
Germany: and Putin, 73; unification of following Cold War, 60; in World War I, 44; in World War II, 30, 82, 149
Gessen, Masha, 147
Gide, André, 11, 114
Global financial crisis (2007–08), 153
Gomart, Thomas, 3
Gorbachev, Mikhail, 41, 62
Gorchakov, Aleksandr, 28
Gordon, Philip, 66
Governance structures, 71–86; isolation and secrecy in, 81–86; polls and legitimacy in, 77–81; Putin's role in, 75–77
Graham, Thomas, 151, 155, 169
Great power: Russia's self-perception as, 13–34
Greene, Samuel, 31, 93, 167
Group of Eight (G-8), 66
Gudkov, Lev, 9, 81, 98, 151, 157

Haley, Nikki, 91
Hermitage Capital Management, 133
Herzen, Aleksandr, 88
Hill, Fiona, 74
HIV, 114
Homosexuality, 107
Human rights, 64, 66, 87–99, 106–07, 109, 172
Hunter, Robert, 28

Ideology in moral framework, 103–06
Imperialism: expansionist policies as defensive measures, 30–34; Russia's self-perception as empire, 25–30
Individual rights, 87–99. *See also* Human rights
Information Security Doctrine (Russia 2016), 54
Insecurity, 23, 27, 36, 80, 165
Internal system of Russia, 69–99; governance structures, 71–86; and individual rights, 87–99; isolation and secrecy in, 81–86; and justice, 94–99; polls and legitimacy in, 77–81; and property rights, 87–94; prospects for change in, 139–57; Putin's role in, 75–77; and rule of law, 94–99
International law, 99
Internet: and cyberattacks, 56, 75; protest role of, 135–37; state monitoring of, 85, 150; threat perceptions exacerbated by, 53

Iraq, U.S. invasion of, 37, 43, 48, 50, 52, 66
Isolationism, 34, 81–86
Ivangorod, Russia, 6
Ivanov, Vladimir, 93, 95

Jensen, Don, 24
Justice, 78, 94–99, 110, 113

Kalb, Marvin, 152
Karaganov, Sergey, 55
Kara-Murza, Vladimir, 133
Karasin, Grigoriy, 50
Keenan, Edward, 120
Kennan, George, 22, 38, 55, 56, 81
Kennaway, A. (Sasha), 71, 94, 97
Khodorkovsky, Mikhail, 90
Kissinger, Henry, 6, 16, 22, 31
Kolesnikov, Andrey, 114, 154–55
Kolpakov, Ivan, 115
Konovalov, Aleksandr, 96
Kosovo, intervention in, 66
Kozyrev, Andrey, 11
Kurilla, Ivan, 4, 29, 139, 142, 144, 151, 171
Kyrgyzstan, color revolution in, 43

Language, 10, 18, 21, 26, 105, 116, 162
Latvia, history of, 122
Lavrov, Sergey, 10, 21, 42, 47, 50, 62, 103, 170–71
Lebanon, Cedar Revolution in, 43
Ledeneva, Alena, 95–96
Legitimacy, 28, 38, 48, 72, 77–81, 122
Leninism, 104
Levinson, Aleksey, 9
Lewis, David, 74
Liberalization: after Cold War, 64–65, 66; cycles of, 139–43; of history, 120, 123–24

Libya, interventions in, 43, 46–49, 52
Liik, Kadri, 171
Lipman, Maria, 115
Listyev, Vladislav, 64
Lithuania, history of, 122
Litvinenko, Aleksandr, 134
London Olympics (2012), 7
"Lost generation," 148–49
Lukin, Vladimir, 67
Luzin, Pavel, 145

Malaysia Airlines MH17 incident (2014), 164
Mankoff, Jeffrey, 17, 149
Marten, Kimberly, 20, 111
Marxism, 104–05
McFaul, Michael, 141
McLaughlin, John, 170
Mearsheimer, John, 30–31
Media: censorship of, 84; and doublethink, 113–14; and "generation of the future," 150; independence of, 84; and protests, 128–29; state control of, 72, 74, 84–85
Meduza (media outlet), 85, 115
Medvedev, Dmitriy, 47, 139, 141
Memory, 6, 42, 60, 120, 129, 147, 150
Merkel, Angela, 35, 106–07
Merridale, Catherine, 115
Middle class, 145, 155
Military interventions: in Abkhazia, 32, 170; in Crimea, 29, 32, 48, 56, 170; in Georgia, 29, 32, 63, 75–76, 82, 170; in Moldova, 32; as political tool, 19; in South Ossetia, 32, 170; in Tajikistan, 32; in Ukraine, 17, 29, 30–31, 32, 39, 48, 53, 63, 170
Military power: and great power status, 15, 18–19; and national security policy, 170; public opinion polls on, 154, 160; respect for, 170;

spending on, 153–54; and threat perceptions, 40, 49–57
Milošević, Slobodan, 43
Mironenko, Sergei, 121
Moldova: election protests in, 43; Russian intervention in, 32
Monaghan, Andrew, 77
Mongols, 10, 71–72, 111, 121
Moral framework, 103–16; and doublethink, 113–16; and ideology, 103–06; and religion, 103–06; truth vs. untruth in, 109–13; Western decadence as threat to, 106–08
Moscow Olympics (1980), 7
Murders by the state, 133–34
Mutual assistance, 22–25
Mysticism, 105

Narva, Estonia, 6
National Defense Control Center (Russia), 19, 72–73
National Guard (Russia), 128, 157
National identity, 15, 93, 119, 124
Nationalism, 8–9, 63, 80, 128, 161
National security policy: after Cold War, 51; continuity of, 160; and expansionism, 26; and Russia's great power self-perception, 18–21; and historical liberalization, 120; internet as threat to, 53–54; and military power, 170; and threat perceptions, 35–58
NATO: and Cold War ending, 67; command and control for, 73; cooperation with Russia's neighbors, 55–56; enlargement of, 21–22, 32, 62–63, 166; restricted contact with Russia, 164; as threat, 37; and Ukraine, 30, 39, 56
Navalny, Aleksei, 78, 131, 135, 151
Nemtsov, Boris, 134
Nemtsova, Zhanna, 151

Neutral countries, 31
Nevinson, Henry, 143–44
Nicholas I, 45
Nicholas II, 45, 144
Nongovernmental organizations (NGOs), 43, 53, 168

Obama, Barack, 15, 48, 168
O'Hanlon, Michael, 31
Oil prices, 15, 42, 75, 80
Olympics (1980 and 2014), 7
Opposition movements, 127–38; internet's role in, 135–37; and political expression, 127–31; repression of, 131–34
Orwell, George, 114
Ostrovsky, Arkadiy, 76

"Panfilov's 28 men," 121
Pan-Slavism, 118
Paranoia, 20, 161
Pastukhov, Vladimir, 113, 146–47, 150
Patrushev, Nikolay, 38
Pavlovskiy, Gleb, 144
Peter the Great, 156
Peter III, 45
Piontkovsky, Andrei, 89, 134, 147, 155
Plokhy, Serhii, 25
Poland: after Cold War, 66; ballistic missile defense in, 166; occupation history of, 122; in World War II, 30
Police, 97, 112, 135
Polyakova, Alina, 27
Pomerantsev, Peter, 99
Power: and Cold War, 59, 63; and "disappointed generation," 147–48; economic, 66, 153, 168; and "generation of the future," 150–51; and governance structures, 72, 78, 80–81; great power status, 8–9,

Power (*cont.*)
  11, 17, 20, 22, 24–25, 28, 156; and individual rights, 90, 92, 94–95; and justice, 95; and "lost generation," 148; and moral framework, 103, 105, 108–09, 112; political, 65, 150, 153; and threat perceptions, 35, 37, 56–57
Propaganda, 33, 56, 78, 114
Property rights, 87–94
Prospects for change, 125–57; internal changes, 139–57; internet's role in protests, 135–37; liberalization cycles, 139–42; opposition and protests, 127–38; optimism for, 139–42; patience required for, 152–57; and political expression, 127–31; and repression, 131–34, 142–45; and social change, 145–52
Protests, 127–38; and color revolutions, 44; of elections, 44, 127, 135, 149; internet's role in, 135–37; and political expression, 127–31; repression of, 131–34
Public opinion polls: on elections, 130; on future of Russia, 64, 136, 151–52; and governance structures, 77–81; on military power, 154, 160; on Russian identity, 9; on threat perceptions, 39
Pushkin, Aleksandr, 14–15
Pussy Riot, 106
Putin, Vladimir: on Arab Spring, 46; on Cold War ending, 59; on containment policy, 167; and cooperation with the West, 41; on election protests, 44; and European politics, 62; foreign policy priorities of, 49–50, 67–68; and Russia's great power self-perception, 13; and internal governance structures, 72–73, 75–77, 140–41; on international order, 50, 51, 161; internet distrusted by, 53; on Libyan intervention by the West, 46; and "lost generation," 148; and Medvedev, 139; Merkel on, 35; negotiation strategies of, 24; on NGOs, 43; personality cult of, 105; and protest movements, 128, 130, 132; public opinion of, 77–81; regime change fears of, 40, 42, 45; on Russia as "major European power," 10; on Russian history, 119; on strike-first strategy, 54; summits with BRICS countries, 16; and Syrian civil war, 48; and threat perceptions, 18, 54, 55; and Ukraine, 27, 112

Qaddafi, Muammar, 45

Reagan, Ronald, 37–38
Realism, 34
Regime change, 37, 40–45, 48, 52–55, 143–44, 155
Relativism, 106
Religion, 85, 103–06, 118
Repression, 6, 113–14, 118, 131, 150, 154
Respect, 11–12, 18–21, 170
Retro-totalitarianism, 147
RISI (Russian Institute of Strategic Studies), 114
Robber capitalism, 89
Rogozin, Dmitriy, 37
Romania, ballistic missile defense in, 166
Roxburgh, Angus, 81
RSFSR (Russian Soviet Federative Socialist Republic), 14
Rule of law, 23, 88, 94–99, 142, 168, 172
Russia: and Cold War, 59–68; cooperation by, 22–25; disruption

by, 22–25; empire self-perception in, 25–30; and Europe, 8–12; expansionist policies as defensive measures, 30–34; great power self-perception in, 13–34; historical perspective, 117–24; internal system of, 69–99; moral framework of, 103–16; prospects for change, 125–57; threat perceptions, 35–58; and the West, 1–12. *See also* Internal system of Russia; Moral framework; Prospects for change; Threat perceptions
Russian Academy of Sciences, 155
Russian Institute for Strategic Studies (RISI), 114
Russian Orthodox Church, 85, 103–04, 118
Russian Soviet Federative Socialist Republic (RSFSR), 14
Russo-Japanese War (1904–05), 153
Rybkin, Ivan, 134

Saddam Hussein, 45
Safronkov, Vladimir, 21
St. Petersburg, 28, 73, 131, 133
Satanovskiy, Yevgeniy, 50
Satter, David, 8, 33, 87, 96, 132, 141
Schröder, Gerhard, 73
Schuman, Frederick L., 159
Secrecy, 81–86
Security dilemma, 21. *See also* National security policy
Self-confidence, 9
Self-perception, 13–34
Serebrennikov, Kirill, 96
Sexuality, 107–08
Seymour, Gerald, 6
Sherr, James, 23
Shevtsova, Lilia, 22
Skaskiw, Roman, 109
Skripal, Sergei, 134

Smirnov, Sergey, 53
Smith, Hanna, 159
Smith, Kathleen E., 143
Smith, Walter Bedell, 5
Soccer World Cup (2018), 7
Sochi Olympics (2014), 7
Social media, 24, 56, 135–37, 148, 150–51
Soft power, 7, 166, 169
Solzhenitsyn, Aleksandr, 8, 128
South Ossetia, Russian intervention in, 32, 170
Sovereignty, 27, 48, 50, 55
Soviet era: defense policy, 20; and "disappointed generation," 147–48; expansionism during, 31; foreign policy, 20; governance structures, 74, 76–77, 81–82, 84–85; historical preservation of, 118, 120–21; history of, 122–23; military spending in, 156; and moral framework, 104, 111, 113, 161; and property rights, 88, 90; reforms during, 143, 145–46, 147; repression during, 131–32; and rule of law, 98; and threat perceptions, 37–38, 41, 43, 54
Stalin, Joseph, 79, 82, 105, 119, 133, 147, 156
Stanovaya, Tatiana, 16, 26–27, 88, 132, 145, 150
Strike-first strategy, 54–55
Sushentsov, Andrey, 72
Suslov, Dmitriy, 17, 27
Suslov, Mikhail, 83
Suspicion, 38, 41, 43, 56–57, 74, 111, 143
Sweden: neutrality of, 31; Russian threats against, 21
Syrian civil war, 17, 29, 46–49, 52
Szamuely, Tibor, 9, 17–18

Tajikistan, Russian intervention in, 32
Tax rates, 95
Television, 113–14, 131, 148, 150
Terrorism, 65
Threat perceptions, 35–58; Arab Spring, 46–49; color revolutions, 43–45; enmity of other nations, 35–40; Libya interventions, 46–49; public opinion polls on, 39; regime change, 40–45; responses to, 49–57; Syrian civil war, 46–49
Three Whales corruption case, 133
Tikhomirov, Lev, 115, 162
Tolstoy, Lev, 26
Tomkins, Stuart Ramsay, 88
Totalitarianism, 60, 64, 124, 147
Traitors, 82–83
Trenin, Dmitriy, 14
Truck driver protests (2016), 127
Trump, Donald, 161, 166
Truth vs. untruth, 104, 109–13
Tsygankov, Andrei, 131

Ukraine: color revolution in, 43; EU cooperation with, 56, 107; gas cutoffs for, 75; history of, 122–23; and Russian expansionism, 26; Russian intervention in, 17, 29, 30–31, 32, 39, 48, 53, 63, 170; sovereignty of, 27; U.S. influence in, 41
United Kingdom, Russian attacks on individuals in, 133–34, 164
United Nations, 66, 168
United States: and Arab Spring, 47; bilateral talks with, 24–25; centrality to Russian foreign policy, 17; and Cold War, 32, 61–62, 66; and color revolutions, 43–44; and confrontation with Russia, 165–67; and containment policy, 167–70; cooperation with Russia's neighbors, 55; domestic policy in, 164; elections of 2016, 24; as enemy, 45; and EU strategic interests, 16; "reset" with Russia, 25, 32, 140, 168, 171; Russian attacks on individuals in, 133; and threat perceptions, 39–41, 44–45, 47–49, 51, 55–56
Untruth, 109–13
Utkin, Sergey, 146

Valdai Discussion Club, 33
Van der Post, Laurens, 5, 110, 119, 145

Warsaw Pact, 16
The West: and Cold War ending, 60; and color revolutions, 43–44; decadence of, 106–08; individual rights in, 87; and "lost generation," 149; Russia compared to, 8–12; and Russian identity, 1–12; and Russia's great power self-perception, 24–25; terminology of, 4; as threat, 49–57. *See also* Europe and European Union; United States
Wood, Andrew, 164
World Cup (2018), 7
Worldview, 4–5, 14, 40–41, 55, 80, 149, 171
World War I, 117, 153
World War II, 15, 30, 82, 114, 121–22, 143

Yanukovych, Viktor, 107
Yeltsin, Boris, 10, 11, 41, 44, 45, 64, 78, 94
Youth, 135, 137, 148, 150–52
Yukos oil company, 90

Zubarevich, Natalia, 5